MAIN EMBANKMENT

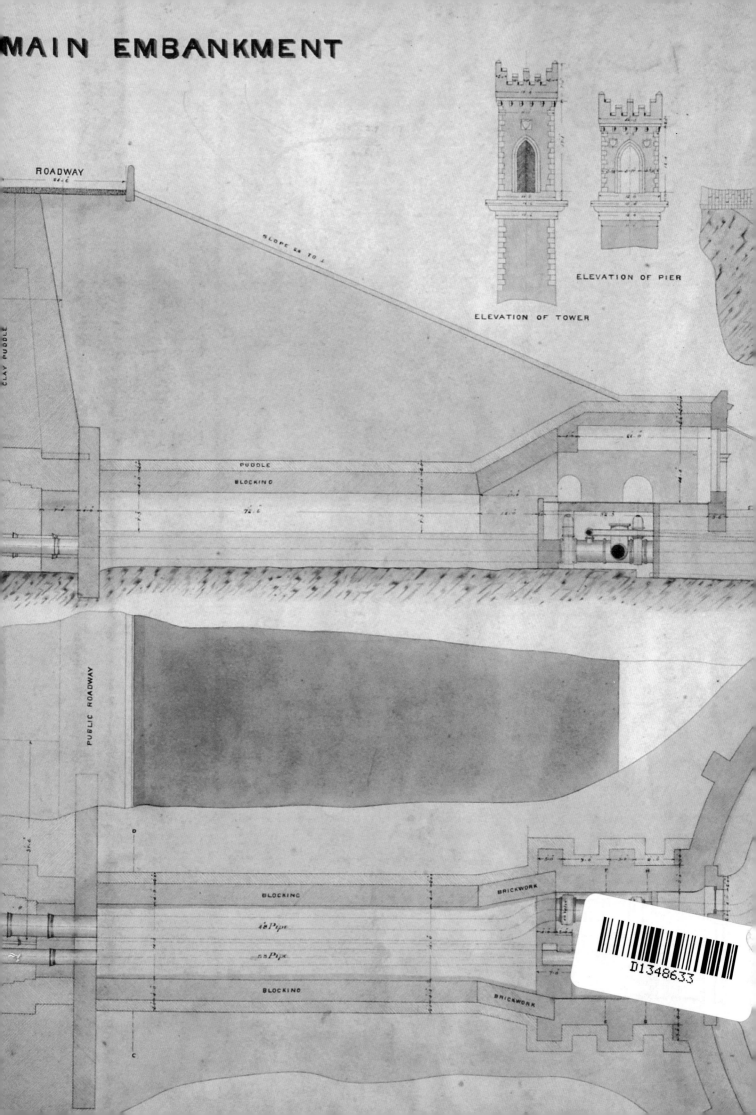

ROADWAY

SLOPE 2½ TO 1

CLAY PUDDLE

PUDDLE

BLOCKING

ELEVATION OF PIER

ELEVATION OF TOWER

PUBLIC ROADWAY

BLOCKING

BRICKWORK

Pipe

Pipe

BLOCKING

BRICKWORK

SECTIONAL ELEVATION OF SCREEN CHAMBER

SCALE ¼ INCH TO ONE FOOT

www.dlrcoco.ie/library

Dún Laoghaire-Rathdown
County Council Comhairle Contae
Dhún Laoghaire-Ráth an Dúin

Public Library Service
Seirbhís Leabharlainne Poiblí

628.1094183

– *Items to be returned on or before the last date below.*
– Tá na hearraí le tabhairt ar ais ar, nó roimh, an dáta
  deireanach atá thíosluaite.

drainage

18. JAN 07.

To those who serve... and still remain unsung

Our Good Health:
A history of Dublin's water and drainage

MICHAEL CORCORAN

Dublin City Council · Comhairle Cathrach Bhaile Átha Cliath

Dublin City
Baile Átha Cliath

FIRST PUBLISHED 2005 BY
Dublin City Council
Dublin City Library & Archive
138–144 Pearse Street
Dublin 2

A catalogue record is available for this book
from the British Library

ISBN: 0 946841 77 2

Designed by Carton LeVert
Printed by Print Media Services
Bound by Library Bindings
Indexed by Helen Litton

Supported by LANPAG
Local Authority Workplace Partnership Group

PICTURE CREDITS

The following images have been supplied by
Dublin City Council:
Diagrammatic maps by GIS Section, © Dublin City Council:
pp 9, 35, 80, 94, 140, 149, 160, 171, 205, 207; Dublin City
Archives at Dublin City Library & Archive: pp 11, 13, 15, 17,
21, 25–6, 30 (A.R. Neville Atlas, all © Dublin City Council);
Malton Prints pp 10, 23, 29; Dublin City Council Maps,
p. 64; © Dublin City Gallery, The Hugh Lane: pp 115–6;
Dublin and Irish Collections at Dublin City Library &
Archive: pp 32 (Post Office Directory), 34, 102, 105, 110,
113, 119 (all Fred E. Dixon Slide Collection); Engineering
Department, © Dublin City Council: pp 22, 45 (right),
70–2, 74–8, 91, 95, 98–101, 120, 123, 128–9, 131–2, 143, 145,
150–1, 153, 155, 158–9, 167–170, 172, 174, 180, 186–7, 189,
191–2, 195, 197, 201–2, 204, 206, 209

Dublin City Council is grateful to the following individuals
and institutions for kindly providing illustrations as follows:
© Edward Chandler: pp 81–3; © Michael Corcoran: pp 139,
141, 144, 147; © Corporation of London, Guildhall Library:
pp 33, 42; © Dave Meehan Photography: pp 8, 18–19, 25
(thumbnail), 31, 47–8, 57, 58, 61–3, 65–6, 68, 93, 108,
124–5, 134, 162, 164, 194, 200 (bottom), 203, 208, 210, 211;
© The Irish Press plc: p. 143; © The Irish Times: pp 182,
184; © the Institution of Engineers of Ireland: pp 40, 92;
© Brian McKeown: pp 79, 86; © National Gallery of Ireland:
p. 96; Courtesy National Library of Ireland, Lawrence
Collection: pp 50–1, 89, 97, 127; © Royal College of
Surgeons in Ireland: p. 45 (left); © Royal Society of
Antiquaries of Ireland, John L. Robinson Lantern Slides:
p. 52; © Sisters of Charity Caritas: p. 37; © Martyn Turner:
p. 198; © Terry Willers: p. 200 (top)

Contents

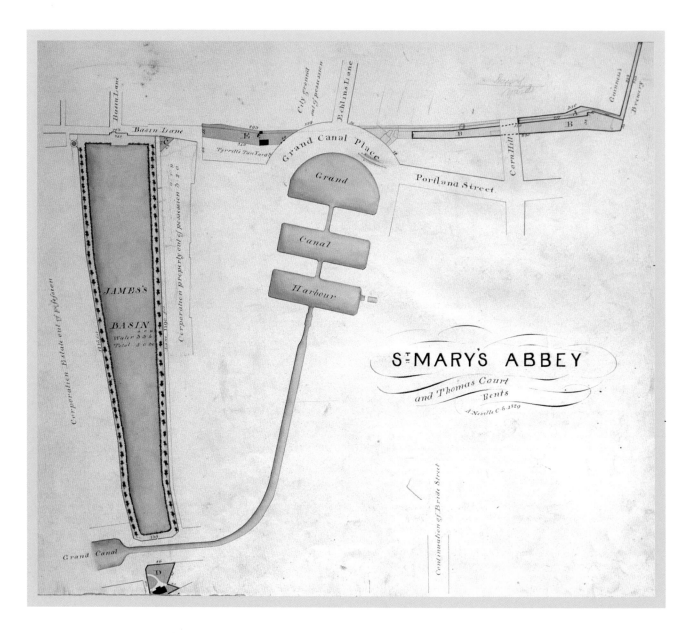

**Grand Canal Harbour
and James's Street Basin.**

A.R. Neville, 1829

Foreword

It gives me great pleasure to welcome you to the history of Dublin's water and drainage. The availability of water and its associated infrastructure is a critical element in the development of any large urban area, and Dublin is no exception. Dublin City Council is proud of the fact that it is responsible for the sourcing, treatment and delivery of this essential service to the citizens of Dublin.

The proximity of water brought many benefits to dwellers in the Middle Ages. In addition to safety and a water supply, a river also provided fertile flood plains for growing crops, a means of transport to get produce to market and the line of defence against invading armies. Two of the greatest fears for people living in urban areas were the fear of fire and of plagues. The presence of water greatly alleviated the former fear but it was not until the latter half of the nineteenth century that the connection between water and diseases such as cholera and typhoid was confirmed. The introduction of a clean water supply and a good drainage system eliminated such plagues in a very short time. It is a credit to people such as Sir John Gray, Dr Cameron and Parke Neville who, amidst strong opposition, pursued relentlessly to a successful conclusion in 1867 the Vartry Water Supply Scheme. The citizens of Dublin owe a great debt of gratitude to these people for the clean wholesome supply, which is still in operation today.

In recent years, the city and the region have greatly expanded and so have the population's expectations. The water and drainage systems are now taken for granted, to such an extent, that people only become aware of the service when it ceases to work. This service can only be achieved through the dedication of a workforce which makes itself available twenty-four hours a day, three hundred and sixty-five days a year. The members of this workforce are the unsung heroes who appear when flooding or broken water mains manifest themselves.

The balance between supply and demand has at times been tenuous, and the impacts of droughts are well documented. The relationship between the development of the water supplies and drainage systems, and the strains exerted by the demands of a growing city, are recorded here. Michael Corcoran, the author of this book, worked in the Council for forty-eight years, twenty-four of which were in the Drainage Division. He brings, as a result, a unique insight to the content of the book. He is also well versed in the history of Dublin and is already the author of *Thro' Streets Broad and Narrow* – the story of Dublin's trams. I congratulate and thank him for all the work and dedication employed in bringing this story to the public forum.

We are grateful that the publication of this book has been generously assisted by LANPAG, as part of the partnership process within Dublin City Council.

While the start of a new century can create trepidation and uncertainty about the future, this history of the water and drainage systems of Dublin helps in renewing our confidence that the capability of those who provide the water services is more than adequate to meet the future needs of the people of Dublin.

John Fitzgerald
Dublin City Manager
Autumn 2005

Introduction

Michael Phillips,
Dublin City Engineer

Dublin City, like most large urban areas, was founded in its present location because of the presence of water. The location of the River Liffey provided a safe haven for Viking boats, the numerous tributaries were a source of drinking water and, in general, a plentiful supply of marine life was available for food.

Throughout the Middle Ages, the city grew and shrunk depending on wars, economic times and plagues. Through all this time, the city still required a water supply, the provision of which had to contend with everyday demands of industry and agriculture. All these issues are dealt with in the book, but they emerge particularly in the latter part of the nineteenth century, with the introduction of the Vartry Water Supply Scheme, which was the foundation stone of the present day water supply system. The Vartry Scheme was followed a short time later by the construction of the Waste Water Treatment Works at Ringsend. The development and expansion of these services in the twentieth century was very much dependent on the availability of finances, and the areas where development was proceeding. The introduction of Development Plans facilitated the strategic planning of water and drainage services. In addition, the introduction of the EU Standards meant that major investment was required in all aspects of sourcing, delivery, collection and treatment. The introduction of modern technology in the early 1990s has had a major impact both on the methods of working, and particularly in conserving and optimising the use of available infrastructure.

Increased environmental standards and climate change have set new challenges and demands which must be accommodated. In addition, the increase in public participation in relation to implementing strategies requires in-depth public consultation in order to alleviate concerns. At the same time, the public perception of water as a plentiful resource will have to change. Rivers, drinking water and wastewater have to be considered as a valuable and limited resource which requires to be managed in a sustainable manner. Industry has already commenced playing its role through the 'Polluter Pays Principle'. Achieving a balance between all the competing needs is critical to obtaining the required sustainable solution.

New standards, such as the Water Framework Directive and the public awareness programmes, are endeavouring to educate and raise the level of awareness. The existing long-term strategies for water and drainage illustrate how seriously Dublin City Council takes its responsibilities in planning to ensure that the present and future generations of Dubliners are adequately provided for where water is concerned.

The story of Dublin water and wastewater systems, like most public sector services, is also about the people who provided the services. These people, at all levels of the city administration, endeavoured to provide a service even when the monetary resources were scarce. In trying to commit the story to print, it was important that not only the technical achievements but also the ethos of the workforce down through the years would be highlighted. In this respect, the Council is very fortunate to have had within its ranks for so long a time, a person of the calibre of Michael Corcoran. Throughout his career in the Drainage Division, he has been a dedicated historian and this is apparent in his management of the records and drawings.

His loyalty to the Council in Dublin is not only illustrated in this book, but within the legacy that remains in the department from which he retired. The production of this book has really been a labour of love for Michael, and Dublin City Council is indebted to him for it.

In writing a book such as this, the challenge is to successfully strike a balance between the necessity to be technical on the one hand and the need to tell a good story on the other. I believe the author has accomplished this task with skill, and I wish you an enjoyable read.

Michael Phillips
City Engineer
Dublin City Council

Acknowledgements

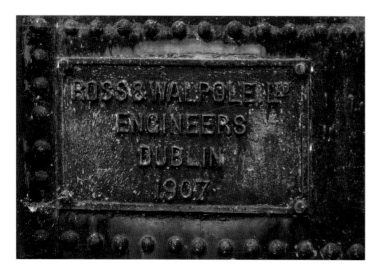

**Nameplate Leeson Street
Valves: Ross & Walpole
Ltd, Engineers, Dublin,
1907/DM.**

Several organisations have opened their archives
and records for the compilation of this history.
I wish to thank them for their help and forbearance,
as follows: Dublin City Library and Archive;
Electricity Supply Board; Fingal County Council;
Howth Estate Archives; the Institution of Engineers
of Ireland; Royal College of Surgeons in Ireland;
South Dublin County Council.

Many individuals, especially my friends and
colleagues, have given generously of their time and
expertise to read this work at various stages of its
compilation. They have supplied much vital
information, filled in gaps, and corrected several
errors. My sincere thanks go to: John Callanan;
Leo Collins; Dermot Coyle; Padraig Doyle; Ned
Fleming; Clifton Flewitt; Captain Christopher
Gaisford-St Lawrence; Con Harrington; Brendan
Keane; Tom Kinirons; Brian McKeown; Tony
Mahon; Gerry O'Connell; Mary O'Doherty; Joe
Rooney; Martin Ryan; Patrick Ryan; Paddy Shine.
Special thanks are due to Kevin O'Donnell who
wrote most of chapter 10 relating to the water
service in the period 1920–1970; and to Larry
Brassil and Matt O'Brien for their in-depth
knowledge of the Borough of Dun Laoghaire.

The illustrations were provided mainly from
the collections of Dublin City Council at the
Engineering Department and at Dublin City Library
and Archive. My special thanks to John Maguire of
Dublin City Council's GIS section, for providing
the fine series of diagrammatic maps for the book.
I am also sincerely grateful to many other kind
people who helped to provide illustrations for the
text, including: John Callanan, the Institution of
Engineers of Ireland; Chris Corlett and Colette
Ellison, Royal Society of Antiquaries of Ireland;

John Fisher, Senior Archivist, Guildhall Library London; Sister Magdalena Frisby and Sister Marie O'Leary, Sisters of Charity Caritas; Bernadette Galloghly, Senior Librarian, Dublin City Public Libraries; Liz Forster, Administrator, Dublin City Gallery, *The Hugh Lane*; Eithne Massey, Senior Librarian, Dublin and Irish Collections; Louise Morgan, Reprographics Section, National Gallery of Ireland; Mary O'Doherty, Librarian and Archivist, Royal College of Surgeons in Ireland; Colette O'Flaherty, Assistant Keeper, National Library of Ireland; and Peter Thursfield, The Irish Times. The historian Edward Chandler kindly permitted us to reproduce photographs from his collection, while the artists Martyn Turner and Terry Willers respectively allowed us to reproduce some of their cartoons.

My sincere thanks go to the Dublin City Librarian, Deirdre Ellis-King, for facilitating the production of this book by her staff, and to Dublin City Archivist Mary Clark and Divisional Librarian Alastair Smeaton for overseeing this process. I am particularly grateful to City Archives staff members, Andrew O'Brien who worked with me in making the final selection of photographs for this book out of the hundreds available to us, and Padraic O'Brien who helped me to track down salient facts as the deadline approached.

This book would never have emerged without the inspiration and support of the Dublin City Engineer, Michael Phillips. Initially intended as a history of drainage, at his suggestion it was widened to encompass water-supply so that we would cover the twin elements which are essential for public health. His commitment and encouragement have been forthcoming at all times and he has been most assiduous in sourcing funding for the project. My heartfelt thanks go to him and to his management team, especially Tim Brick, Tom Leahy, Tim O'Sullivan, Brian Smyth and Battie White. Finally, this work is dedicated to the hundreds of people who have shaped the water and drainage services of Dublin down the ages. Some have left their name and fame as a legacy and these have been recorded in the pages of this history. Others may be unnamed and unknown but these too have left a foundation of good health for us to enjoy today, in the form of good quality water and drainage. This history is a tribute to all of them, past and present, and to their essential but often unsung endeavours.

Michael Corcoran
Dublin
Autumn 2005

Since the mid-nineteenth century, continuous social progress, better health and increasing life expectancy have revolutionised the human condition. In 2005 our lifestyles are still being progressively enhanced by ever expanding knowledge and improved technology. Better funded services and – a matter for optimism – a growing respect for the environment, which affects our lives more than we as yet fully realise, are further positive factors. An absolutely crucial element in all this progress has been the development of the water supply and drainage systems that are indispensable to our continuing good health.

Public health engineering is not new and there are many examples of water supply and drainage systems constructed to serve cities in the ancient world. For example the Palace of Minos at Cnossus, dating from about 2000 BC, possessed a system of drainage, Nineveh had its sewers more than 3,000 years ago, and about 588 BC the Cloaca Maxima of ancient Rome was built. The ancient Roman Empire had many aqueducts: one of the most spectacular features the three-tier, 275m long, 49m high, Pont du Gard, which was part of a 50km aqueduct that supplied water to the city of Nimes.

Despite the foregoing, public health engineering in the modern world has been developed mostly during the last one hundred and fifty years. Considering the highly organised sanitary services of today it is not easy to form a mental picture of the conditions that prevailed in the United Kingdom and Ireland considerably less than two hundred years ago. In 1837 when Queen Victoria came to the throne:

> The householder stored his filth as he liked, or got rid of it as he could. From early in the century water-closets (such as they were) had begun to be used in the better houses; but nearly all these houses had cesspools – commonly cesspools which both leaked and stank; and in towns a cesspool of that sort would generally be in the basement of the house. Nuisances injurious to health abounded everywhere; and against such nuisances, however flagrant, there was no sort of summary jurisdiction (Sir John Simon, *English Sanitary Institutions,* 2nd edn, 1897).

As we will see, the discovery of the link between drinking water from wells contaminated by faecal matter and the occurrence of waterborne diseases in humans was discovered in the mid-nineteenth century. This led to the development in urban areas of piped water systems supplied from uncontaminated sources. As knowledge has grown about the significance for human health of the chemical and bacteriological constituents found in water, the developed world has devised treatment processes to remove harmful contaminants. Nowadays mains water is habitually filtered and sterilised to ensure that harmful bacteria are eliminated. Water is managed on a catchment basis and forward planning by the larger water authorities has practically eliminated the possibility of source or quality failure. The EU in its Drinking Water Directive has set down standards to be observed throughout the Union.

Modern sanitation may be said to have originated with the development of main piped water supply, which made practicable for the first time the installation of the water-closet (WC). This invention, although not new, was previously out of the question for most people because of the large quantities of water required for its operation. The WC is one of the most important inventions in the history of modern civilisation because it is directly responsible for the reduction of the death rate due to water-borne diseases, such as typhoid, to a small fraction of what it used to be.

The contrast between the developed and the undeveloped world is stark. Water is essential for life yet many millions of people around the world face water shortages. Drought regularly afflicts some of the world's poorest countries, while millions of children die every year from waterborne diseases.

In our relatively comfortable world, public services, especially those that comprise the most fundamental and hidden infrastructure, are taken for granted by the vast majority of people. Getting fresh water, one of the elements essential to our very existence, by simply turning on a tap is so ordinary as to never cost us a thought. And the equally straightforward dispatch of health-threatening wastewater to the drainage system is just one more undemanding action in our daily lives.

Unthinking acceptance makes us oblivious to the ingenuity, skills and commitment of the pioneers who thought out and laid down vital but concealed public services. Always evolving, their work continues today, as it will in the future. As to the past, even eminent historians admit their ignorance of those who established and developed these essential services. This is a matter of some regret because those intrepid innovators are clearly worthy of a most honourable place in history.

Although the internet has made information more widely and easily accessible, the story of our public services – particularly the less glamorous ones – is still somewhat obscure. This is partly due to the fact that public works and their accompanying procedures in times past were seen as so mundane that they attracted minimal interest. People who engaged in public works in those times tended not to record in permanent form facts and events that seemed insignificant at the time they occurred – indeed to some extent this remains true to this very day. Unfortunately when those people retired or changed careers, the record of how work was organised and carried out during a particular period disappeared with them.

Until the significance of archival material came to be appreciated, it was considered tidy and efficient to dispose of old paperwork. Irish people are said to have been more reluctant than other races in the past to keep written records. There was also the catastrophic loss of irreplaceable records in the devastation of the Custom House in 1921 and the Four Courts in 1922. Other less well-known disasters occurred as well, such as the destruction in 1923 of the *Freeman's Journal* offices, which housed a large photographic archive.

In the Republic of Ireland, the exclusion of technology from our written history and culture further attenuated the volume of surviving material. Thanks to the work of archaeologists and historians, information about our earliest water service is reasonably accessible. However, events that took place after the onset of the Industrial Revolution around the mid-eighteenth century have attracted far less attention. Before today's widespread and ever growing interest in social and local history began, the story of drainage and wastewater – a much less attractive subject than water supply – was to be found only in widely dispersed papers, reports and drawings.

In practice, water and drainage systems are totally interdependent. Taking information from wide variety of sources, what follows is an attempt to outline the history of these services without which modern society simply could not function. The material assembled here attempts to tell, in chronological sequence, the story of Dublin's water supply and drainage services. In doing so it also attempts to set against a wider historical background the many individual schemes undertaken in the city over the past 300 years.

A rarely acknowledged fact is that no public service can be looked at in isolation. Every utility and public service that underpins modern living is complementary to all the others and therefore all individual services appear at various junctures throughout this history. Hopefully, this introduction to Dublin's most fundamental utilities will lead to a wider appreciation of civic and social progress. The evolution and geography of the various networks and installations described here can be readily divided into several clearly defined periods and areas. Different social and economic conditions prevailed in these periods and places during which the water and drainage services evolved, and looking at how each of them developed in contemporary conditions can help to form an overview of local history.

A corollary to the complementary nature of the various public services is their necessary inattention to administrative boundaries. It is not possible to describe the Dublin city water supply and drainage networks without looking at those of the adjoining local authorities that are inextricably connected with those of the city. The most important instance is that of Dun Laoghaire. Dun Laoghaire is often regarded as simply another Dublin suburb and this is unfortunate because the former borough, now part of the larger Dun Laoghaire-Rathdown County Council, had a population of some 50,000 shortly after its establishment in 1930, making it the third biggest town in the then Irish Free State. Because its water and drainage services are closely connected to those of Dublin, neither they – nor services in the adjoining areas of Fingal, South Dublin, Kildare and Wicklow – can be omitted from this book.

Reading what follows should also help to relegate the myths surrounding 'the rare old times' and 'the good old days' to an ignoble chapter of shame where they properly belong. The vast majority of people from the generations that lived in the earlier years of this narrative were cruelly repressed by ignorance, poverty and perverse social structures. As time passed, their social and economic conditions became less oppressive but progress was slow; every advance was but grudgingly conceded by those who wielded power. Improving health and life expectancy are important themes in this book, as are social and financial betterment. Looking back through these pages at the miseries suffered until comparatively recent times by our forebears will surely make us realise that we are lucky to live in an age that, for most people, is more comfortable than at any other time in human history.

Irish history is conspicuously selective in the people and pursuits privileged to populate its pages. Most history books give the impression that positive engineering outcomes such as water supply and drainage happened naturally. Through several generations the ingenuity and labour of engineers, scientists, administrators, craftsmen and general workers have created and improved our essential infrastructure. But historians have to a large extent been unmindful of them or have ignored them. This is regrettable, because the contributions of these disregarded individuals to the benefit and well-being of every citizen were monumental, and we owe them an incalculable debt. Dubliners owe more to Sir John Gray, Sir Charles Cameron and Parke Neville than to James Joyce, Sean O'Casey or Samuel Beckett! This volume endeavours to start making long-delayed amends.

Brief biographical notes on some of the leading figures in the story of Dublin's water and drainage systems are set out in this narrative. There is of course a host of individuals whose mundane daily diligence built, operated and maintained the systems. A few of them are named as representative of their many colleagues whose identities are lost to history. Dean Swift, within whose neighbourhood so many of these people lived and worked, described them presciently when he wrote:

> Men who live and die without a name
> Are the chief heroes in the sacred list of fame.

PROTOCOLS

Because both technical and general readers will come upon this text, the author has included enough engineering detail to satisfy the former while hopefully not alienating the latter. Important technical terms, which can be off-putting for the general reader, are defined when they first appear.

One of the fundamentals that should be explained at the outset is Ordnance Datum (OD). When the original Ordnance Survey was completed in the late 1830s all levels in Ireland were related to Poolbeg Datum. This referred to the low water level of an ordinary spring tide recorded at the Poolbeg lighthouse on 8 April 1837. Known as Poolbeg Datum (PbD), this was superseded in 1970 by Malin Head Datum (MHD).

Some further simple protocols are observed in this work. When a particular theme is followed through to its conclusion, a chronological step backwards is sometimes necessary to introduce the next topic. All the major schemes, their outstanding features and associated networks, are described. That effective systems must evolve methodically is obvious, but this did not always happen. This was especially so when planning, once regarded with deep suspicion, was either ignored or practised capriciously. Hence a few inconsistencies!

Before the change to the metric system in the 1970s, most drawings, documents and construction works were measured in imperial units. Although imperial usage has now all but ceased, old drawings and reports will always contain imperial dimensions and acquaintance with them is therefore essential for anybody reading engineering or architectural history. For the years up to 1972, when the metric system was introduced in the Irish Republic, imperial measurements are quoted, with some metric equivalents given for easy reference. Metric dimensions are quoted for work carried out from 1972 onwards. It should be noted that millimetres rather than centimetres are quoted, in accordance with the ISO standards laid down in the 1970s.

Again for easy reference a few equivalents are quoted in this and the following paragraphs. An inch is equal to 25.4 millimetres; a foot (12 inches or 12") equals 304.8 millimetres. A metre contains 39.37 inches or 3.28 feet. A mile is the equivalent of 1,609 metres, a kilometre being 0.621 of a mile. An acre is 0.4046 of a hectare, which contains 2.47 acres. Chains and chainages are words encountered in old reports and drawings. Sixty-six feet long, the chain was used by land surveyors and engineers as an instrument and unit of measurement, and the term chainage still describes lengths or distances from an established point.

It should be borne in mind that the dimensions of the metric units that replaced imperial ones are not exactly the same – the 9-inch (9") diameter pipe, for example, was followed by a 225mm rather than a 229mm unit. The metric dimensions quoted in this document therefore are for standard units: the 4-inch (4") pipe is now 100mm, the 6-inch (6") is 150mm, and the 12-inch (12"), or one foot, is 300mm.

Costs and prices are quoted in the currency used at the time of the event described. It is worth remembering that at least four types of currency were used over the period covered in this work. The figures given for earlier projects bear little comparison with those in force at the time of writing, because modern costs and wages are totally different to those that prevailed fifty, or a hundred or more years ago.

An Irish pound, thirteen of which equalled twelve English ones, existed until 1826 when the two currencies were amalgamated. Curiously Dublin Corporation persisted with the old system in its accounting for another two years. The 1826 financial parity continued after the establishment of the Irish Free State and the introduction of distinctive Irish notes and coins in 1928. It also lasted through the change to decimal currency in 1971 and survived until the Irish pound was floated independently in 1979. To allow for ready if anachronistic comparisons, pre-1971 prices, wages etc in this history are quoted in pounds (£), shillings (s) and pence (d), the Euro equivalent following in brackets.

To say that what happens today will be history tomorrow is a cliché. So, to make the Dublin water supply and drainage narrative as complete as possible, developments taking place or planned at the time of writing are included in these pages.

THE PODDLE

The origins of Dublin as the Gaelic Ath Cliath and
the Viking Dyflynn or Dubh Linn are so well
recorded as not to need any detailed description
here. The Liffey was tidal as far inland as what is
now Islandbridge, so the Poddle was an important
but suspect source of fresh water for the early
settlers – both rivers were used for waste disposal.
Because the Romans never established colonies
here, nothing even remotely like their sophisticated
water supply or drainage systems was seen in
Ireland before the arrival of the Normans around
1170. At that period the embryonic city of Dublin
lay west of the Poddle and was centred on the area
around High Street.

Dublin received its first charter from Henry II
in 1172 and was still a small city in the sixteenth
century, only 46 acres in extent and surrounded by
a wall with 45 towers. The maximum population
within that wall has been calculated at 8,000, or 174
persons per acre. This was two and a half times the
population density of the late nineteenth century,
when Dublin's overcrowding and slum problems
were among the worst in the world, the city being
described at that time as the Calcutta of Europe.

The growing city became better regulated once
the Normans, whose concepts of civic management
and amenities were a considerable improvement on
what had gone before, became established. One of
their early achievements was the provision of a
public water supply that was clean by the standards
of the time.

Although the subject of much conjecture there
is some evidence that a pre-Poddle water supply
was based on Coleman's Brook. This watercourse,
part natural and part artificial, flowed parallel
to the Liffey from a River Camac millrace.
It entered the Liffey at what is now Merchant's
Quay and is said to have served Viking Dublin.
Part of the Coleman's Brook culvert was reconstructed in 1990.

Writing in the journal of the Kilkenny Archaeological Society (5th S, Vol. 1, 1890–1891) Henry
F. Berry MA confirmed that prior to the mid-
thirteenth century Dublin's water was in great part
supplied by the Poddle. This river was described
as rising from a spring in the neighbourhood of
Tymon, County Dublin, and flowing through
Kimmage and Harold's Cross to the Liberties. Its
actual source is where the Tallaght Hospital now
stands and it is known as the Tymon Stream down

FUN.—*August 18, 1866.*

DEATH'S DISPENSARY.

OPEN TO THE POOR, GRATIS, BY PERMISSION OF THE PARISH.

Contaminated water supplies. *Innocent children and unsuspecting adults drink from a pump overseen by Death – an allegory reflecting poor quality water in early European cities.*

to the confluence with the City Watercourse and thereafter as the Poddle.

In a writ issued on 29 April 1244 Maurice Fitzgerald, Lord Justiciar of Ireland, commanded the Sheriff of Dublin, with the advice of the mayor and citizens, to appoint without delay twelve freemen as jurors or inquisitors. Their purpose was to identify the place at which water could most conveniently be taken from the Poddle and conducted to the city at the cost of the citizens, who had undertaken to pay for the work. Any damage that might be caused by the works was to be notified to the justiciar and repaired at the king's expense. Finally anybody who opposed the work was to be suppressed by force and attached to appear before the justiciar at the next assizes.

An agreement was made with the Priory of St Thomas, which owned a weir on the River Dodder at Balrothery. This weir raised the river level high enough to permit its diversion by a canal to the head of the Poddle. The quantity to be drawn off was limited to that which could pass through the axle ope of a wagon and the monetary consideration was five marks. This must have been one of the earliest examples of a river diversion scheme. Development since the 1970s has all but obliterated

this canal, but the Balrothery Weir was restored in the 1980s and survives in good condition after nine centuries of service.

At the Tongue Field, north of the present Sundrive Road, the flow was divided by a cutwater called the Stone Boat, two thirds of the volume going via the present Harold's Cross, Blackpitts, Patrick Street and Dublin Castle route to the Liffey. This was known as the Earl of Meath's Watercourse and in former times it supplied the manors of Thomas Court and Donore, also called the Liberties. In time this course became increasingly contaminated with waste and sewage, making it unfit as a source of domestic water.

In *The Rivers of Dublin* (Dublin Corporation, 1991) C. L. Sweeney records that the Poddle has fifteen branches and diversions, as well as a plethora of names by which parts of it have been known over the centuries. It also served more than fifty mills and other commercial enterprises, which inevitably led to pollution.

THE CITY WATERCOURSE

The one-third portion of the Poddle water diverted at the Tongue Field went into a channel known as the City Watercourse. It flowed at a higher level than the Earl of Meath's Watercourse, via the present Rutland Avenue and Dolphin's Barn Fire Station, under the Grand Canal (from 1756) and on through Dolphin's Barn to James's Street. A cistern or basin, which in more modern times would be called a reservoir, was constructed near James's Street. This cistern served the more elevated parts of the city and it is recorded that in 1660 and again in 1671 lead mains were laid from it and other works were carried out to improve and extend the public water supply.

Work on the 1244 scheme appears to have been carried out expeditiously because instructions were issued on 18 November 1245 to have a supply laid on to the new King's Hall at Dublin Castle. A length of lead pipe excavated in Castle Street in 1787 may have been part of this conduit laid down more than 500 years earlier by order of Henry III.

It took nearly ten years to supply the majority of the citizens from the reservoir or basin that contained the supply for the city. The earliest distribution system consisted of open channels along the sides of Thomas Street and High Street. People wealthy enough or lucky enough to enjoy their own individual supply were served by a very restricted link known as a quill – Dublin was one of many cities that used the size of various types of quills to measure domestic connections in the early days of their public water systems. The water from the quills was at best an intermittent trickle. The conduit, a more copious if less convenient source of supply for the majority of the population, was located in High Street near the present Synod Hall (now Dublinia).

During his mayoralty in 1308 the munificent John le Decer erected at his own expense a marble cistern in the Cornmarket. Le Decer, who was noted for his generosity to the church, charity to the poor and contributions to civic improvement, also built a bridge over the Liffey.

A far less pleasant occurrence in the fourteenth century was the arrival of the Black Death, a highly contagious and fatal plague that ravaged Europe and struck Dublin in 1348. The most virulent form of a disease that visited Dublin several times between the late eleventh and early seventeenth centuries, the Black Death was also known as the plague or the pestilence. It was transmitted from rats by fleas and killed an estimated 14,000 of the Dublin area's population between August 1348 and January 1349. The figure quoted here does not, however, accord with estimates of population for the period and is therefore open to question. While drugs and medicines unknown at the time could probably have saved lives, a pure water supply and effective drainage would certainly have been major factors in at least curtailing the spread of the Black Death and other pestilences.

Under the thirteenth century agreement made with the Priory of St Thomas a down payment of five marks and an annual rent of one mark were to

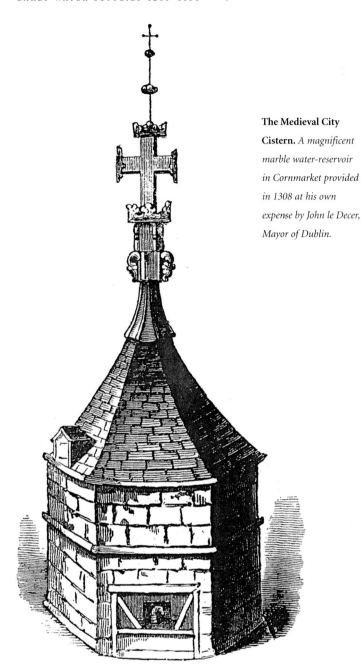

The Medieval City Cistern. *A magnificent marble water-reservoir in Cornmarket provided in 1308 at his own expense by John le Decer, Mayor of Dublin.*

be paid to the monks. In 1259 an inquiry found that the city had drawn twice its allocation of water but failed to pay any rent. The bills for improvements carried out on the Balrothery weir in 1555 also remained unpaid seven years later. In the early nineteenth century Andrew Coffey, the then waterworks superintendent, reconstructed the weir, and the present sluice gates and bypass channels date from that time. Following Hurricane Charlie in August

The Tongue. *Also known as the Stone Boat, this was built in 1555 and divided the river Poddle from the City Watercourse*

1986 major repairs were again made to the weir and this very historic structure remains as a link with the distant beginnings of our water supply.

Reverting to 1555, in that year a structure called the Tongue was built at the division of the Poddle waters, just downstream from the present Sundrive Road. A concrete successor to the first Tongue, and also known as the Stone Boat, it still divides the stream proportionately. In deference to the presence of the Tongue, a neighbouring licensed premises has adopted The Stone Boat as its public title.

Pipes made of lead were first used to distribute the water in the thirteenth century, and for a long time afterwards lead was the only material employed for this purpose. As late as 1671 there is a record of expenditure on such pipes. However, wooden pipes – hollowed out tree trunks, usually of oak, elm or fir – were in almost universal use by the middle of the eighteenth century. The elm pipes came from trees at Oxmantown, a finite source later supplanted by purchases from further afield, as far away as Scandinavia. Ideally wooden pipes were not less than 12 inches (304mm) in diameter and came in lengths of between 16 and 20 feet (4.8–6m).

During its primacy in supplying water to Dublin

the City Watercourse and its extension into the city were blocked from time to time. According to Hollinshed's Chronicles, in 1534 the followers of Silken Thomas 'cut the pipes of the conduits whereby [the city] should be destitute of water'. In 1597 the Talbot family of Templeogue stopped the supply in pursuance of a dispute with the owners of mills that were powered by the river. And during the Cromwellian occupation of Dublin in 1649 Royalists led by the Marquis of Ormond again blocked the Poddle. The Parliamentary forces under the command of Colonel Jones were thus deprived both of drinking water and power for their corn mills.

Various regulations were introduced over the years to improve and ensure the quality of the water. Allowing animals to graze beside the open watercourses, dumping of any sort and washing of clothes were among the numerous proscribed malpractices. In the case of offending animal owners, fines could be imposed at a fixed rate per beast for every day the nuisance continued. Maintaining an uncontaminated supply relied heavily on the goodwill and common sense of the citizens, but dealing with stupid, irresponsible or malevolent individuals was always a problem – and obviously it would have been impossible to police the City Watercourse constantly.

A detailed account of the Poddle system was given in a paper entitled 'The Inception of the Dodder Water Supply', read to the Old Dublin Society on 14 January 1952 by V. Jackson MICEI. It was published in the *Dublin Historical Record* (Vol. XV, No. 2).

THE BRADOGUE

The earliest settlements on the north side of the Liffey were probably on the high ground around Stoneybatter and Arbour Hill. Later, the Christian-ised Norse inhabitants of Dublin are believed to have been forced by the occupying Normans to move across the Liffey to this area. Originally Ath Cliath, it later became known as Oxmantown. The district relied for fresh water on the Bradogue stream which, rising out of springs in Cabra and Grangegorman, flowed east and south to join the Liffey at what is now Upper Ormond Quay. The Bradogue, with its associated streams and branches, is comprehensively described by C. L. Sweeney in *The Rivers of Dublin*. A slab or stone (steyn) along the river's course was known as Bradogue Steyn, corrupted into English as Broadstone.

Providing an acceptable water supply for this area did not become urgent until the late seventeenth century. Around 1670 a water main was laid on the old bridge across the Liffey to give a Poddle supply to the north side, supplementing what came from the Bradogue and local springs. All of the Bradogue watercourses and branches became part of the foul drainage network in the nineteenth century.

DAWN OF THE MODERN ERA

Modern Dublin began to take shape during the 1660s, with massive development following in the course of the succeeding century. Great new streets and squares were built south of the Liffey and the previously underdeveloped north side also started to expand. Providing a water supply (and later, drainage) for the growing city posed problems that have taxed the resources of Dublin Corporation and its successor, Dublin City Council, continuously ever since.

Following the restoration of the monarchy in 1660, James Butler, twelfth Earl and first Duke of Ormond (1610–1688), returned as viceroy and attended to Dublin's most pressing needs after twenty years of unrest and Cromwellian stagnation. Water was a priority and in 1663 a new code of regulations came into force. This set out the terms and conditions of supply together with rates and charges – and transgressors could expect to have their supplies cut off.

The flow in the Poddle and the City Watercourse fluctuated seasonally and was also adversely affected by mill owners and others who drew off water without considering the rights of others. To overcome abuses and provide for increasing demand, a larger city basin was constructed in 1670. There was also, in 1681, an early, crude and unsuccessful

Plan showing growth of Dublin 1200–2003.

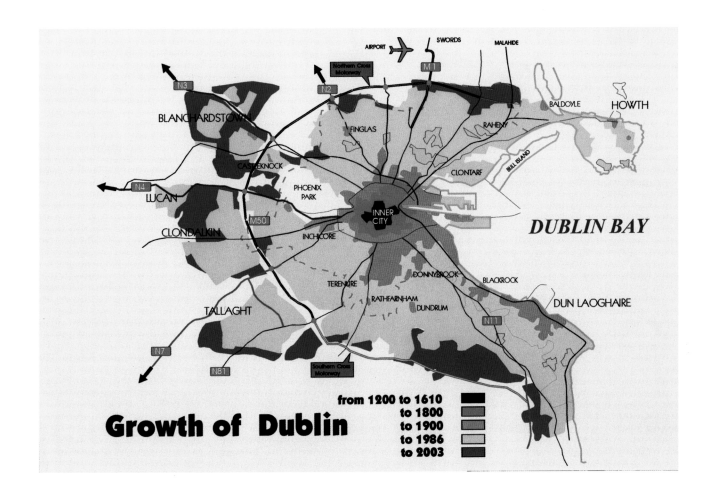

Growth of Dublin

from 1200 to 1610
to 1800
to 1900
to 1986
to 2003

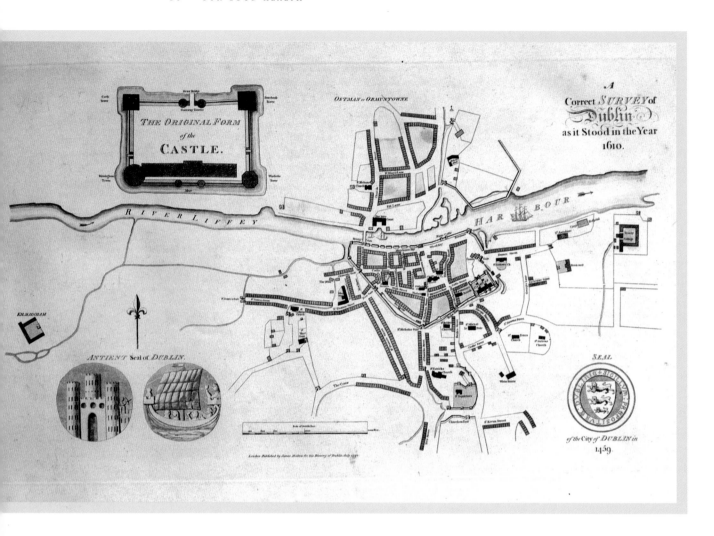

The earliest map of Dublin. *Produced by John Speed in 1610, this was published in a revised edition by James Malton during the 1790s.*

instance of a public-private partnership when the operation of the system and the collection of revenue were leased out.

During the fifteen years on either side of 1700 Dublin experienced developments of far reaching importance. The city began to cultivate a distinct industrial base, much of it following the arrival of the Huguenots in 1685. In the same year the city saw what was arguably its first newspaper (*The Dublin News Letter*). In the 1680s the Royal Hospital at Kilmainham became the precursor of the many splendid buildings that would earn great distinction for Dublin during the next 150 years. Two further developments that would confer huge future benefits on the city were the establishment, in 1708, of the Ballast Board (distant ancestor of the Dublin

Port Company) and the beginning of land reclamation that would eventually create the North and South Lotts.

Dublin Corporation, or City Assembly as the ruling municipal body was known until the 1840s, delegated various functions to commissions or boards. Thus water was the responsibility of the Pipe Water Establishment (later a commission), which also oversaw paving and other functions. Ultimate authority and responsibility of course remained with Dublin Corporation.

Industrial pollution became a serious problem as early as 1718, when people complained that the public water supply was unfit. The cause was traced to effluents from a tucking mill and a paper mill on the Poddle. When challenged, the mill owners

adopted a hostile attitude, arguing that the corporation had no powers to prevent the discharges. When
this indeed turned out to be the legal situation, the
Irish Parliament in 1719 enacted legislation 'for
cleaning and repairing the watercourse from the
River Dodder to the city of Dublin, and to prevent
the diverting and corrupting the Water therein'.
With the city's rights to the watercourse reaffirmed,
the corporation was enabled to proceed against
the polluters.

In 1682 the population of Dublin was recorded
as 58,000 by Sir William Petty; other sources of
the period put it at 60,000, a figure that doubled
to 120,000 by 1722. It was also estimated that the
number of inhabited houses grew by 4,000 between
1711 and 1728. However, in the experience of this
writer, population numbers should be treated with
some caution. Conflicting estimates can be produced
by selective extrapolation from accurate statistics,
right up to the present day. Apart from human
error, differences can arise because of the criteria
adopted for various sets of statistics. Other factors
that affect estimates include what individual com-
pilers regarded as the city boundaries at the time.

The new basin, also called the Great Cistern, was at
a higher level than its predecessor and was therefore
capable of providing a greater volume of water at
increased pressure. Located on the site of the
present Basin Street flats and school it extended
from Brandon Terrace on the south to Basin Street
Lower on its north end. From the basin, a lead main
10 inches in diameter was laid into James's Street,
and three mains of 6 inches diameter extended into
the city to distribute water to upwards of 90 streets.
The outstanding architect Colonel Thomas Burgh
(1670–1730) was an adviser on the new basin project.

While the old basin at St James's Gate had a
meagre storage capacity and excess water was
wasted, its 1721 successor represented a major step
forward in water conservation. The city's first real
impounding reservoir, its storage capacity was
500,000 hogsheads of water – which represented up
to three months' supply. There were approximately
50 gallons in a hogshead, making the volume of the
basin around 25 million gallons. In the early nineteenth century the basin was described as being
1,210 feet (369 metres) long, its width varying from
225 to 250 feet (68–76 metres).

**Part of the City
Watercourse.**
*Running from Dolphin's
Barn to the City Basin,
this area was known as
'The Back of the Pipes'.*

Delphins Barn Lane

Water Course from Dolphin's Barn to Mr Taaffe's Ground 1565 feet

Back Water Course

THE CITY BASIN

As the city grew the thirteenth century basin
became ever less capable of supplying water and by
the early eighteenth century it also needed extensive
repairs. In 1721 the corporation constructed a new
basin (Bason in the spelling of the time) or
reservoir at James's Street. The City Watercourse,
suitably raised by embankments and masonry, was
diverted into this new reservoir. This arrangement
led to the area extending from Dolphin's Barn up
to the present Grand Canal becoming known as
'The Back of the Pipes'.

In his archaeological report on the
basin (August 2002) Patrick Ryan of the city
archaeologist's department records that the
project so exhausted the civic finances that the
corporation had to borrow £1,000 at 6% interest to
pay for the work. Landscaped with gravel walks and
trees, the basin became an attractive area to visit
and enjoy, and was also a venue for concerts and
fireworks displays.

Some householders sank wells as a source of
water, but these were liable to pollution leaching
from the numerous cesspools that were so nauseating
a feature of eighteenth-century and nineteenth-
century urban life. The barrels and other receptacles
widely used to gather rainwater for domestic use

posed a much reduced health hazard in comparison to the wells. Other users depended on enterprising private suppliers, who delivered to their customers' storage facilities from barrels.

With a constantly growing number of water users in the expanding city, the corporation's two water rent collectors became very overworked. Water revenue was a most important source of municipal finance and a third collector was therefore appointed in 1724. A vigorous campaign to collect arrears was undertaken and water charges now became due every six months instead of yearly.

In 1735 the architect Richard Cassells in his 'Essay towards supplying the City of Dublin with Water' estimated that 6,507 out of a total of 9,789 premises, or more than 66 per cent, benefited from a domestic water supply. Colonel Thomas Burgh was also interested in the subject of water, and was the author of an essay carrying the same title as that produced by Cassells.

Unscrupulous privateers outside the city habitually treated the City Watercourse as their own private property. A pamphlet in the Library of Trinity College, written in 1735 by Richard Cassells, tells of an examination carried out on the watercourse that found the channel to be badly choked with weeds. There was seepage through the banks and in some places above Dolphin's Barn the banks had been breached and the openings stopped with sods. These openings were effectively sluices that could be removed in summer so that water would run in small channels through the adjoining fields for irrigation or other purposes.

A serious threat to the Poddle water supply occurred in 1739 in repugnant circumstances. In August of the previous year, a particularly brutal and gratuitous murder was committed by Lord Henry Barry of Santry, for which he was tried in April 1739 and condemned to death. His uncle, Sir Compton Domville of Templeogue, through whose land the City Watercourse flowed, threatened to cut off the water supply if his nephew was executed. Unsurprisingly Barry was reprieved, emigrated and was re-granted his estates in 1741.

COPING WITH INCREASING DEMAND

Over a period of more than fifty years after 1721, various works were carried out to improve the supply from the City Watercourse and the City Basin. By 1735 the Poddle supply was woefully inadequate for the needs of the citizens. Writing in 1829 Andrew Coffey recorded that several essays had been published in 1735 about mitigating the constantly deteriorating state of affairs in that year. One of the essayists was James Scanlan, who had acquired considerable experience of waterworks abroad and whose ideas appealed to the authorities in Dublin. The result was his appointment in 1739 as waterworks engineer.

It should be remembered that in those times the title 'engineer' did not mean that the bearer had any professional qualification. In former times the appellation of engineer loosely described anybody who designed, built or made complicated structures such as bridges or machinery, including pumps and locomotives. From the mid-eighteenth century onwards the title became more strictly defined, with institutes and universities awarding degrees. The Institution of Engineers of Ireland (IEI) was founded in 1835. The title 'engineer' is also applied to the highly qualified fitters and mechanics that build and maintain extremely complicated machines and other equipment.

James Scanlan made several improvements to the water supply from the City Basin and paid particular attention to the needs of the growing north side of the city. In accordance with his programme the corporation acquired, for £3,500, the mills and weirs at Islandbridge and by 1745 a supplementary supply was obtained from the Liffey at that location. This Islandbridge supply was pumped up by a water wheel, described as a 'powerful water engine', which delivered the water through two 6-inch wooden mains to the north side of the city.

A crisis occurred in 1788 when the bridge over the Liffey at Islandbridge collapsed, severing the two 6-inch mains. Timber staging was quickly erected however, enabling the supply to be reinstated

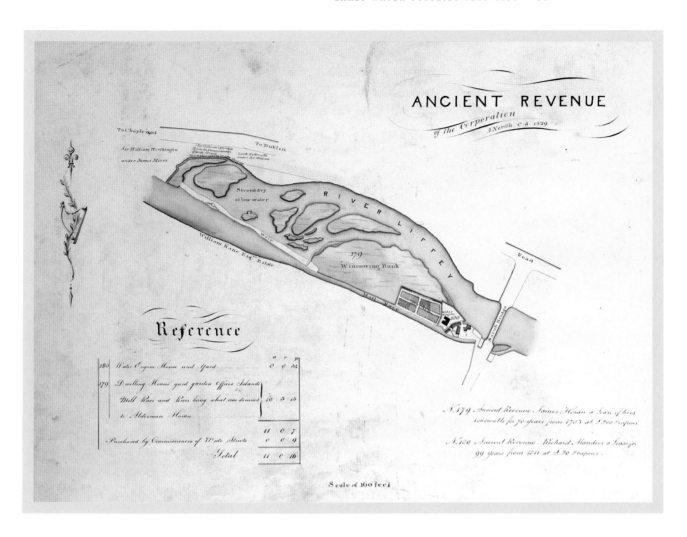

without undue delay. When the water engine at Islandbridge wore out, it was not repaired or replaced, but the Pipe Water Establishment did not immediately abandon Islandbridge as a supplementary source of water.

Despite the ingenuity of Scanlan and others who tried to satisfy the city's growing demands, the Poddle supply became ever more hopelessly inadequate. Even after the Islandbridge source became operational the overall quantity of available water was still insufficient, being required to service some 185 streets. Even though the increasingly archaic system was incapable of further expansion the unsatisfactory situation continued to deteriorate for another forty years.

During those four decades of severe water

shortage the authorities had to contend with enterprising citizens who illegally drew off water for onward sale. Known as hucksters, they went to considerable lengths to evade detection and protect their business. Hugh McFarran of Patrickswell Lane (today's Nassau Street) was a huckster whose exploits were reported in the *Dublin News Letter* of 24–28th November 1741. On being confronted by civic dignitaries and waterworks officials, he produced a firearm and attempted to shoot the lord mayor. A struggle ensued during which McFarran brandished a knife with which he tried to stab the mayor. The *Dublin News Letter* recorded, however, that he was overpowered, 'tied with a rope and sent to Newgate where he now remains to receive the punishment due to such offenders'.

Map of Islandbridge.

A powerful water-wheel or engine was located here on the river Liffey and delivered water supplies to the north side of Dublin.

As the scarcity of water became ever more critical, various scams were perpetrated by those who were always ready to rip off the community at large. In 1775 there were well-founded suspicions of collusion between waterworks turncocks and property owners or occupiers acting as hucksters. The turncocks, who were responsible for opening and shutting valves, were believed to have been leaving their implements or keys in the premises of hucksters overnight, facilitating the manipulation of valves and the illegal extraction of water. The water thus diverted went into tanks from which it was sold on to others who had no supply of their own. Following investigations, the use of the tanks was banned and the turncocks were ordered to retain personal possession of their keys at all times.

Reports that survive from the period also tell of exasperated people behaving in a manner akin to that displayed in modern road rage scenarios. On 16 May 1775, during a bitter dispute about water rights – which was not resolved until 1784 – Pipe Water Establishment employees arrived to disconnect supplies from what is now St James's Gate Brewery. An infuriated Arthur Guinness is said to have snatched a pickaxe from a member of the work gang and directed some very colourful language at George Gee, the pipe water director. The sheriff was called and had to warn an angry brewery worker that he was in danger of spending the night in the notorious Newgate Gaol if he did not moderate his behaviour.

As technology improved and the demand for water connections increased, it later – much later – became a legal requirement to have a storage cistern and ballcock as part of every plumbing installation. In the meantime many of those who resided in Dublin's splendid eighteenth-century houses derived some benefit from a municipal piped water supply, albeit this was available only at ground floor or basement level. Pressure was negligible, the supply was erratic and the water was anything but pure by modern standards. Some houses had the wells (already referred to) and survivors of some of these ancient wells, long since back-filled or slabbed over, are still discovered occasionally in the course of building work, usually at the rear of Georgian houses.

While hanging out washing in Cranmer Lane (off Haddington Road) in the year 2000, a woman lost her footing and fell. She found on recovering herself that the footpath beneath her clothes line had disappeared into the ground. When the city drainage division was summoned to investigate the large and mysterious hole, the area engineer and local routemen found it to be about 2.79m (nine feet) deep and three quarters full of very clear water. The missing stones from the footpath were clearly visible at the bottom of the well, which was obviously much deeper than the local drainage network. Further research established that many of these wells had continued to supply horses and other animals with water long after better sources became available for their human owners.

The governing elite of the eighteenth century, which often inflicted great cruelties on the poor and uneducated lower classes, was sometimes responsible for acts of considerable kindness. Charles Duke of Rutland, who was lord lieutenant from 1784 to 1787, had at least two monumental fountains erected in Dublin to provide water for the poorer denizens of a prosperous city. One of these fountains was at the front of the Royal (later Collins) Barracks in what is now Benburb Street. This fountain, which bears the date 1785, was later removed to a location within the military complex. At the time of writing the intention is that it will be returned to its original site as part of the National Museum's enhancement plans for Collins Barracks.

Opposite the front of the National Gallery in Merrion Square West is the second Rutland fountain, erected in 1791 and restored in 1975 as a contribution to the celebration of Architectural Heritage Year. It retains the two lions' heads from the mouths of which the water flowed. The Rutland fountains were but examples – certainly the most extravagant – of communal water supply programmes carried out at different periods over the course of the following century and a half (see further references to these in Chapter 4).

Another imposing structure is the fountain that stands near the junction of James's Street and Steeven's Lane. Bearing the date 1790, this obelisk, which was at one time the terminus of a cross-town tram service from Fairview, was restored in 1988 as part of city's millennium celebrations.

CANAL WATER – IRON PIPES

Construction of the Grand Canal, which Dublin Corporation anticipated would be a reliable and plentiful source of water, began in 1756. The city entered into a contract with the Grand Canal Company in 1765 to purchase 'an ample supply of water', which was in fact surplus water conveyed from the country. It was expected that this water would be available within a year but a succession of incidents delayed the opening of the canal, thus postponing the new supply.

Water from the Grand Canal first flowed into the City Basin in August 1777. It did not however become available to the public until the following year. In the meantime the corporation was empowered by an Act of 1775 to levy a water rate. Ten per cent of its pipe water rents were to be paid to the Grand Canal Company. Frequent disputes arose around this issue, particularly in relation to late payments, and continued for nearly thirty years.

In 1776 it was decided to appoint a waterworks superintendent who would have full control of the system and all staff. The first incumbent was William Mylne, an engineer, who was responsible for the vast amount of work carried out during a period of major urban development. Mylne, who was highly regarded, was paid a salary of £140 per annum and had a house 'at the City expense'. He resigned in 1786 but was persuaded to return to work and remained in the service until his death in 1790. A tablet in St Catherine's church in Thomas Street bears the following inscription:

> To the Memory of William Mylne, Architect and Engineer from Edinburg, who died aged 56 years, March 1790, and whose remains are laid in the Church-yard adjoining. This Tablet was placed by his Brother Robert Mylne of London, to inform Posterity of the Uncommon Zeal, Integrity and Skill, with which he

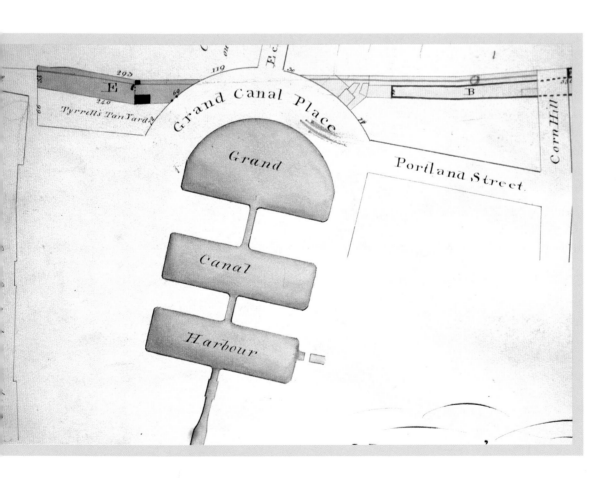

The Grand Canal Harbour. *This supplemented Dublin City's water-supply from 1778 onwards, providing fresh water sourced from the countryside.*

formed, enlarged, and established on a Perfect System
the Water-Works of Dublin.

St Catherine's was extensively refurbished in 2000.

James Johnston, who took over the post of
waterworks superintendent in 1790, was succeeded
in 1804 by the long-serving and forceful Andrew
Coffey, whose annual salary was £250 in 1805.
Coffey (1748–1832), first employed in the waterworks in 1774, was the father of Aeneas Coffey who
achieved fame as a distillery engineer.

Patrick Ryan notes that in 1802 the canal supply
was cut off as a result of a late payments dispute.
By that time the City Watercourse was capable of
supplying only a fifth of Dublin's growing demand
for water, a situation that greatly strengthened
the negotiating position of the Grand Canal
Company. Legal posturing and intensive bargaining
took place between 1802 and 1804 leading to the
corporation's agreement to pay 15% of all its water
supply income to the canal company. One of the
few references to the ordinary workers in the
Pipe Water Establishment is to be found around
this time when, in 1805, they were issued with
uniform caps and badges carrying the words 'Pipe
Water Works'.

In 1803 the eminent Scottish engineer John
Rennie (1761–1821), who carried out several major
public works in Ireland, was consulted about the
water supply. He noted that the Royal Canal, work
on which had been started in 1790 but was not
completed until 1817, flowed into the city from a
higher level than the Grand Canal and he believed
that it could provide enough water to satisfy
Dublin's needs. Rennie, who was noted for courteous
professionalism, received the freedom of the city in
1804. Andrew Coffey, however, believed that the
north city could best be served by a Liffey supply, to
flow from Islandbridge to a pumping station near
the present Heuston Bridge.

A steam engine to power the Liffey pumps was
purchased for £1,560 5s 3d (British) from Boulton
& Watt of Birmingham but was never installed. It
was sold in 1807 to Jameson's Bow Street distillery
and in 1808 the first Liffey water supply system was

finally shut down. In *The Liffey in Dublin* (Gill &
Macmillan, 1996) Professor John de Courcy noted
that 150 years were to pass before the river would
again supply water to Dublin. Much later – in the
1980s – following decades of disuse at Bow Street
a steam engine that may have contained parts of
the Boulton & Watt machine was dismantled and
reverently re-erected in University College Dublin
at Belfield.

By 1806 the supply of water was found to be
'totally insufficient' for the needs of the citizens. The
corporation therefore entered into 60-year contracts
with both the Grand Canal and the Royal Canal
companies to secure, as far as could be reasonably
forecast at the time, an ample and uninterrupted
water supply.

Increasing instances of leakage were a serious
problem with the wooden mains. The failures led to
more and more complaints from ratepayers and
arguments, initially with the Grand Canal Company,
about the difference between the quantity of water
extracted and that delivered to users. Leakage from
water mains has been a perennial problem and
nearly two hundred years were to pass before this
seemingly perpetual curse was tackled methodically
(see Chapter 13). In the early nineteenth century,
problems with leakages were compounded by the
rapid rate of deterioration of wooden pipes.

Timber for conversion into pipes was processed
and stored in a depot at Barrack Street (today's
Benburb Street). In *The Liffey in Dublin* Professor
de Courcy describes wooden pipe technology.
Imported timber was transferred to rafts at the
highest point on the Liffey that ships could reach
and brought to the Gravel Walk Slip, an inlet
upstream of the present James Joyce Bridge. The
timber was hollowed out and stored, in water if
possible, until needed. To get the best out of
wooden pipes they had to be kept damp at all times.
In use from the 1660s, the importance of the
Barrack Street depot was eventually undermined by
technology. As the Industrial Revolution progressed,
a growing range of new materials and manufactured
items became available. Cast iron pipes, made by

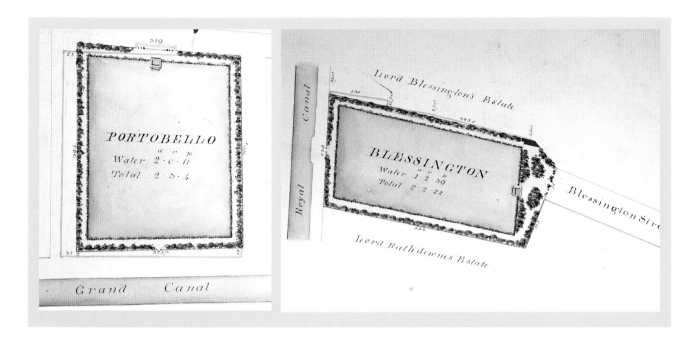

the Arigna Ironworks and available by 1797, were used in some Dublin streets and found to be satisfactory. By 1814, John and William Clarke of Ringsend were also manufacturing metal pipes. The new technology was acknowledged statutorily in 1809 legislation, known as the Metal Mains Act. This authorised the corporation to carry out extensive new works, and levy additional water rates. During the next twenty years most of the old wooden mains were excavated or abandoned, metal being substituted. A report of October 1828 stated that sixty-two miles of metal mains had been laid, with less than one mile of wooden pipe remaining to be replaced. Some of these mains, usually 7½ inches in diameter, remained in service until the late twentieth century.

In that same year of 1828 Andrew Coffey was suspended for three months for alleged irregularities in the stores and accounts of the Pipe Water Establishment. Richard Crofton, who was appointed to replace Coffey, was storekeeper and therefore accountable for what was in stock. He later admitted that 'errors' had been made by 'somebody else'. Coffey was vindicated and restored to office, his salary at that time being £400 per annum.

THE PORTOBELLO AND BLESSINGTON STREET BASINS

From what was originally called the First Lock at Griffith Bridge, also known today as Suir Road Bridge, the Grand Canal went to James's Street (Grand Canal Place) along the line of the present linear park and tramway. During the 1790s an important new section of canal was constructed from the First Lock (Suir Road) to Portobello and Ringsend. In time this length of waterway, which joined with the Liffey, became the main line. The original route to Grand Canal Place, reduced to the status of a branch, fell into decline; this was especially so with the introduction of rail and, later, mechanical road transport.

Beside the new canal cut to Ringsend a second water supply basin, more than two acres in extent, was constructed upstream of Portobello Bridge on the site of the present Warren and Martin Streets. The building of this basin was recommended by James Johnston in April 1801, but work did not begin until 1806 and the project was completed in 1812. This reservoir, also known as the Richmond Basin, supplied water to the south-eastern area of the city, and to Portobello Barracks. The Grand

Plans of Portobello Basin (left) and of Blessington Street Basin (right). *The former supplied Grand Canal water for the south-eastern suburbs, while the latter provided water from the Royal Canal for the north side of the city.*

Blessington Street Basin (right) with its Victorian gate-lodge (above). *Today this is a tranquil city-centre oasis with its own thriving population of wild fowl.*

Canal would henceforth cater for the south side, while the Royal Canal became the main source of water for the north city, supplied on terms similar to those agreed with the Grand Canal Company. From 8 to 12 feet deep, the Portobello Basin was supplied from an overfall gauge weir 38 feet long on the canal. Eight 7½-inch and two 7-inch pipes conducted the supplies out of this basin

Since 1880, via a 12-inch main, the Grand Canal has also supplied the water for the lakes in the splendidly refurbished St Stephen's Green. This work was paid for by Lord Ardilaun, whose statue looks across from St Stephen's Green towards the College of Surgeons. The 12-inch main returns to the Canal at Percy Place and there is an overflow from this system into the city drainage network at St Stephen's Green North. Canal water was also used intensively by the many distilleries and breweries that once flourished in the south-west of the city, and is still supplied to Guinness's Brewery for washing out.

Between the end of Blessington Street and the Broadstone branch of the Royal Canal (long since closed), a basin, suggested eleven years earlier to serve the north side of the city, was completed in 1814. A gauge weir similar in design and size to the one at Portobello serviced this basin, approximately 1.75 acres in extent. Blessington Street Basin had six 7½-inch pipes (replaced by a 16-inch main in 1893) to supply the north side of the city, which expanded steadily, especially after 1830. It was also the source of water for the Bow Street Distillery, the flow to which was limited to 180,000 gallons per day in 1932. Happily the Blessington Street Basin has survived and is now a peaceful and much-appreciated environmental amenity.

Peter Clarke, author of *The Royal Canal, the Whole Story* (Elo Press, 1992), wrote in *Technology Ireland* in April 1993, that the Royal Canal had 76 locks along its 90-mile route. It suffered from an inadequate supply of water due to the raising and lowering of boats and in dry summers it was hard

pressed to fulfil its commitments to Dublin Corporation. As a result, in some years the canal was closed to navigation for lengthy periods.

A striking example of how something later proved to be hazardous is deemed desirable before its dangers are recognised can be found in *History of the City of Dublin* (Warburton, J., Whitelaw, J. and Walsh, R., 1818). This extract speaks for itself:

The city, formerly dependent on the reservoir, called the bason, in James's Street, and the Liffey, has now an ample supply of excellent water from the Grand and Royal canals; and its water-works, which embraced above sixty miles of wooden pipes becoming decayed, and the necessity of constant repairs producing perpetually returning derangement and disorder in the pavements, the system has been abandoned, two additional reservoirs have been constructed contiguous to the canals, metal mains are laying through the principal streets, and as the revenue of the Pipe-water Committee is now abundant, it is hoped that in a short time no city in Europe will be better supplied than Dublin with that prime necessary of life, good water.

The City Assembly, as the city's governing body was known until the 1840s, consisted of an upper house comprised of the lord mayor, 2 sheriffs and 24 aldermen. The lower house had 124 common councilmen, 28 sheriffs and their peers, and 96 representatives of 25 civic corporations or guilds which became increasingly obsolete with the passage of time. The Pipe Water Committee in 1818 is recorded as consisting of the lord mayor, sheriffs, treasurer, 12 aldermen and 24 councillors. This massive administration, which routinely prefaced its reports with a paragraph praising itself, claimed to be responsible for a water supply to every house at a cost of $\frac{1}{2}d$ per day. The hovels in which so many citizens eked out miserable existences obviously did not figure in these statistics.

That there was, however, some awareness of the plight of the poorest and their need for access to water is obvious from the appointment in 1827 of

Portobello Basin.

Originally a reservoir on the Grand Canal, and now mainly in-filled, today it is a haven of peace in a busy residential and commercial area

the Commissioners for Fountains. This body, which had the distinguished Scotsman Alexander Nimmo as its engineer, bore the responsibility for providing fountains in the poorest parts of the city.

Waterworks entries in directories and other publications in the early nineteenth century usually had a closing sentence as follows: 'In all cases of fire, application for water to be made at City Assembly House or Stores at Barrack Street'. In pre-Dublin Fire Brigade times (before 1862) fire fighting was in the hands of the parishes and insurance companies. They relied on primitive manual pumps and, long before the telephone was invented, it is not difficult to understand the fear people had of fire and how much valuable time was wasted in following the procedure just described.

Because there were few valves and no hydrants, an excavation was frequently necessary to reach the main, which often had to be broken to obtain the urgently needed water. This inefficiency and its associated horrors are fully described in *The Dublin Fire Brigade* (Tom Geraghty and Trevor Whitehead, Dublin City Libraries, 2004).

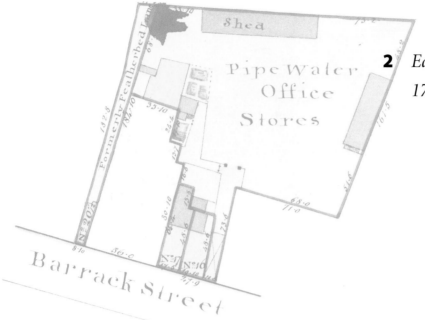

BEFORE THERE WERE SEWERS

In the first half of the eighteenth century the lack of a drainage system was one of the many unpleasant features of life in Dublin. The full effect of this may be savoured from Dean Swift's poetic description of a street in the aftermath of a heavy shower:

> Now from all parts the swelling kennels flow
> And bear their trophies with them as they go;
> Filth of all hues and odours seem to tell
> What street they sailed from, by their sight and smell;
> Sweepings from butchers' stalls, dung, guts and blood;
> Drowned puppies, stinking sprats, all drenched in mud;
> Dead cats and turnip tops come tumbling in the flood.

By the time of Swift's death in 1745 Dublin's spectacular growth was well under way. But despite their grandeur the city's impressive Georgian houses and magnificent public buildings still had but the most primitive sanitary arrangements, even in the late eighteenth century. The majority of houses depended almost exclusively for their domestic drainage on commodes, chamber pots and slop buckets, which were emptied into a covered cesspool in front of each house. The word kennel used by Swift in the passage quoted above is an archaic variant of the word channel, describing an open sewer or street watercourse.

In a sophisticated era paradoxically notorious for its lack of hygiene – chamber pots were brought into dining rooms after meals – such crude public toilets as existed were politely known as houses of easement or, more earthily, bog houses. A tragedy that occurred in one of these public conveniences in 1741 was reported in the *Dublin News Letter* of 22–26 September:

> Last Tuesday as some children were playing in a yard in George's Lane (now South Great George's Street) one of them (a little boy) ran into the Bog-house to hide, when a board gave way, by which he fell in, and was suffocated.

In London in 1775 Alexander Cummings took out a patent for a water closet (WC) and this was improved upon three years later by Joseph Bramah (1748–1814), a man who was responsible for significant advances in drainage, fire-fighting and hydraulic technology. Bramah's domestic WC became increasingly used towards the end of the eighteenth century, and he established a company to manufacture them. Stephen Halliday in *The Great Stink of London* records that Bramah made 6,000 closets in the thirteen years up to 1797.

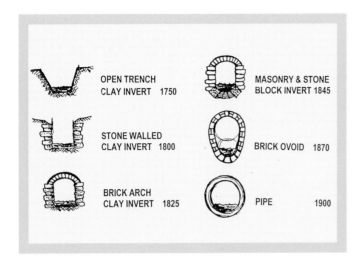

OPEN TRENCH CLAY INVERT 1750	MASONRY & STONE BLOCK INVERT 1845
STONE WALLED CLAY INVERT 1800	BRICK OVOID 1870
BRICK ARCH CLAY INVERT 1825	PIPE 1900

Diagram showing cross-section of typical sewers, 1750–1900.
A variety of shapes were used for early sewers, while materials used in construction ranged from clay to masonry, from stone blocks to brick.

A widely believed urban myth ascribes the invention of the water closet to Thomas Crapper (1836–1910) who was born in Yorkshire more than sixty years after Cummings's patent was registered. Crapper became a very successful plumber whose several patents included three relating to water closets. The mistaken belief that he invented the WC may be due to the fact that his business flourished when waterborne drainage systems were becoming widespread and his name appeared prominently on his products.

Physical reminders of the absence of sanitary accommodation in the eighteenth century can still be seen at the rear of many Georgian houses in Dublin and elsewhere. These are the cantilevered extensions at half-landing level on the back walls of the buildings, designed to house WCs, baths and wash hand basins. They were constructed when a high-pressure water supply, mains drainage and greatly improved sanitary ware became widely available from the 1860s onwards. In 1879 Parke Neville, the city engineer, estimated that there were 7,800 WCs in Dublin.

In the absence of comprehensive sewerage systems, domestic drainage arrangements based on Bramah's principles discharged to the cesspools and simply exacerbated conditions that were already obnoxious and inimical to public health. The growing use of WCs and the widespread absence of

cisterns and ball cocks led to complaints about water wastage – and the level of arrears in payments – in December 1798.

An alternative to the WC that had its devotees was the dry closet. This was replete with numerous unpleasant complications surrounding the removal and treatment of its contents. At one time, dry closets were thought of as the future standard. However, they lost out in urban areas with the establishment of modern water supply systems. With copious supplies available to service them, waterborne drainage systems became the universal norm. But dry closets did not disappear completely and isolated examples could still be found, mostly in areas remote from sewer systems, well into the 1950s.

In the eighteenth century it was assumed, wrongly, that the liquid in cesspools would filter through the ground, into which the wells for drinking water were also sunk. But the clay and limestone strata of Dublin were so dense that the contents of the pools were retained until they were full. This meant that the cesspools had to be opened up and cleared periodically – a grossly unpleasant procedure for everybody involved, and one that 'exposed in the public streets a highly putrid and offensive mass'.

In areas without domestic drainage or cesspools the waste was habitually thrown out of windows, very often upper floor windows. The more responsible occupants of a house would shout a warning before discharging the contents of a receptacle out of the window, but others failed to do so and unwary passers-by were sometimes drenched in a shower of ordure. Lumps of excrement wrapped in newspapers were another hazard from above and were known as 'tenement pigeons'.

Most of Dublin's important eighteenth-century streets and the parallel lanes running behind them had surface water drainage channels which discharged to the nearest watercourse or river. In time, overflows from the domestic cesspools were also connected to these channels, exacerbating the situation described so memorably by Dean Swift and resulting in river pollution.

The surface water channels or any other conduits that would carry effluent away were effectively used as sewers. In some places, existing open drains were being deepened and improved by 1750 and, as the eighteenth century progressed, random rubble or stone sidewalls with earthen inverts (floors) became normal for new sewers. The next step was to cover the sewers with slabs and, during the first quarter of the nineteenth century, many conduits had brick arches built above them, thus creating the recognisable antecedent of a modern sewer. Dublin's oldest sewers were built by different developers, and several changes of size could be found even under one length of a street. This writer recalls this in a particular sewer he travelled in Lower Mount Street before its reconstruction many years ago.

In a historical prelude to his report on Dublin drainage published in 1880 (Chapter 7) the English engineer and sanitarian Sir Robert Rawlinson commented that:

> such sewers were … formed from time to time without any reference to a general plan; and have, consequently, been constructed in defective form and of the roughest materials. Having been commenced and gradually completed in an irregular manner, they were not true either in line or gradient, many of them were square on cross-section, having flat, rough and irregular bottoms, the sides being built of rubble; they were also porous, and consequently allowed any filthy fluids passing into them to taint the soil below, and on both sides.

They were in reality no better than the cesspools they were intended to replace.

CONTRASTS IN LATE EIGHTEENTH-CENTURY DUBLIN

Dublin enjoyed a satisfactory level of employment in the closing years of the eighteenth century. The food industry flourished, as did breweries and distilleries, and crafts such as tailoring, metalwork and jewellery. Up to 11,000 people were reputed to work in the weaving industry while coach building and its associated trades, in which Dublin excelled, accounted for large numbers of highly-skilled men. The building industry also accounted for much employment. But the publisher William Woodfall's assertion in August 1785 that 'there never was so splendid a metropolis in so poor a country' helps to

Opulent Dublin during the 1790s. *Elegant ladies and gentlemen perambulate in St Stephen's Green, presided over by an equestrian statue of King George II in the distance.*

underline other realities of contemporary life – and the contrast was not merely between urban and rural scenarios.

Although Dublin was so ostensibly wealthy in the late eighteenth century, its splendid streets, squares and public buildings were in reality a façade. Behind the elegant houses there were lanes and alleys, yards and waste ground. Here subsisted hordes of wretched people, unhealthy and unskilled, illiterate and frequently unemployable. Their total destitution, unrelieved by any form of social welfare, worsened the lawlessness that has always been a feature of urban life – all this in a society where the more prescient among the upper classes feared violent revolution of the type that was about to explode in France.

Among the immediate threats to the prosperity of Dublin's industrialists and businessmen in the 1780s were social unrest and a shortage of skilled labour. There was also bitter rivalry between apprentices in various trades as well as serious mutual antipathy between apprentices and students, leading to regular pitched battles in the streets. Premature, and often violent, efforts by journeymen and apprentices to organise and take industrial action were met by harsh sanctions. Apprentices were effectively the chattels of their masters and individuals frequently rebelled against the virtual slave status they endured. Severe laws were enacted to counter the escalating industrial strife that eventually led to a more egalitarian atmosphere in which trades unions could at least be contemplated.

With the declaration of American independence fresh in people's minds, the prospect of a coalition between militant workers, nationalists and revolutionaries, was always a possibility. Sir Boyle Roche, a member of the Irish parliament, and a master of mixing metaphor and malapropism, expressed the very real fears of many privileged people in one of his most famous outbursts: 'If French principles should take root in Ireland we should come down to breakfast one morning to find our bloody heads upon the table staring us in the face'.

The Parish Watch system, in operation since 1714, became progressively less capable of dealing with either industrial unrest or spiralling criminality. In *Dublin Hanged* (Irish Academic Press, 1994) Brian Henry describes vividly what agitation, crime and punishment were like in late eighteenth-century Dublin. He narrates how in 1786 the ramshackle Parish Watch was replaced by a single citywide police force. Unfortunately, this quite efficient body became a victim of political pressure surrounding issues of cost and taxation and, after only nine years of operation, it was succeeded by a revived watch system.

Severe punishment of wrongdoers rather than efforts to improve the lot of the lower classes was the prevailing policy. Footpads, who would today be called muggers, were numerous. Once arrested and tried, crude justice usually guaranteed that they would not re-offend: Henry records that 242 felons, including thirteen women, were hanged between 1780 and 1795. On 23 July 1785 five of these hapless miscreants were publicly hanged in a cruelly botched multiple execution at Kilmainham. The penalty of transportation was also imposed, sometimes as an alternative to a death sentence. For non-capital crimes, public whipping through the streets along specified routes was a punishment regularly inflicted.

UNDERGROUND RIVERS, ESCAPES AND ARCHAEOLOGY

In 1780 a new prison, situated south of Green Street Courthouse on the site of the present park and called Newgate after the Thomas Street establishment it replaced, came into use. During the suppression of a riot on 6 July 1790 a group of fourteen Newgate inmates dug their way out of the prison and into a sewer which was in fact the culverted River Bradogue. Brian Henry records that five of the prisoners were poisoned by sewer gas and that three more were recaptured at the outfall to the Liffey at Upper Ormond Quay, but six others escaped to freedom and future lives that were of limited duration.

Although well documented, the Newgate escape is not nearly as famous as incidents involving patriots who used the Poddle to abscond from Dublin Castle. Like the Poddle, the less prominent Bradogue has a complicated network of branches and diversions, but all of these have for many years been part of the foul sewer system. The Poddle, on the other hand, has regained its status as a river after a long period of serving as a foul sewer. But, whether river or sewer, the Poddle was a security risk – an escape route – since Dublin Castle was first built.

Members of the Dublin city drainage staff frequently investigate reports by people who firmly believe in the existence of mysterious tunnels built under Dublin for various, usually sinister, purposes. Some of the stories involve escapes such as that from Newgate: underground rivers like the Bradogue can easily be woven into folklore. The abandoned Bradogue culvert was unexpectedly uncovered beneath Chancery Street during road and drainage works in the 1970s, leading to several fanciful

stories that invariably featured both heroes and villains. C. L. Sweeney records in *The Rivers of Dublin* that it was twelve feet wide and six feet high with a flat arch and only about two feet of cover. It was backfilled and will probably be exposed again in some future archaeological dig.

Sweeney also records an example of archaeology frustrated by a discovery made near the Bradogue culvert, this time in the yard of the Fruit and Vegetable Market at Chancery Street. A large waste collection area, lower than the surrounding ground level, was prone to filling with rainwater and so the city drainage division was requested to insert a gulley in its floor and connect this to the nearest sewer. When the drainage crew excavated for this work they found three large slate-stone slabs. 'They curiously lifted them', records Sweeney, 'only to gaze in wonder at a skeleton stretched underneath in a stone chamber. The gulley connection was made at speed and the floor quickly reinstated after the sarcophagus was reassembled and before inquisitions held up the job'.

Present-day Green Street Courthouse (above) with (below) Newgate Gaol.
Designed by Thomas Cooley and opened in 1780, Newgate Gaol housed many Irish patriots, including Oliver Bond, Napper Tandy, Robert Emmet. It was demolished in 1839.

Front 177

NEW GOAL FRONT

STARTING A MODERN DRAINAGE SYSTEM

Walled medieval towns were dangerously unhealthy places in which to live. There were various ordinances that prohibited littering and fouling, but enforcement was at best uneven. Hygiene and healthcare were unknown to the vast majority of the population and, apart from the occupiers of some large buildings, nobody enjoyed the benefits of a planned drainage system.

Whether paved or not, many of the streets served also as open drains and were depositories for every conceivable variety of filth. Scavenging (sweeping and cleansing) was poorly organised and inadequately supervised. There were endemic diseases and frequent plagues and the mortality rate was horrifying. Many of those who survived infancy died young in any case; the unhealthy environment, poor diet and primitive medicine all left people utterly vulnerable to whatever ailments prevailed at any particular period.

When the city (almost entirely on the south side of the Liffey until the mid-seventeenth century) began expanding beyond its walls and into adjacent early suburbs, the situation hardly improved, albeit by then open drainage channels were present in some streets. This situation as we have seen contrasts incongruously with Dublin's reputation in the closing years of the eighteenth century as one of the most elegant cities in Europe, the second largest in the British Empire, and the fifth largest in Europe.

Legislation passed in 1773 and 1774 laid the responsibility to provide an orderly public drainage system for Dublin on a 'Corporation for paving, cleaning, lighting, draining and improving the streets'. This corporation or board was appointed on 2 June 1774 and lost no time in getting down to business; its inaugural meeting took place on 6 June in Navigation Board House. Adjourned for two days, the resumed meeting on 8 June began to deal with the 'nuisances at present subsisting in the several Streets, Lanes and Alleyways of this City'.

Richard Manders' seal and signature from his lease of the water engine at Islandbridge. *A wealthy Dublin baker, Manders was Lord Mayor in 1801–02, and used the water engine to provide energy for his mills.*

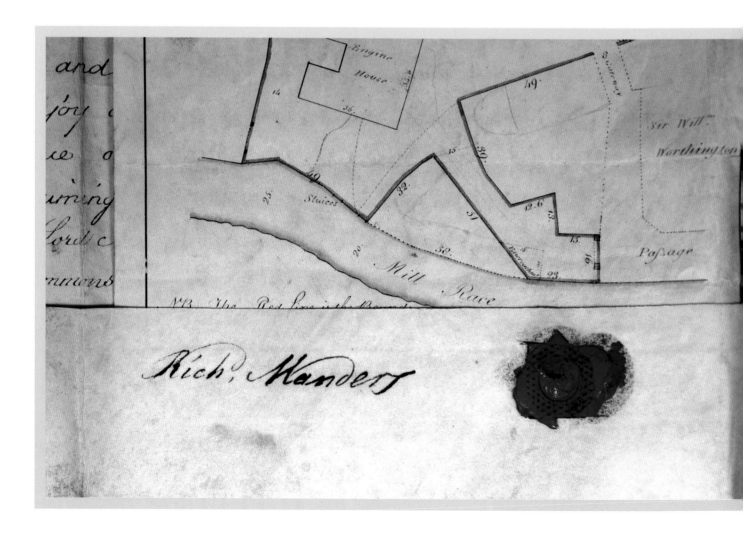

The Board began its work by carrying out paving and then addressed drainage, taking action against people who had diverted the contents of their cesspools to the channels and sewers that were initially intended to carry off only surface water.

In time, it became obvious that more powers were needed and in 1807 the board's duties passed to five 'Commissioners for Paving, Cleansing and Lighting'. As was the case with their predecessors, the commissioners performed several additional duties, including the licensing of various trades and other activities. They met daily at No. 1 Dawson Street and their staff included a secretary, treasurer and supervisor. Sackville Street and Marlborough Street, which had separate arrangements of their own, were omitted from the commissioners' remit.

When a sewer was needed in an existing street, the commissioners served notices on the householders, summoning them to a meeting at which they explained their plans and levied charges. Tenders – 'proposals' – were invited to carry out the work, a typical example being the drainage of South William Street. Following the commissioners' meeting of 20 March 1812, notice was given that contractors' proposals would have to be lodged by 3 pm on Friday 3 April, plans and specifications being available for inspection in the meantime at the Paving Office. In this instance four tenders were received and the contract was awarded to Richard Bergan, whose quote, the lowest, was £14 5s (€16.70) per linear perch. The perch, which fell out of general use in the nineteenth century, is equivalent to five metres.

In 1816, the annual expenditure of the Commissioners for Paving, Cleansing and Lighting was stated to be somewhat in excess of £52,000 (€60,960). In 1818 Warburton, Whitelaw and Walsh in their *History of the City of Dublin* stated that:

> Covered sewers of enlarged dimensions, and terminating in their general receptacle, the Liffey, are constructing where wanting, under the direction of the enlightened judgement of the first commissioner, Major Taylor, whose firmness was necessary to resist much opposition and obloquy.

Major Taylor was one of those who strove to eliminate the corruption that was virtually endemic in public bodies of that time. There were so many boards and commissions, all raising revenue by a variety of methods, that inefficiency, waste and financial misappropriation were inevitable. Serious questions were too often answered unsatisfactorily. The commissioners were replaced in 1827 as a result of financial discrepancies, at about the same time that irregularities in the Pipe Water Establishment were also being investigated. The financial purging, reform and democratisation of public bodies, together with the allocation of expanded responsibilities and their funding, absorbed vast amounts of time, energy and political negotiation – and legislation – throughout the nineteenth century.

For many years, doctors and public health officers experienced intense frustration when trying to persuade people to practise even the most fundamental principles of hygiene. The majority of people, however, accepted disease and the high death rate fatalistically. Infant mortality was dreadful, and only a minority of people could expect to survive beyond their forties. It was widely believed that epidemics were a punishment from God, especially on the lower classes, whose poverty was seen by many as a crime in its own right. To those above them, the hapless lower strata of society were the general service classes, tolerated only to be exploited as required.

If they considered the commissioners' plans too costly or simply did not understand the need for sewers, householders sometimes refused their cooperation – and money – for drainage works. A case in point was Capel Street, where a partially completed sewer was filled in and it was not until 1853 that this important thoroughfare was properly drained. Even prestigious Sackville (O'Connell) Street had operational cesspools as late as 1816. As already noted, Sackville and Marlborough Streets had hitherto escaped the writ of the paving commissioners, claiming their own autonomous drainage arrangements, but these now came under the control of the commissioners.

A continuous flight from the country into the towns gained momentum around 1750 with the onset of the Industrial Revolution. Destitute rural people migrated to towns in the hope of finding employment – and occupied every available hovel or cellar. Although far less industrialised than cities in Britain, Dublin also experienced this ingress, which was further encouraged by the growth and prosperity of the Georgian city. The already high numbers of destitute migrants became even greater in the wake of the 1798 Rebellion, and Dublin's population in 1800 was officially quoted as 172,084 people.

POVERTY, OVERCROWDING AND ILL-HEALTH

Dublin fell into decline as a capital city when the Act of Union came into force in 1801, its troubles exacerbated by several factors beyond the control – or conscience – of the civic authorities. The abolition of the Irish parliament and the city's attendant loss of status was a severe blow. The departure of numerous wealthy and influential people to London adversely affected the city socially, economically and physically, the effects being felt quite rapidly. A simple set of statistics illustrates the scale of the decline the Act of Union caused to Dublin's economy and status. In 1800, 270 peers and 300 MPs lived in the city, but by 1820 only thirty-four peers and five MPs remained.

The difference in the numbers of people needed to serve and supply the establishments of 1800 and 1820 was very great. The chronic poverty of the lower orders now enveloped much of the servant class, which lost so much opportunity for employment following the exodus. The city's already unhappy circumstances were further exacerbated by the recession that followed the battle of Waterloo in 1815.

Several recently prosperous areas began their steady downmarket slide, while those already in decline sank further into decay. This depressing process was most marked in the Liberties, already crushed economically by the decline of the weaving

trade. Formerly elegant houses began their inexorable degeneration into slum tenements, further exacerbating and extending the toxic overcrowding and other public health problems that already existed. The city centre became ever less attractive behind the still gracious principal streets, although some prestigious new building work, for example in the area of Mountjoy, Merrion and Fitzwilliam squares, continued well into the nineteenth century.

Such development as took place after 1800 was largely attributable to Dublin's extensive business and professional population which continued to expand and provide services that were always in demand. There was also a substantial civil service and military establishment whose remits, like those of the other sectors mentioned, covered the entire island of Ireland. As the nineteenth century progressed, the professional and middle classes became more numerous, increasing wealth and purchasing power among certain sectors of the population.

The home of a prosperous family in the late eighteenth and early nineteenth centuries has been brilliantly recreated at No. 29 (at one time No. 30) Lower Fitzwilliam Street. Built in 1794, this house was occupied until 1806 by Mrs Olivia Beatty, the widow of a prominent Dublin wine merchant. Several owners and 122 years later, the house was acquired as offices by the Electricity Supply Board (ESB) in 1928. In a unique partnership between the ESB and the National Museum it was sensitively restored in 1991 and furnished in the style of the period during which Olivia Beatty lived there, and it welcomes visitors. In his *Number Twenty-Nine* (ESB/National Museum, 2001) Curator Kieran Burns tells the story of the house and gives a vivid description of Dublin and its better-off citizens in the years between 1790 and 1820.

Traffic congestion in Dublin is not a modern phenomenon. It was certainly a problem more than two centuries ago and became particularly acute in the first decade of the nineteenth century. Obstructions were frequently caused by road openings made to facilitate water and drainage work. These were referred to by Warburton,

Whitelaw and Walsh in 1818 as 'interrupting in a disagreeable and dangerous manner the communication of the streets'. Kieran Burns observed that, with all the excavations they encountered, people moving into new houses in Georgian Dublin frequently found themselves in the middle of active building sites.

A Bill promoted in 1807 to provide for the more effectual improvement of Dublin and its environs prescribed building ledges in the sewers to carry water mains, thereby reducing the impact of too many road openings. Waterworks engineer Andrew Coffey objected strenuously to this proposed requirement on several grounds, including his well-founded belief that repairs to water mains in sewers would have to be carried out 'in a vapour of torches and the noxious effluvia of putrid filth, dangerous to life and to the water supply'. He campaigned vigorously on the issue and mustered enough support to have the offending clause dropped from the legislation.

Coffey, who served as waterworks engineer from 1804 until his death in 1832, appears to have been a conscientious and practical professional. Some

confusion about his age arises from his appearance as an expert witness for Dublin Corporation in an 1825 court case. In the preliminary evidence his year of birth was stated to be 1758. But when answering counsel's questions he gave his age as seventy-seven, which indicated that he was born in 1748. He was therefore eighty-four when he died in 1832.

Coffey lived at Pembroke (now Sarsfield) Quay, near the Waterworks Stores at Barrack Street, today known as Benburb Street. His skills extended to fashioning the darts thrown by the lord mayor during the Riding of the Franchises ceremony. This ritual confirmed the extent of the corporation's authority, the furthest points to which the mayor could throw the darts marking the municipal boundary, an especially important matter along the shoreline. Andrew Coffey was succeeded as waterworks engineer by the distinguished architect John Semple. Semple was dismissed in 1842 by the newly-created Dublin City Council, not through any fault of his own but as part of a general purge of officials who had been appointed by the preceding Dublin City Assembly.

THE DRAINAGE POVERTY BAR

Having to charge for its work left the Paving Board and its successor, the Commissioners for Paving, Cleansing and Lighting, powerless to improve the abominable sanitary conditions in the increasingly overpopulated and underprivileged areas. The socially conscious Rev James Whitelaw (1749–1813), who became Rector of St Catherine's in Thomas Street in 1788, described the conditions endured by local people. His *Report on the Population of Ireland* records the situation that prevailed in the Liberties in 1798. In the narrow streets of this district with houses so crowded together that some had no back yards, he encountered squalor so total as to be virtually incomprehensible two centuries later.

As Georgian Dublin was being constructed, the fashionable streets around St Stephen's Green and Merrion Square became the addresses at which many people wished to live. Migration from the Liberties eastwards was part of this trend and so previously desirable houses in the districts west and southwest of the Castle went downmarket, being let in tenements to poorer people. A whole district that, only a few years previously, had been an attractive place in which to live, now became the poor quarter of the city.

Frequently, as many as four families shared one apartment. Whitelaw recorded that up to sixteen persons of various ages and both sexes were in one room less than fifteen feet square, stretched on a wad of filthy straw, swarming with vermin, and without any covering save the wretched rags that constituted their wearing apparel. No. 6 Braithwaite Street contained 108 souls, and a survey made twice in Plunkett Street revealed that there were 917 occupants in thirty-two adjoining houses. The local population included working manufacturers, petty shopkeepers or others engaged in trade, the labouring poor and beggars.

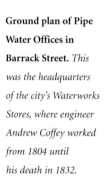

Ground plan of Pipe Water Offices in Barrack Street. *This was the headquarters of the city's Waterworks Stores, where engineer Andrew Coffey worked from 1804 until his death in 1832.*

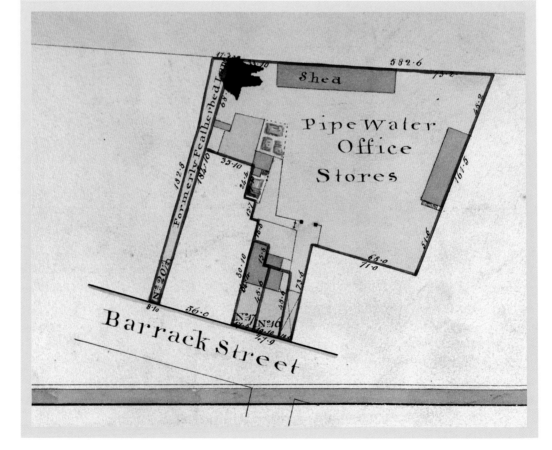

This crowded population … is almost universally
accompanied by a very serious evil – a degree of filth
and stench inconceivable, except by such as have visited
these scenes of wretchedness. There are few or no
necessaries, and, of course, into the back yard of each
house, frequently not ten feet deep, is flung, from the
windows of each apartment, the ordure and filth of its
numerous inhabitants; from whence it is so seldom
removed that it may be seen nearby on a level with the
first floor; and the moisture that after heavy rain oozes
from this heap, having no sewer to carry it off, runs
into the street by the entry leading to the staircase, for,
strange as it may appear, it is a fact that there is not one
covered sewer in that populous portion of the Liberty
south of the street called the Coombe.

Sadly Rev Whitelaw died aged sixty-four as a result
of illness contracted from the poor to whom he
ministered.

Living conditions continued to worsen as
growing numbers of destitute, undernourished
people squeezed into ever more overcrowded living
quarters. That there was awareness of the crying
need for water in the most depressed parts of the
city was recognised in the appointment of the
Commisisoners for Fountains in 1827 (as recorded
in Chapter 1). In 1832, more than eighty water
fountains were installed in the more impoverished
parts of the Liberties. Unfortunately, while the
fountains were of considerable benefit, the water
they supplied was neither constant in flow nor of
great purity.

While the 'public health movement' of the time
was strongly pressing the desperate need for action,
the formidable and public-spirited Dr Thomas
Willis (1790–1881), apothecary and social
campaigner, lent his considerable influence to the
movement for reform. He published his searing
report on St Michan's Parish, around the Church
Street area, in 1845, and followed up with evidence
to the parliamentary committee on the Dublin
Improvement Bill 1847. Changes were already
gathering momentum however, and the 1848
Nuisances Removal Act and the 1849 Dublin

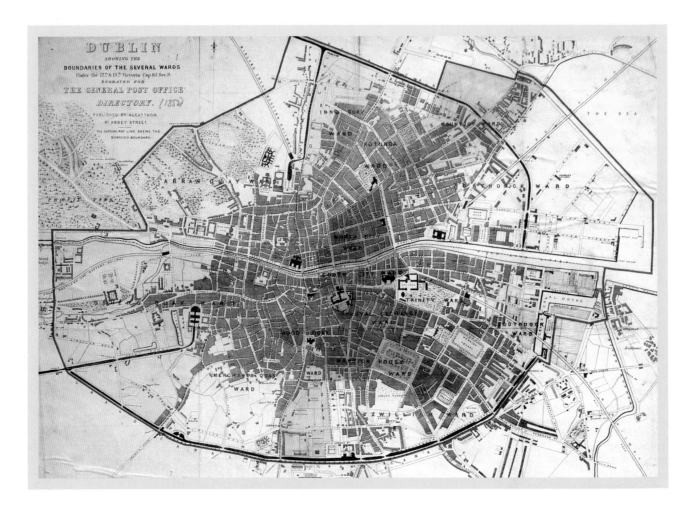

Map of Dublin, 1840.

Showing the enlarged city boundaries which closely followed the line of the Royal and Grand Canals.

Improvement Act laid solid foundations for future progress. Meanwhile Willis (alluded to again in Chapter 3) uncannily – and probably unwittingly – wrote a virtual paraphrase of Rev William Whitelaw's narrative, just quoted, from almost half a century earlier:

> …it is not an infrequent occurrence to see above a dozen human beings crowded into a space not fifteen feet square. Within this space the food of these wretched beings, such as it is, must be prepared; within this space they must eat and drink; men, women and children must strip, dress, sleep. In cases of illness the calls of nature must be relieved; and when death releases one of the inmates, the corpse must of necessity remain for days within the room … the results … are – that every cause that can contribute to generate contagion exists here in full vigour, and that disease, in every aggravated form, with all its train of desolating misery, is rarely absent.

Such were the appalling physical and social conditions awaiting the urgent attention of those who would so unstintingly implement the improvements to be promoted by the new regime that began in the 1840s.

**REFORMING THE CORPORATION –
CITY HALL**

Although a long-drawn out and tedious process, the first effective steps to the democratisation of urban local authorities were taken with the passing of the 1840 Municipal Corporations Act. The existing City Assembly mounted stubborn but unavailing opposition to the progress of this measure. This grotesquely undemocratic and self-perpetuating body (described in Chapter 1), represented obsolete and irrelevant medieval guilds and did not administer the city in the interest of all the citizens. It was now abolished and replaced by the new City Council, which met for the first time in November 1841.

The new council, consisting of the fifteen aldermen and forty-five councillors, was elected by those qualified to vote and chose the lord mayor from among the members. While the franchise was admittedly restricted, it was a vast improvement on what it replaced and was widened as time passed. Meetings of the reformed corporation were initially held in the Assembly Rooms (the Civic Museum until 2003) in South William Street.

The Royal Exchange, Thomas Cooley's masterpiece on Cork Hill, was purchased by the corporation in 1852 for use as the City Hall. An Act of George III had been passed on 27 May 1768 'for promoting the trade of Ireland by enabling the merchants thereof to erect an exchange in the city of Dublin'. Completed in 1769, the former Royal Exchange underwent substantial interior alterations by the corporation over the years, numerous offices, partitions and a new staircase being installed. Nearly a hundred and fifty years on, following the transfer of most City Hall staff to the Civic Offices at Wood Quay, the building was meticulously restored as nearly as possible to its original condition.

THE CITY BOUNDARY IN 1840

Delineating the area over which the new corporation exercised jurisdiction had begun in 1763 when a commission was established to construct a circular road around the city. The work took more than thirty years to carry out, but by the end of the eighteenth century, today's North and South Circular Roads were virtually complete and were regarded as the city boundary. When the commission began its work the canals were still in the future, but in the first two decades of the nineteenth century both the Grand Canal and the Royal Canal were complete,

Dublin's City Hall
c. 1867. *Originally the*
Royal Exchange, it
became the City Hall in
1852 and was dominated
by a statue of Daniel
O'Connell, which is now
inside the building.

skilled employment brought to other cities. Its already limited taxation base consequently resulted in low levels of municipal finance, a situation exacerbated by a reduction of £100,000, or one sixth, in the Griffith revaluation of 1854. Furthermore, many progressive municipalities throughout the United Kingdom included revenue-earning and socially beneficial utilities like gas and (later) public transport among the services they provided. In Dublin both gas and public transport were in the hands of commercial concerns, and the corporation's attempts to acquire the gas undertaking proved abortive. The genesis of the very successful electricity service later provided by the corporation is outlined in Chapter 8.

BEYOND THE BOUNDARY: THE TOWNSHIPS

In the early nineteenth century local government in County Dublin outside the city boundary was administered by the Grand Jury system. Catering for the needs of the rural and land-owning elite, this arrangement was totally unsuitable for growing urban areas.

Dunleary was a hamlet with a small harbour served by a short pier that was used chiefly by local fishing boats. The growing settlement was renamed Kingstown in honour of George IV when he embarked at Dunleary in 1821. Construction of Kingstown Harbour commenced in 1817 by the great Scottish engineer John Rennie and was completed in 1842. Work on the harbour attracted hundreds of labourers and their families into the area. The influx was accommodated in slum conditions in the Glasthule and York Road districts.

As the town developed, including the rail link to the city and the introduction of a steamship service to Hollyhead, the working population multiplied. No cottages or sanitary provision was made for the workers until late in the century. The consequent overcrowding, lack of clean water and adequate drainage contributed to the death toll when cholera struck; the worst outbreaks were in 1831 when there

forming an oval outside the circular road. From 1840 the canals constituted much of the municipal boundary, making Dublin a compact but artificially restricted city for the next sixty years.

From the southeast the boundary began at the mouth of the Dodder, which it followed to Ringsend Bridge, then ran along Ringsend Road, Barrow Street and Grand Canal Street to Macquay Bridge. The Grand Canal marked the boundary as far as the present Suir Road, then it ran along South Circular Road, Conyngham Road and Infirmary Road to bring it to the North Circular Road gate of the Phoenix Park. It next followed the North Circular Road to Phibsboro' Church, through which it turned north and continued along St Peter's Road to the Royal Canal. It went east with the canal to Jones's Road where it turned north again to Clonliffe Road, which it followed to Ballybough Bridge. The River Tolka formed the boundary to Annesley Bridge before it took off on a southeasterly line to a point on Tolka Quay about 890 yards (813 metres) east of the East Wall Road junction. From there it ran south to the Liffey, turning west at a point opposite the former coastguard houses on Pigeonhouse Road and so back to the Dodder.

Although it had some industries Dublin lost out in not being able to attract the level of investment the Industrial Revolution and its high levels of were thirty-two deaths, in 1861 when 124 people died, and again in 1872.

Under the provisions of the 1828 Lighting of Towns Act and subsequent legislation, townships were established to encourage residential and business development. Commissioners, whose objectives included the installation of high quality street networks, together with essential services and amenities such as water, drainage and public lighting, administered and promoted these townships.

Kingstown became the first district in County Dublin to take advantage of the 1828 Act when a number of wealthy inhabitants established a township in 1834. This coincided with the opening of Ireland's first railway, the Dublin and Kingstown, running from Westland Row (now Pearse) Station. Eighteen notable residents were approved as town commissioners to supervise 'lighting, paving, cleansing and watching' and otherwise improve the township.

The 1828 Act did not remove the responsibility for roads and bridges from the Grand Jury. However, following their absorption of Glasthule in 1855, accountability for local roads and bridges was transferred to the Kingstown Commissioners by an Act of 1861. In the competition to offer better lifestyles and addresses to prospective residents in its more exclusive districts, Kingstown claimed the title of the Premier Township

To reduce the cost of obtaining local Acts of Parliament, the Town Improvement (Ireland) Act became law in 1854. The township of Blackrock, which also embraced Williamstown, was established in 1860 and Monkstown was added in 1863. The 1854 Act also facilitated the establishment of Dalkey in 1863, and Killiney and Ballybrack in 1866.

Of the ten contiguous townships established in the Dublin area up to 1880, five – Pembroke, Rathmines, New Kilmainham, Drumcondra and Clontarf – immediately adjoined the city boundary. Pembroke (set up in 1863) covered Ringsend, Sandymount, Ballsbridge and Donnybrook. Rathmines, oldest of the five and established in 1847, later took in Rathgar (1862), Harold's Cross (1866) and Milltown (1880). New Kilmainham (incorporated in 1868) contained Inchicore, while Drumcondra (1878) included Glasnevin, and Clontarf (1869) embraced Marino, Killester and Dollymount.

The richer townships outside the city were financially better able, but often unwilling, to provide as

Map showing the Dublin Townships, late nineteenth – early twentieth century.
The Townships were self-governing suburbs, which had all been absorbed into Dublin City by 1930.

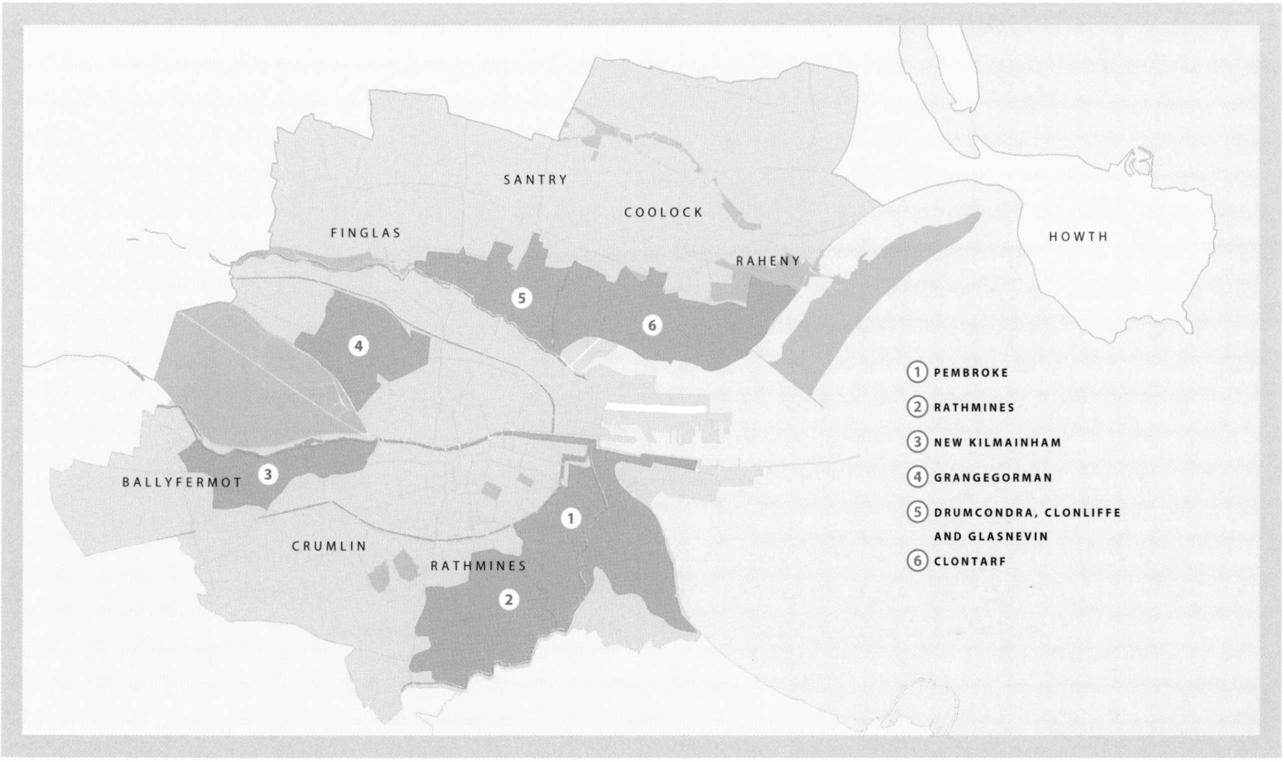

1 PEMBROKE
2 RATHMINES
3 NEW KILMAINHAM
4 GRANGEGORMAN
5 DRUMCONDRA, CLONLIFFE AND GLASNEVIN
6 CLONTARF

wide a range of public services as the far less wealthy Dublin Corporation. Rathmines adopted and practised an attitude of hostility to Dublin City, its needy citizens and impecunious corporation. Paradoxically, despite its relative poverty, the corporation provided more comprehensive services than its neighbours did. Rathmines in particular failed to live up to its obligations, especially in matters of public health. The entire story, with all its depressing details, is fully related by Séamus Ó Maitiú in *Dublin's Suburban Towns* (Four Courts Press, 2003).

In the late 1860s the population of Dublin City was, officially, about 255,000 people. The next census, in 1871, gave the populations of the townships then existing in the Dublin area: Bray, 6,087; Killiney and Ballybrack, 2,290; Dalkey, 2,584; Kingstown, 17,528; Blackrock, 8,089; Pembroke, 20,982; Kilmainham, 4,956; Clontarf, 3,442. The population of Rathmines at the time of the 1871 census was 20,982, by coincidence exactly the same as that of Pembroke. Ten years later Rathmines was estimated to have 24,000 people, while Pembroke had 26,000.

Although not a township or urban district, Dublin Port is an area of prime importance to the city. It is controlled by a body that exercises some of the powers of a local authority and some that few others enjoy – it has, for example, its own police. When the East Wall, now East Wall Road, was completed in the late eighteenth century, it was bounded on one side by the sea. As the port began its rapid growth, especially after the establishment of the Port and Docks Board in 1869, continuous land reclamation has left East Wall Road well inland, and created a huge area that takes its water supply from the city and discharges its sewage to the city drainage system.

In so far as public health, housing and drainage were concerned, poorer districts immediately outside the municipal boundary, but which later came under the jurisdiction of the townships, suffered at least as badly as similar districts within the city. There were areas of great deprivation in places such as Ballybough, Kilmainham, Irishtown

and Ringsend. The scale and depth of the destitution was so great as to almost overwhelm those who laboured incessantly to ameliorate the conditions of the poor.

Mother Mary Aikenhead (1787–1855), who founded the Irish Sisters of Charity in 1815, gave evidence to a Royal Commission established in 1833. She described the horrors she and her colleagues encountered thirty-five years after the Rev James Whitelaw's account of conditions in the Liberties (Chapter 2) and thirty years before the Pembroke Township came into being.

> It would be heart-rending to describe the misery which we daily witness. Many in the prime of life are reduced to debility from want of food, subsisting for 48 hours on one meal, without sufficient clothes to cover them, their wretched furniture and tattered garments being pledged as a last resort …. Last summer the cholera morbus broke out again in the villages of Sandymount, Irishtown, Ballsbridge and Ringsend and raged for five weeks with great violence. We found many in the agonies of death without the means of procuring even a drink and many perished without medical aid …. The lanes and streets are filled with filth in Ringsend and Irishtown; there are no sewers … the poor must buy even the water they drink; it is of the worst description and tends to promote disease as much by its scarcity as by its poor quality.

COMMUTERS, WORKERS AND EMPLOYMENT

Always attractive as residential and sometimes as business locations to those who could afford to live in their more upmarket districts, the townships inevitably exercised a debilitating influence on Dublin's population statistics, rateable valuation and municipal finances. The city's population actually fell by 4,000 to 251,000 during the second half of the nineteenth century when many who could afford to do so moved to the new townships.

Commuting by moderately prosperous people was progressively encouraged with the growing availability of affordable public transport. One

Contemporary portrait of Mother Mary Aikenhead. *Founder of the Irish Sisters of Charity in 1815, her order tended to the poor of Dublin and she personally witnessed the horrors of the cholera epidemic in 1832.*

result of this was the building of upper class houses outside the city boundary. Such development generated valuable rates income and created a sense of community activity that was lost to the city.

From 1834 onwards the Dublin and Kingstown Railway encouraged commuting from Pembroke, Blackrock and Kingstown. Railway services to Malahide (1844), Howth (1846) and Bray (1854) followed. There were also infrequent horse buses serving select destinations including Rathfarnham and Clontarf, but the fares, as on the trains, were too high to benefit working people.

In the nineteenth century Dublin was predominantly a centre of administration, business and commerce, with a growing middle class. While near the bottom of the rigidly stratified social and economic pyramid, certain occupations were regarded as essential to preserving the system and therefore more worthy of consideration than others. Artisans, mechanics and daily labourers were cited in the Tramways Acts as being specifically entitled to concessionary fares following the introduction of horse trams in 1872. But even these fares were beyond the means of the vast surplus of casual labourers and the destitute, whose plight was hopeless and whose numbers were maintained by the flight from the land of the victims of successive rural catastrophies. Only emigration and the savage mortality rate kept the numbers of these unfortunates at a manageable level.

DOUGHTY CAMPAIGNERS

Change, however slow, was on the way since the 1840s, triggered by distinguished personalities with strong social consciences. The philosopher Jeremy Bentham (1748–1832) promulgated the doctrine of utilitarianism, which stated that every action should result in the greatest good for the greatest number. His disciple Sir Edwin Chadwick (1800–1890) aroused public opinion in the 1840s with his public health campaign, part of which called for a pure public water supply and self-cleaning water-carriage sewers.

Chadwick, whose 1842 *Report into the Sanitary Conditions of the Labouring Population of Great Britain* shocked public opinion and greatly influenced people in Dublin, was an inspiration for Dr Thomas Willis, who has already been encountered in Chapter 2. The enormity of what had to be tackled is described starkly by Willis in his *Hidden Dublin: Facts connected with the Social and Sanitary Condition of the Working Classes* (1845), about the parish of St Michan's just north of the Liffey.

> There is one large sewer running through the centre of the parish, and very nearly its entire length, through which the water of the River Bradogue runs; there are very few private or branch drains. A large proportion of the houses have not necessaries, and those that have are in very few instances connected with a sewer, but must be emptied by carrying out through the house. There are no public necessaries, nor urinaries; water closets are scarcely known, unless in public buildings; there may not be above a dozen in the entire district. There is a great want of water, not from any absolute scarcity, it being supplied to the district for about four hours on three days each week. Of those houses let to weekly tenants, not one in ten has the water conveyed into it by branch from the street main. The tenants in such cases are dependent for their supply on the public fountain, which is often at a considerable distance from their residence. The water is not constantly on in these fountains. The wretched people have no vessel to contain a supply; the kettle and broken jar are the only ones to be seen in these abodes of misery. Nothing marks their poverty more than when congregating round the public fountain, struggling to have their little supply. There are many lanes and courts in which a tumbler of water could not be had fit for drinking. Even for the purpose of cleanliness a scanty supply is with difficulty to be had, and appears of such value that it is rarely thrown out until after being put to several uses. I have frequently noticed this filthy stuff remaining within the rooms, and have been invariably told that it was yet wanted. It had first been used, perhaps, to wash the man's shirt, and some little white linen; it was then used to wash coarser things, and even again put in requisition to mop out the room floor, or

stairs. These facts are not confined to the very poor. The most offensive stench to be met with is that which emanates from these filthy suds; and I find that when these rooms or stairs are ever washed, it is with this noisome semi-fluid poison.

It was against this topographical and social background that local democracy was born and Dublin's modern water and drainage systems began their evolution. The several irreversible developments that accompanied the Industrial Revolution and presaged egalitarianism included the rise of the increasingly better-educated and more prosperous middle classes. These people, who multiplied during the Victorian era, persistently sought a better quality of life – for everybody – than had been available hitherto. The pure water and good sanitation advocated by the public health movement which was active at the time were but two of the new standards the movement sought, encapsulated in the proverb 'Cleanliness is next to Godliness'.

The enormity of the problems taken over by the reconstituted corporation of the 1840s was staggering. An anonymous historian, writing in 1906, looked back sixty-six years. He observed that

when, as the result of the Municipal Corporations (Ireland) Act of 1840, the reformed Corporation took in hands the control of the city's affairs, it inherited all the evil consequences of long-continued neglect and mismanagement, not to say corruption. It was not until after the lapse of some years that it could venture upon anything more than palliative measures.

Further progressive statutes, particularly the Dublin Improvements Act of 1849, created circumstances in which essential public services could be provided or improved most effectively. What were now needed were people of vision, energy and courage to carry out public works on an unprecedented scale and Dublin was fortunate to have such individuals ready to improve the lot of its long-suffering citizens.

ENTER PARKE NEVILLE

The appointment of Parke Neville as Dublin's first full-time city surveyor was a significant and providential event. Previously the functions of the city surveyor had been undertaken on a part-time or consultancy basis. Two members of the Neville family, Parke's grandfather and father, were engaged in the role of city surveyor in the first half of the nineteenth century: Arthur Richards Neville from 1801 to 1828, followed by his son Arthur Neville, who continued in that post until his death in 1856. Detailed research on the Neville family, previous city surveyors and other prominent officials, has been carried out by the city archivist Mary Clark, whose findings have been published in the *Dublin Historical Record* and *Quay Issues*, a Dublin City Council staff journal.

Parke Neville was born in 1812. His education included being articled to Charles Vignoles (1793–1875), one of the leading engineers of his day. He was employed on several railway projects in Ireland, worked in England for a time and then studied architecture. In the 1840s he helped his father, Arthur Neville, as an assistant city surveyor. Later President of the Institution of Civil Engineers and Vice-President of the Institute of Architects, he was also active in several scientific and literary societies.

A contemporary described Parke Neville as being

of sterling character, upright and straightforward in his dealings with his fellow-men and most conscientious in the performance of his public duties, which were discharged with unswerving fidelity. He was slow in forming an opinion; but when once formed he maintained it with energy and determination.

In April 1851, the city's infrastructural services, including water and drainage, came under the control of Parke Neville, who was appointed as borough engineer and local surveyor, and tackled his daunting remit vigorously. Neville was noted for forward thinking, a talent not universally appreciated in some crucially important mindsets of the

**Photograph of Parke
Neville, first Dublin
City Engineer.**

*The first Dublin City
Engineer, Parke Neville
was described as 'of
sterling character…
most conscientious in
the performance of his
public duties'.*

1850s. He was also willing to develop theory and practice empirically in what at that time were pioneering branches of engineering, and now had to co-ordinate the activities of what were hitherto autonomous entities.

There were two Commissioners for Paving, Cleansing and Lighting in 1850. They were named in Henry Shaw's *Dublin Pictorial Guide and Directory* as Richard Smyth and Lieut-Col Sir George Morris. Their offices were at 23 Mary Street where they had a staff of nine. From 1 January 1851 the commissioners' functions came under the aegis of the corporation and the new city surveyor. This post was combined with that of the newly established position of city engineer in 1857.

Neville also assumed control of the quaintly titled Pipe Water Establishment, which had its offices at the City Assembly House in South William Street. Five office staff and five collectors were based there, while the Establishment's stores were at Barrack Street (now Benburb Street). The Establishment Secretary and Supervisor was Sir Drury Jones Dickinson. It took some time for all the services to be combined and there seems to have been some degree of less than willing co-operation. For a time, Neville operated from his own private office in York Street but by 1853 he had the water and drainage services under his direct control in City Hall.

The magnitude of what faced Neville was starkly catalogued by a distant successor, E. J. Bourke, who was city engineer more than a hundred years later. Writing in 1960, Bourke listed the terrible problems the reformed but semi-insolvent corporation took over in 1851. It inherited huge debts, especially those of the Wide Streets Commissioners and the Pipe Water Establishment. The street surfaces were bad, the cleansing services poor, and domestic refuse collection was practically non-existent. Inadequate and defective stone drains purported to remove surface water, and there was no waterborne house drainage system 'as we know it'. More importantly, the city had an inadequate water supply.

In 1856, No. 1 of the three principal and numbered committees of the corporation had charge of paving, lighting, cleansing, wide streets, sewerage and improvements. Committee No. 2 was responsible for pipe water and the execution of sanitary powers. The functions of the committees were subsequently changed or re-organised more than once as the city officials tried to provide improved services.

DR JOHN SNOW AND SIR JOSEPH BAZALGETTE

Potential epidemics of many killer diseases were a constant fear for the vast majority of the population in the nineteenth century. The pestilential tenements or worse than primitive hovels in which unfortunate citizens barely existed, lacked the three public services most essential to public health: clean water, drainage and cleansing, which covered waste removal and street sweeping. The combination of bad housing and poor diet allowed maladies almost forgotten today to wreak havoc on peoples' health.

While medical science was advancing steadily, modern concepts of hygiene and public health were in the earlier stages of evolution. Superstition and misinformation were still rife – and the discovery, let alone acceptance, of many precepts now regarded as fundamental were away in the future. Miasma (noxious odours in the atmosphere) rather than contaminated water was widely believed to be the cause of much illness and innumerable deaths. The smells which permeated everything included those emanating from a general lack of hygiene: from sewage, polluted rivers and watercourses, urban piggeries and urban dairy cattle, animal rendering factories and smoke from the coal burned in industrial and domestic fires.

Improving public health and hygienic awareness was of the highest priority. In London, the pioneering anaesthetist Dr John Snow (1813–1858) was convinced, as early as 1849, that contaminated water rather than noxious vapours caused cholera. This fatal disease, which struck terror into the people of these islands in the second quarter of the nineteenth century, had come from the east to Europe in the

Sir Joseph Bazalgette: image by George B. Black, lithograph on paper, 1863. *Bazalgette is famous as designer of the London Main Drainage Scheme but he also acted as consultant for early Dublin drainage and produced drawings for interceptor sewers.*

1820s and first appeared in Dublin on 23 March 1832. Always a threat during the next half-century, there were further serious outbreaks in 1848–1849, 1853–1854, 1864 and 1866.

In 1854 Dr Snow proved his contaminated water theory to his own satisfaction when, in a detailed study, he traced an outbreak of the disease to a public water pump at Broad Street (now Broadwick Street) in Soho. This pump delivered water affected by the dangerously polluted River Thames. Snow's advice given to the local authority on 7 September 1854 has passed into folklore as 'Take the handle off the Broad Street pump'. A distinctive kerbstone now marks the pump's site.

A public house, appropriately named the John Snow, stands on the site of his surgery, commemorating the father of the science of epidemiology and his great achievements. Snow is also credited with pioneering the use of map pins to mark groups of locations clearly in his 1854 survey. Unfortunately it

took several years for his cholera theory to be fully proved and universally acknowledged. In the meantime, however, a growing volume of informed opinion supported his position. Finally, in 1883, the distinguished German bacteriologist Robert Koch (1843–1910) identified the cholera bacillus and proved conclusively that it was waterborne. By the time of the 1864 outbreak in Dublin, the connection between the disease and contaminated water was better understood.

As in other things, contemporary relativities are important in comparing water sources and quality. Dublin's water came from what should have been, by the standards of the day, acceptably clean canals. But, in 1835, the corporation had reason to complain to the Royal Canal Company about painting its vessels with gas tar and allowing manure to fall from boats into the water.

Nevertheless, unsatisfactory as Dublin's water supply was by modern standards, its quality was certainly better than that which so concerned Dr Snow in London. There, as with the Liffey in Dublin, the Thames was the receptacle for the city's sewers. Despite this, several water companies were extracting water from the Thames for human consumption. This scandal and how it was so brilliantly dealt with by Sir Joseph Bazalgette (1819–1891) is told in Stephen Halliday's *The Great Stink of London* (Stroud, 1999). Sir Joseph acted for a time as a consultant to Dublin Corporation, and drawings showing his proposals for interceptor sewers in the city are preserved in the city's drainage division archives.

Interceptor sewers are a most important component of sewer systems, and from this point will be met frequently in this book. They are major conduits, pipes or tunnels laid along strategic routes to take drainage from sewers that formerly flowed into rivers.

Apart from the difference in size of the two cities, the drainage comparisons between mid-nineteenth century Dublin and London were striking. In both places, the lack of a main drainage system cried out for drastic action. But, while Dublin's municipal engineering services were integrated under the aegis of one authority, London's were still hopelessly fragmented. The only authority in a position to impose a solution in London was parliament and, although it established the Metropolitan Board of Works in 1855, it did little else for another three years, when the weather created an absolute imperative for immediate action.

During the extremely hot summer of 1858 the nauseating stench from the Thames became overpowering and permeated every part of the Palace of Westminster. Parliament was galvanised into giving Joseph Bazalgette the resources he needed and work on the great London Main Drainage Scheme became a priority. Meanwhile, Dublin was anxious and probably better organised administratively than London to solve its drainage problem. The solution, a main drainage system very similar to what would now be realised in London, had been suggested by Parke Neville for Dublin in 1853, but more than forty years were to elapse before the work would begin – and take ten years to complete.

One comparison between London's interceptors and those that would eventually be built in Dublin was the matter of scale. Building the London interceptors enabled Bazalgette to construct the splendid Embankments, but Dublin was fortunate in already having the quays – virtually smaller embankments – under which to lay its intercepting sewers. Meanwhile Neville, in a report dated 23 March 1877, pointed out that the then recently completed London Main Drainage served a population of 3.5 million in an area of 74,200 acres; this represented a population of forty-seven persons per acre. At that time Dublin, including the Rathmines and Pembroke townships, covered 6,300 acres, with a population of 400,000; the population density here was sixty-three persons per acre.

MAPOTHER AND CAMERON

Among the hazards tolerated as a result of the nineteenth century's widespread ignorance of hygiene were several that are thankfully forgotten today. In densely populated areas consisting of appalling housing conditions, piggeries, slaughterhouses and knackers' yards abounded. There were in addition numerous dirty dairy premises – with cows in filthy yards at the rear – frequently selling milk that was adulterated: pasteurisation and testing were in the future. Above all, there was a vast equine population, each horse excreting an average of 14lbs (6.53kg) of dung per day, much of it deposited on ill-paved streets. None of these horrors could begin to be tackled in the absence of clean water and an effective drainage system.

Once the imperative of a pure water supply was recognised, rapid progress was possible. This depended as much on the sanitary engineer as on the medical profession, a close working relationship between the two being essential. Parke Neville collaborated closely and most effectively with successive chief medical officers, first Dr Edward Mapother and then Dr (later Sir) Charles Cameron.

Born in Fairview, Edward Dillon Mapother (1835–1908) was one of Parke Neville's many contemporaries who were regrettably all but forgotten following independence. But their enormous contributions, both to their chosen professions and to the City of Dublin, have been of lasting benefit to every citizen. A remarkable characteristic shared by all these individuals was a consuming interest in the vast range of educational and learned bodies in which they participated enthusiastically. The personification of this hunger for knowledge, Edward Mapother was appointed to the Chair of Hygiene at the Royal College of Surgeons in Ireland in 1864. In the same year he became the city's first chief medical officer.

Mapother quickly identified a major essential in the improvement of public health – a comprehensive sewerage system. He contrasted the state of the Liffey in 1864 with what could be achieved by the construction of interceptor sewers. In a paper read to the Section of the History of Medicine of the Royal Academy of Medicine in Ireland on 12 November 1997, Mary O'Doherty MA, quoted Mapother:

With regard to another fertile source of stench we may promise ourselves a most essential improvement in the sewerage of our city – namely, that the refuse shall not be discharged into the Liffey, to decompose upon its shores at low water and emit the most poisonous exhalations, but shall be carried in two main sewers parallel to the river and cast into the sea as far out as practicable … No parsimonious spirit will prevail when it is remembered that the thousands expended will be repaid in scores of human lives and hundreds of sicknesses prevented. Between our unrivalled quays there will then course a pellucid and health giving, instead of, as at present, a poisonous stream.

Edward Mapother departed for London in 1888, where he became deeply involved in research. His even more famous successor, Charles Cameron, was born on 16 July 1830 of a Cavan mother and Scottish father. He studied both chemistry and medicine and joined Dublin Corporation as an analyst in 1862. Cameron's duties in this post were combined with those of medical officer in 1874. He was also a professor at the Royal College of Surgeons and became Dublin's chief medical officer in 1880. Cameron was yet another of those polymaths who contributed much to pursuits outside medicine and public health and was a noted authority on art.

In *The Emergence and Development of Public Health Medicine in Ireland* (2,000 Years of Irish Medicine) Dr Emer Shelley MSc refers to the 1866 cholera epidemic, which claimed nearly 1,000 victims. She relates how Cameron called the attention of the corporation's Sanitary Committee to the high incidence of the disease among people who drew water from a pump in Duke Lane, off Duke Street. Sewage was found to be present in the water and, like the Broad Street pump in London in 1854, this source of water was closed. By 1868, pure water from the Vartry scheme would be available from public pumps and fountains.

Charles Cameron, who was noted for his extraordinary energy and magnanimity, campaigned relentlessly to eliminate disease, raise the standard of public health generally and provide decent housing in Dublin. His tremendous efforts earned him a well-deserved knighthood in 1885, and the Freedom of the City on 30 September 1910, two years before his official retirement. Cameron gave fifty-nine years of unstinting service to the people of Dublin, working until his death in 1921 at the age of ninety-one. Sir Charles's memory is deservedly honoured in the name of Cameron Square in Kilmainham and Cameron Street, off Cork Street.

SEEKING MORE AND BETTER WATER: CANAL CARTEL

In 1854 the corporation consulted the engineer Thomas Hawksley of London about improving Dublin's water supply. Abundance, cleanliness and high pressure were the desired criteria. Hawksley recommended that the Grand Canal Company should provide six million gallons per day, taken from the vicinity of the Twelfth Lock. Situated at Lock Road, south of Lucan, this is 210 feet above Datum and could have delivered water at a reasonable pressure. The Twelfth Lock on the Royal Canal, which is at Blanchardstown and 195 feet above Datum, was suggested as the source of a further four million gallons per day.

Inevitably disagreements about payments arose and, because of other urgencies and a lack of finance, the subject lay in abeyance for another four years. Meanwhile it became increasingly recognised that the water supplied from the canals was polluted and therefore dangerous to health. Despite this and Dr Snow's grim conclusions about contamination, talks with the canal companies were re-opened in 1858.

The negotiations again centred on the price at which the canals would provide an adequate and guaranteed supply of water from levels that would ensure high pressure. A serious disadvantage of the canal water supply systems was their lack of pressure, with the result that water could be piped only into ground floors or basements. The imminent widespread introduction of domestic water systems,

sometimes called indoor plumbing, and the need to build at higher levels than those of the canals would obviously necessitate new arrangements.

When the canal companies declined to consider any progressive arrangement, the corporation decided to obtain powers that would enable it to secure its own independent source of pure water. Thomas Hawksley and Parke Neville recommended the Coyford scheme, which would extract an adequate supply from the River Liffey near Newbridge. Their plan was adopted and steps were taken to promote the necessary Bill in the 1859–1860 parliamentary session.

Upon realising that the corporation was serious in its intentions, the canal companies and the railway interests connected with them – the Royal Canal was now controlled by the Midland Great Western of Ireland Railway Company – opposed the Coyford scheme. They claimed that there was no other source of supply equal to theirs for quality

and economy. Further tortuous negotiations took place and the Coyford scheme was abandoned in favour of a canal plan.

Parliamentary powers had been sought to carry out the Coyford scheme but the canal interests, having seen it off, reverted to their previous stance, refusing to give guarantees on quantity and pressure. Much precious time was wasted by these cynical manoeuvres. It was next proposed by those antagonistic to the corporation's plans, that the government be asked to appoint a royal commissioner who would examine all the proposals for improving the city's water supply, and that whichever scheme was recommended should be accepted by all parties. This was agreed, and the recently knighted engineer John Hawkshaw was appointed as commissioner.

In the mid-nineteenth century, installing water and drainage systems assumed ever-greater importance. Consulting engineers specialising in these sectors were in constant demand and co-operated

Dublin's first Chief Medical Officers: Edward Dillon Mapother (left) and Sir Charles Cameron (right). *Mapother advocated a comprehensive sewerage system for the improvement of public health. Cameron campaigned relentlessly to eliminate disease and provide good-quality public housing in Dublin.*

closely with their colleagues in the public services. These specialist consultants became highly experienced and could quickly assess needs and problems in widely differing circumstances. They earned widespread respect and fame and were routinely appointed by parliament, government departments and other public bodies to advise on local schemes and proposals. Their reports were the genesis of most of the schemes that have evolved and grown into modern water and drainage systems. Dublin benefited greatly from reports drawn up by these consultants, inspectors and royal commissioners.

Sir John Hawkshaw visited Dublin in August 1860 and examined all the proposed supply schemes in detail. These were six in number: the Grand and Royal canals; Lough Owel and Lough Sheelin; the River Dodder; the River Dargle and Lough Bray; the River Liffey; and the River Vartry. Among the submissions made to Hawkshaw there were several from leading medical doctors, all severely critical of canal water quality. Dublin Corporation adopted a strictly neutral public position during the commissioner's hearings.

In April 1860 John Frederick Bateman, a well-known engineer who was presumably aware of the ongoing controversy in relation to the water supply to the city, addressed a letter to the lord mayor. In it he outlined a proposal for a new supply of ten million gallons per day from an impoundment on the upper Liffey at Cloghleagh near Ballysmuttan Bridge. Being convinced of 'the exquisite purity, in a chemical point of view' of the mountain water, he did not consider any treatment necessary. The supply would gravitate to Dublin through the Crooksling Gap, partly in a 2.5-mile long tunnel, and terminate in a service reservoir at Tymon Castle, southwest of the city.

To demonstrate his confidence in his proposals, Bateman offered to construct the scheme and operate it for a period of five years at his personal

financial risk for the sum of £185,000. This must surely be one of the earliest examples of a DBO (design-build-operate) project. The Cloghleagh scheme was revived about 1970 to provide a water supply for the new town of Tallaght but later abandoned when it became obvious that it could not yield the required quantity (Chapter 10). It is sometimes referred to as the Ballysmuttan scheme.

The speedily compiled Hawkshaw report of 20 October 1860 confirmed that Dublin's water supply was bad and there was urgent need of a greatly improved system. Sir John identified the Vartry as the best source of this sorely needed and superior supply. He acknowledged that a satisfactory service for the city and suburbs could be obtained from the Liffey by the Coyford or Ballysmuttan schemes, or from the Dodder. However, difficulties could be foreseen with the milling interests on those rivers.

Among the Vartry scheme's advantages was the ease with which the conduits coming into the city from the south could supply the municipal townships of Bray, Killiney, Dalkey, Kingstown, Blackrock and Pembroke. This consideration greatly influenced the far-seeing commissioner in deciding which of the alternative schemes he would recommend. The Rathmines Commissioners' reasons for not taking Vartry water will be found in Chapter 6.

In the 1850s, Dublin's daily water consumption was higher than that of some cross-Channel cities, being quoted as thirty-seven gallons per head in December 1857. The James's Street Basin provided 4.472 million gallons, 2.886 million came from Portobello, and 3.181 million from Blessington Street. Regarding consumption per head, it should be borne in mind that the average figures do not distinguish between domestic and industrial use and most individuals would have used less water than the figures suggest.

4 *The Vartry Water Scheme 1861–1920*

OVERCOMING OPPOSITION

The result of the Hawkshaw Commission was unexpected and the estimated cost of the favoured Vartry scheme higher than expected. Nevertheless the corporation decided, at a meeting held on 23 October 1860, to promote a Bill in the 1860–1861 parliamentary session empowering it to undertake the massive project. Parke Neville, with Thomas Hawksley as consultant, prepared all the necessary drawings and other documentation. Richard Hassard, the first engineer to draw up details and costings for a Vartry scheme and who was later involved in the Bohernabreena (Chapter 5) and Howth (Chapter 9) water supply schemes, appears to have felt deprived of due credit for his work. In a paper read to the Institution of Civil Engineers of Ireland on 13 March 1861, he claimed his rightful place in the Vartry story *(Proceedings*, Vol. VI, 1863).

One of the greatest benefits ever conferred on Dublin, the Vartry water scheme was built between 1861 and 1868 and is still a source of great pride to Dublin City Council. It was described in detail by Parke Neville in his book, *A Description of the Dublin Corporation Waterworks*, published by John Falconer of 53 Upper Sackville Street in 1875. From this primary source, together with papers researched and presented by Eamon (Ned) Fleming, currently superintendent at Roundwood, comes much of what follows.

It was expected that those who had frustrated earlier schemes would honour their promise to accept Sir John Hawkshaw's findings, but this did not happen. Instead, they now resurrected the Cloghleagh Scheme as a competing plan, but this was seen as a smokescreen for their real object of thwarting any project that would deprive the canals of revenue. A bitter parliamentary contest ensued, extending over five weeks in the House of Commons and a further six days in the House of Lords. In the face of this acrimonious opposition, the Corporation Bill was finally carried.

SIR JOHN GRAY

A name that will forever be associated with municipal progress and exemplary standards in public life is that of Sir John Gray (1816–1875), indefatigable chairman of the corporation's waterworks committee. Parke Neville recorded that success in overcoming the most inveterate opposition to the Water Bill was due mainly to the skill,

Sir John Gray, bust by
Sir Thomas Farrell at
Roundwood Reservoir.
Gray was a doctor,
a journalist and a
conscientious member of
the city council, who
secured parliamentary
approval for a supply
of clean water from the
Vartry River for
Victorian Dublin.

vigour and tenacity of the then Dr John Gray. Neville was indeed fortunate in having Gray's friendship and powerful backing, which he publicly acknowledged.

A medical doctor by profession and proprietor of the *Freeman's Journal*, Gray was a principled politician and conscientious city councillor who was acutely aware of the city's urgent needs. He was ably supported by two aldermen, R. H. Kinahan and George Roe. During the progress of the Water Bill, Alderman Kinahan, who was in failing health, was advised to return to Ireland but refused to desert his colleagues at Westminster. He subsequently became seriously ill in one of the parliamentary committee rooms and died the following day. Following its passage through parliament, the Dublin Corporation Water Bill received the royal assent on 21 July 1861. As soon as he became certain that the Vartry project would become a reality, Gray pre-empted any possibility of land speculation in the Roundwood area. He bought the land that would be needed for the scheme and transferred it

to the corporation at no profit to himself.

Seventy years later, Michael Moynihan, city engineer, wrote:

> In the public life of the city at that time was one very strenuous man who could not be taught to spell the word 'fail'. He had behind him an honourable reputation, the influence wielded by a Member of Parliament who was free of party ties, and the support of the powerful journal which he owned. The citizens of Dublin have raised a noble monument to the memory of Sir John Gray. It was nobly earned, for to him is due the Vartry supply of water to our city.

In addition to the main purpose of obtaining water from the Vartry, the Act also made Dublin Corporation responsible for the public water supply in South County Dublin and North Wicklow. A flat rate of 1*s* 3*d* (one shilling and three pence) in the pound – the equivalent of 8 cent today – was to be levied on rateable valuations for this service in what became known as the extra municipal districts or areas.

Statutory charges precisely set out in legislation enacted prior to 1914 became a constant source of trouble in later years. With costs and prices falling during the forty years up to 1914, there were few problems in those decades. However, with the outbreak of the Great War and consequent inflation, it became impossible to maintain services at the rates that had been set by statute forty or fifty years earlier. New legislation was frequently cited as the only solution to the severe difficulties in which many public service providers found themselves.

Towards the end of the abortive negotiations with Royal Canal officials that preceded the Vartry scheme, a very small sum separated the corporation's offer from the canal company's demand. This later led to the observation that 'looking back, the citizens of Dublin may congratulate themselves that even by the small margin of £200 a year they were saved from the Canal waters'.

GEOGRAPHY

The River Vartry rises at the base of the Great Sugar Loaf mountain and flows southwards by the Devil's Glen and Ashford into the Broad Lough, which discharges into the sea at Wicklow town. The length of the Vartry from rise to sea is seventeen and a half miles and its total catchment area is 34,890 acres (14,119 hectares). In 1861 there were five mills along the river.

On obtaining the necessary powers, the corporation immediately proceeded to carry out the work. The first stone was laid at the site of the future Prince of Wales Reservoir, Stillorgan, on 10 November 1862 by the lord lieutenant, the Earl of Carlisle.

The point selected on the Vartry as the site of the embankment to form the great storage reservoir is about seven and a half miles from its source and one and a half miles southeast of Roundwood. The level of the water at this point was 632 feet above Ordnance Datum and 520 feet above the then highest point in the City of Dublin.

The main embankment, which formed Lough Vartry – the name given to the reservoir – was 66 feet high at its deepest part and the greatest depth of water was 60 feet. It was 1,640 feet long on top and 28 feet wide and has a puddle core. Slow sand filters were constructed with a total depth of 6 feet and 6 inches. The road from Wicklow to Roundwood, which previously passed over land submerged by the reservoir, was carried over the embankment.

At the eastern end of the embankment, the overflow weir was 300 feet long and the level was 6 feet below the top of the bank. When the reservoir was full at this level the area of land covered was 409 acres and was the largest in these islands when it was created. The storage capacity was 2.4 billion gallons, equal to two hundred days supply for the 1860s city and suburban districts.

Two other embankments, the Knockatemple and the Watersbridge, were constructed to carry county roads across the reservoir. A five feet high stone wall, the base of which was on a contour line six feet above the top water line, surrounded the reservoir and works. This wall was eleven miles long and the area enclosed, including embankments, filter beds and lands purchased by the corporation, was 550 acres in extent.

EARTHEN DAMS, RESERVOIR AND TOWER

Both Vartry dams are earthen embankments with puddle clay cores keyed into the underlying rock. The upstream slopes are protected from wave erosion by stone pitching. This consists of roughly dressed stones, typically 18 inches deep, laid on a bed of broken stone on the slope of the dam, the gaps being packed with smaller stones. The stones used for pitching and to build the boundary walls of the waterworks came mainly from material excavated from the overflow channels and by clearing neighbouring fields of large granite boulders deposited during the last ice age.

The granite boulders were split by boring a series of small holes, 2 to 3 inches deep and 4 to 6 inches apart along the grain of the stone using a steel chisel

Vartry Lodge at Roundwood Reservoir.
Built for the reservoir's superintendent, Vartry Lodge still fulfils its original function.

known as a jumper. A wedge or plug was then driven between two hard pieces of steel called feathers and a succession of sledgehammer blows resulted in a clean break.

The downstream slopes of the embankments were grassed. This dam type – often known as a Pennine Dam – was extremely popular in Britain from the nineteenth century to the mid-twentieth century. Its great advantages were that, properly constructed, it was extremely watertight and nearly all construction material could be obtained within the reservoir site.

Work began with the diversion of the river to create a dry working area and prevent flooding of the site by storms during dam building. This was done by temporarily damming the river upstream and diverting it to an eduction tunnel or culvert that ran under the site of the dam and discharged to a newly constructed downstream channel, which returned the river to its original course.

Building the dam proper then commenced with the stripping of all topsoil and excavation of a cut-off trench down to rock level along the centre line of the dam. The trench was cut into the rock until sound material was reached and then filled with puddle clay. This is obtained by mixing the right clay thoroughly with water (puddling) and remoulding the mixture into a putty-like substance.

Suitable stone-free clay was excavated from within the reservoir site and brought to the dam where it was laid along the line of the embankment in a thin layer. Water was added and gangs of labourers armed with spades cut and cross-cut the surface of the clay and then heeled it in, remoulding it and working it into the underlying layer to form a putty-like homogenous mass. The men wore special waterproof boots with steel tipped soles and heels that were greased to prevent the clay sticking to them.

When the dam was finished, a draw-off tower was built near the upper end of the eduction tunnel. Cast iron pipes were laid from the tower through the tunnel, which was then sealed. The supply pipes were brought up inside the tower and intakes at different levels were provided so that water could be drawn off at the level of best water quality. The larger scouring pipes, used to draw down the reservoir, have only one low-level intake.

To cater for storm flows when the reservoir was full an overflow was provided. In the lower reservoir this consisted of a 300-foot long weir, built on its own low dam set to one side of the main dam and discharging to a purpose-made channel. In the upper reservoir, there was a tapering circular shaft with a tunnel at the bottom leading to the channel.

The geological formation of the entire Vartry drainage area is lower Silurian and Cambrian slate, except on the hilltops to the west. It yields a peculiarly soft pure water. In contrast, the untreated raw water supplied from the canals was extremely hard, and left heavy calcium deposits in the mains. Almost colourless during the greater part of the year, the quality of Vartry water was, understandably, regarded very highly. A slow sand filtration system, which was not included in the original plans submitted to parliament, was installed at Roundwood to remove suspended matter. Curiously, in the 1860s, the beneficial biological action of these filters was unknown – the science of bacteriology was still nearly a quarter of a century away. Few other towns or cities enjoyed the benefits of water purification at that time.

On 30 June 1863, the waters of the River Vartry were turned through the tunnel by the lord lieutenant. On the same occasion, Dr John Gray, chairman of the waterworks committee and who declined the lord mayoralty, was deservedly knighted. Sir John's memory is permanently and publicly honoured by the statue that looks down O'Connell Street from the plinth on the north side of the Abbey Street junction. This monument was paid for by public subscriptions and Parke Neville donated the profits from his book about the Vartry water scheme to the fund. Gray Street and Gray Square in the Coombe area also honour the memory of Sir John Gray.

The eduction tunnel, which has two discharge pipes, was first used to pass the river water while the embankment was under construction. One of the

VARTRY. CALLOW HILL. 538. W.L.

**Callow Hill at
Roundwood Reservoir.**
*Showing original filter
beds on the Vartry
River, which are still in
use today and remain
as effective as when they
were first built.*

discharge pipes, 33 inches in diameter, carried the
city supply, while the second, 48 inches in diameter,
was intended to act as a sluice if the water level in
the reservoir needed to be lowered.

Water was taken from the Lower Reservoir
through the 33-inch discharge pipe to the treatment
works, situated directly downstream of what is now
called the Lower Embankment. Purification
consisted of slow sand filtration through beds of
specially graded sand. Today, chemical disinfection
follows, chlorine gas killing off any residual patho-
genic organisms. Fluoride and lime are added to the
filtered water, the first to prevent dental caries and
the latter to correct the natural corrosiveness of the
raw water. As originally built, Roundwood had
seven filter beds (Nos 1–7). Three additional filters
(Nos 8–10) were constructed in 1873 to cope with
increased demand.

THE LEAK – DISASTER AVERTED

In his paper 'On the Water Supply to the City of
Dublin' read to the Institution of Civil Engineers in
February 1874, Parke Neville described, calmly and
clinically, a frightening train of events that had
occurred seven years earlier. In the course of his
research, Ned Fleming, the present superintendent
of Roundwood, found a more graphic and atmospheric contemporary account written by Richard
Walsh, a corporation engineer who had been on the
scene and whose manuscript 'Construction of the
Vartry Waterworks' is in the National Library
(Manuscript 19814).

In November 1866, during the first filling of the
reservoir, a 48-inch throttle valve broke in the
eduction tunnel, which carries the water from the
reservoir to the filter beds at Roundwood. A wooden

Unveiling of Gray bust at Roundwood Reservoir, 1881.
This remarkable series of magic lantern slides, from the John L. Robinson collection at the Royal Society of Antiquaries of Ireland, is published here for the first time. It shows the members of Dublin Corporation's Waterworks Committee assembled for the unveiling ceremony and enjoying themselves by posing on the plinth beforehand.

plug was fitted by divers to the upstream end of the pipe in December to facilitate repair work. In January 1867, a leak that threatened the safety of the dam appeared in the tunnel and the plug then needed to be removed to lower the level of water in the reservoir. The leak, which was first noticed on 31 January, increased alarmingly. Richard Walsh wrote:

> They endeavoured to plug up the hole but it broke out afresh in another place….
>
> 4th (February) Monday: Mr. Andrews came into town, told Mr. Neville there was a leak in the Main Bank at Roundwood. On the 5th Tues. was so alarmed that he at once telegraphed for Bateman, Duncan and Sir J. Gray. The last two arrived on Thurs. at 1 a..m. and went over the Bank by torchlight …. (The Andrews referred to in the report was James Andrews, an assistant water-works engineer who died in 1894.)

A veritable plague of vicissitudes followed, greatly increasing the fears of the engineers. During the second week of February, when every strenuous effort to solve their problems was thwarted, and the situation was at its worst (the plug remained firmly stuck in position as the leak worsened), Walsh wrote:

> The prospect is indeed gloomy, we are all very sad. The rush and roar of the waters, the splash of stones, the darkness, the hot, dank air, the spray of the leak dashing through the joints of the ashlar, the hammering and shouting of the men, the flickering lights glancing about in the darkness and gloom and the dread and danger that hung over our heads as the Bank might have burst in a moment and then Have Mercy on us O God. Neville has fallen off a plank, is much cut on the head, full 20 ft we had to carry him up to bed and send for the carriage, 1 a.m. 10th, Sunday.

Great crowds came from Dublin and Wicklow on that Sunday to see what was happening. Following a day of continuing turmoil and gloom on the Monday, Parke Neville's condition deteriorated and a doctor had to be summoned, and Mrs Neville came from Dublin to be with him on 14 February.

Work continued almost without a break until 1 March, by which date the plug had been removed from the eduction pipe and the leak was finally stemmed.

Richard Walsh has chronicled, in very human language, events that could have proved disastrous for the Roundwood works. How catastrophic they could have been for the local population was described by Padraig Jenkinson in the *Ashford and District Historical Journal* (No. 3) for July 1993.

As soon as news of the Roundwood leak reached Ashford, people began to fear a disaster similar to that which had recently overtaken Sheffield. Above that city was the new Dale Dike Reservoir, very similar in construction to Roundwood. The filling of Dale Dike reservoir was almost complete on 10 March 1864 when the dam collapsed and was swept away by three million tons of water. Extensive areas of Sheffield were destroyed and 241 people lost their lives. Because Roundwood contained three times more water than Dale Dike, the panic of the Ashford people is readily understandable. Jenkinson records that for three weeks Ashford and surrounding districts were literally depopulated as people fled from their homes. When repair and reconstruction of the Roundwood dam were well under way, Mr Bateman, the consulting engineer called in by Parke Neville and Sir John Gray, said 'I am certain that when the existing leak is repaired the bank will be safe for all time'.

The structures associated with the Vartry works were executed in cut stone with attractive embellishments. The drawoff towers and the view of the treatment works from the embankment on the lower dam continue to be admired by day trippers from the city.

Ned Fleming, the present superintendent at Roundwood, records that while other local authorities followed a policy of depopulating catchments – Belfast displaced over 400 families in the Carrickfergus area alone – Dublin did not. However, it took the precaution of diverting the drainage of Roundwood village out of the catchment by canal or drainage ditch, still maintained for that purpose.

Dublin City Council scrutinises all proposed developments in the gathering grounds of its reservoirs and opposes those considered to be a hazard to water quality.

The Dublin Waterworks Acts are noteworthy for their preferential treatment of wealthy land owners, who were represented in parliament. Special clauses were inserted in the proposed legislation during its passage in the House of Lords to protect their interests. Daniel Tighe was paid £5,000 compensation for losses due to the reduction in flow of the river through his estate. Following the Vartry leak, he sued the corporation because of the possibility of the dam failing and obtained a further £12,061.

THE ROUNDWOOD-CALLOWHILL TUNNEL

On leaving the filters, the treated water passed – and still does – through two and a half miles of tunnel. This tunnel, six feet high and five feet wide, was constructed through hard greywacke and quartzite. The tunnel and shafts took more than three years to complete. A huge engineering feat in the Ireland of the 1860s, it merits further description.

Construction of the tunnel, which takes a curvilinear route under hills to the east of the reservoir, began on 4 January 1863. Twenty-one shafts, 600 feet apart, were sunk along the route and the tunnel was driven in both directions from these. Several formidable difficulties, all described by Parke Neville, were overcome in the course of the work before the last heading was opened out in September 1866.

Drilling and blasting was the procedure followed from each shaft. One miner held a long steel chisel (jumper) to the rock face while a colleague hammered it to form a borehole about 18 inches deep. About ten such holes were bored in each face, which were then packed with blasting powder and fired. When the shattered rock was removed, drilling started again. Because of the hardness of the rock, each hole took up to three hours to bore and so blunted the jumpers that as many as forty had to be used for each 18-inches deep hole.

The miners were also hampered on several occasions when they encountered seams of crushed, water-bearing rock. Water from the rock face was directed back to the shaft from where it was removed using a horse-powered hoist or gin. The quantity of water encountered during the work made the substitution of steam power for horse gins necessary in order to drive the pumps at several of the shafts.

Progress was very slow because of the various difficulties; the tunnel advanced by less than four feet per week. In an effort to speed things up, two different types of tunnelling machine, representing the latest technology of the time, were tried. Although neither was particularly successful, they are of considerable interest because they were among the earliest examples of attempts to mechanise the excavation of hard rock in tunnels. Both machines used the then novel technology of compressed air drills, driven by steam engines.

The first machine, invented by Dubliner George Robert Low, was designed to work two drills simultaneously at the rock face. However, because of the small size and rectangular shape of the Vartry tunnel, only one could be used. It was found as a result of the trials that faster progress could be achieved with three shifts working around the clock.

Fred Beaumont, an Englishman, devised the second machine. Parke Neville observed that 'the experiment continued for about eight months at great expense to the inventor'. Beaumont's machine had a series of chisels or jumpers fixed to the perimeter of a slowly rotating disc which cut a continuous groove the full five feet diameter of the machine. Simultaneously a hole was bored in the centre of the disc into which charging powder could be packed and fired to break up the isolated disc of rock.

Although Beaumont's machine failed at the Vartry, due to the hardness of the granite and the limitations of metallurgy at the time, he continued to develop rock-boring machines and achieved considerable success. In 1881 two seven-foot diameter machines he designed performed very successfully in the earliest attempt to construct a tunnel from England to France. When eight hundred metres (more than half a mile) had been completed, the British military authorities stopped the project because they feared that England could be too easily invaded from the continent. Beaumont chose the same stratum and depth for this tunnel as that selected more than a century later for the present Channel Tunnel.

The Roundwood to Callowhill tunnel, which in places is more than 160 feet below ground level, has eight airshafts along its length. The shafts were originally surmounted by towers, but these were removed for security reasons during the Second World War.

CALLOW HILL-STILLORGAN

From the end of the tunnel at Callow Hill break-pressure tank, a 33-inch diameter main was laid for a distance of seventeen miles to Stillorgan, passing through three further break-pressure tanks at Kilmurray, Kilcroney and Rathmichael. These tanks, sometimes called surge tanks, balance the pressure in a pipeline and guard against the possibility of damage by a 'water hammer' – the destructive force created by a sudden change in water pressure. Because these tanks were located on the maximum hydraulic gradient, they involved no loss in the maximum discharge capacity of the trunk main.

Distributing reservoirs, originally named after the Prince of Wales, were constructed at Stillorgan. Covering an area of more than twenty-six acres, each of the two reservoirs has a capacity in excess of 43 million gallons. In 1885, storage at Stillorgan was increased to 177,231,000 gallons when an additional reservoir of 94,213,000 gallons capacity was built. It was named after Sir John Gray, the father of the scheme.

At Stillorgan, the pipes coming from Roundwood can discharge into the reservoirs or directly into the screen house. This octagonal building is located at the south-eastern angle of the lower reservoir and has screens of copper wire gauze. Valves in the building enable the water to be drawn from the reservoirs or from either side of the screens. Two 27-inch diameter mains (since supplemented by additional pipelines) take the water onwards from Stillorgan to the city.

The main contractor for the Vartry scheme was William McCormick of London and Derry. The pipes were supplied and laid by Eddington and Sons of Glasgow. Spencer Harty, later to become city engineer, was in charge of work on the Vartry scheme during its construction period. A feature of the scheme – and of most major engineering works executed before 1900 – was that the work was done by men using picks and shovels, horses and carts. Working conditions were cruel and primitive, with health, safety and welfare only as good as the employers and engineers allowed.

WATER DISTRIBUTION:
THE EXTRA MUNICIPAL DISTRICTS

Under the provisions of the 1861 Waterworks Act, Dublin Corporation became the statutory water supplier for large areas of South County Dublin and North County Wicklow. These areas were known as the extra municipal districts; their water charges were set out in the Act but afterwards modified to the detriment of the corporation through the machinations of various vested interests and, in one instance, venomous spite (see Chapter 6). Details of the different rates charged to various townships are set out in detail in the January 1960 report of E. J. Bourke, city engineer. Supplies were taken off the main coming into Dublin to serve Greystones and Bray, and Wicklow Town was served direct from the works at Roundwood.

Water for the townships that benefited from the Vartry scheme was delivered to their boundaries, the necessary delivery mains and local networks being financed and laid by the township commissioners. Killiney, Dalkey, Blackrock, Pembroke, New Kilmainham and Clontarf were early beneficiaries. Drumcondra followed after its establishment in 1878.

Groups of valves at Merrion Avenue, Simmonscourt and Leeson Street enabled the two city-bound 27-inch mains to be connected. This was to maintain the supply in case of an accident, when one section of either main could be emptied while the other was being repaired. From Merrion Avenue and Simmonscourt, branch mains supplied water to Blackrock and Pembroke. Between 1891 and 1907 an additional 24-inch main was laid from Round-wood to Stillorgan to compensate for the reduced delivery of the 33-inch trunk main as a result of corrosion and incrustation. This also served Bray, Dalkey and Kingstown (Dun Laoghaire).

WATER IN BLACKROCK, KINGSTOWN AND DALKEY

Prior to the completion of the Vartry scheme, water for Kingstown, which included within its boundaries Sandycove, Glasthule, Glenageary, Sallynoggin and Monkstown, came from local streams and wells. The 1861 Waterworks Act contained several provisions (notably Sections 74–77) dealing specifically with the township and the Kingstown Waterworks Company.

Ostensibly, the Kingstown Waterworks Company was set up under an Act of 1859 to improve the supply in the township. It was overtaken by the 1861 Act, which decreed that Dublin Corporation would henceforth be responsible for supplying water to Kingstown. The Act authorised Dublin Corporation to negotiate with a view to acquiring the Waterworks Company and, in the event of a successful outcome, to work the Kingstown water system exactly as the company had done. E. J. Bourke, city engineer in the 1960s, researched the Kingstown company and was satisfied that it was no more than a paper enterprise and was one of several methods devised to take advantage of Dublin Corporation in pursuit of acquiring cheap water.

Section 38 of the 1861 Act laid down that on commencing to supply water in Kingstown the corporation would have to erect and maintain up to six public fountains 'for the gratuitous supply of water

to such poor persons for domestic purposes only … as the Town Commissioners shall direct'. The fountains were to be so placed, constructed and maintained as to prevent misuse of water, or a continuous discharge. Horse troughs, crucial to transport in the nineteenth and early twentieth centuries, were also constructed and are referred to later in this chapter.

To serve Kingstown's population, which reached 18,586 by 1885, a 15-inch diameter pipe conveyed water from the Stillorgan reservoirs to a point near Monkstown Castle. An 1871 Kingstown map shows this supply in place with 9-inch and 12-inch diameter distribution mains laid to Carrickbrennan Road and Mounttown Upper respectively. An extensive network of small, mostly 3-inch, distribution mains is also shown, extending from Carrickbrennan Road to Castlepark Road and from Upper Glenageary Road to the coast.

A branch main from the Kingstown supply was extended to Dalkey. Unhappily, the elevation of the Stillorgan Reservoir at about 270 feet above sea level was insufficient to serve the higher areas of Dalkey around Mount Salus and Torca Road – at their highest point these areas are about 330 feet above sea level. The Township Engineer, Richard W. Walsh (who worked on the Vartry scheme and wrote the graphic account of the leak in the impounding embankment at Roundwood), advocated the purchase of an American device, a Haliday Standard Windmill, to pump water up to these higher areas. These devices had fallen into disuse by 1900.

It is not clear where such pump or pumps were located but a small reservoir and pumping station, now disused, was constructed at an elevation of about 210 feet at the lower end of the 'Metals', between Dalkey Avenue and Ardbrough Road. A second larger reservoir, also disused, was constructed about half way up this section of the Metals. A third small high-level reservoir at an elevation of about 350 feet, now also abandoned and the site sold for housing, was located above Torca Road and below the public right of way on to Dalkey Hill. This reservoir was served by a 4-inch diameter rising main from the pumping station located at the lower end of the Metals.

Vartry water from Stillorgan could easily have reached both of the lower service reservoirs without pumping but not the highest. These service reservoirs appear to have been abandoned in the 1950s when this area was served by a new intermediate level reservoir (see below). Dalkey Township was actively extending water mains into this area well before the end of the century as revealed by a contract drawing signed by Walsh in 1890 which indicates the intention to lay a 3-inch main along Killiney Road, Dalkey Avenue and lower Ardbrough Road. The 4-inch diameter rising main is shown and the high-level tank is referred to on this drawing.

The townships of Kingstown, Blackrock and Dalkey did at one point consider developing their own supply but the scheme turned out to be too ambitious and the townships entered into contracts with Dublin Corporation. Local distribution networks were probably all in place well before the end of the nineteenth century: an old record drawing shows that Kingstown had an extensive distribution network in 1871. The Killiney-Ballybrack water supply, which was taken off the Callowhill-Stillorgan main at the Silver Tassie, was probably developed earlier from local sources.

Relations between the townships and the corporation did not always run smoothly. The compulsory metering of the water to ensure that not more than the agreed supply was taken was a source of friction. A penal charge imposed on excess water taken over and above the contracted quantity led to litigation between Blackrock and the corporation. The townships often complained that they were not provided with the supply contracted for and the corporation was not satisfied that the townships were controlling waste water.

Costs in excess of the original estimates on the Vartry scheme, the quantities of water supplied to the various townships or extra municipal districts, and the price charged, led to endless controversy and disagreements up to the end of the nineteenth

century. Legislation in 1866, 1874 and 1885 gave rise to expensive litigation and exposed the many ruses the wealthy townships used in order to extract the maximum from the corporation. The loopholes in the 1885 Act, exploited in what the lord chief justice described as double-dealing, were finally closed by yet another Act in 1897.

Among the more bizarre proposals was one to create a 'waterworks partnership'. This would give the townships, which had contributed nothing to the capital costs of the Vartry scheme, some control over the system and a share of any profits the corporation might derive from water rates and the sale of water. Another proposal, especially promoted by Bray, was that the nearer a township was to Roundwood, the lower its water charges should be.

Pipes at Leeson Street Bridge.

Victorian water-mains which drew water from the Grand Canal for distribution to the Dublin Townships.

THE CITY WATER MAINS

The two 27-inch diameter pipes carried the city supply a distance of just over 4½ miles from Stillorgan to Eustace (Leeson Street) Bridge, which until 1901 marked the city boundary. Ornate air valves are mounted on the pipes, which can be seen above the arch on the downstream side of the bridge. Later, two additional mains, each 24 inches in diameter, were laid from Stillorgan to the city.

North of Leeson Street Bridge, the original two 27-inch mains diverged. One went northwest via St Stephen's Green, Kevin Street and the Coombe, turning north through Meath Street and Thomas

Leeson Street Bridge, over the Grand Canal.

People crossing the bridge are completely unaware of the superb cast-iron structure below which was designed as a Victorian water-main.

Street, where it reduced to 24 inches in diameter. It continued by Bridgefoot Street, crossing the Liffey at Queen Street Bridge. In Queen Street, the diameter was further reduced to 18 inches and at North King Street it joined an existing 12-inch main.

The other 27-inch main ran northeastwards from Leeson Street under Fitzwilliam Street, Merrion Square, Holles Street and Sandwith Street to Great Brunswick (Pearse) Street. It then turned west to D'Olier Street, which it traversed to Carlisle (O'Connell) Bridge and into Sackville (O'Connell) Street, where it reduced to 24 inches in diameter. The line continued northwards to Cavendish Row, where it reduced further in size to 18 inches. Finally,

on reaching the junction of Frederick Street and Dorset Street, it joined an existing 12-inch main.

This 12-inch main ran westward under Bolton Street and North King Street where, at the junction of Queen Street, it met the main that had taken the other route from Leeson Street via Stephen's Green and Thomas Street. Thus was formed a great encircling artery from which all the minor distributing mains were fed. At every street intersection, screw valves enabled the water to be cut off when repairs were necessary.

The total length of new mains laid in Dublin, and of old ones taken up, cleansed and re-laid, was 50 miles. With 60 miles of existing mains, this brought the total mileage to 110 miles.

ADJUSTING TO A HIGH
PRESSURE WATER SUPPLY: PLANNING
FOR EVERY EVENTUALITY

Before the Vartry water scheme became operational, the corporation warned householders that the supply would be at high pressure. All plumbing should therefore be examined comprehensively and upgraded where necessary in preparation for the increased pressure. Quite simply, existing fittings were incapable of dealing with high pressure and would leak or fail as soon as the pressure increased. Few people paid any heed to the warnings and Parke Neville observed that when the water was laid on, street by street, 'the commotion it caused was great, and the rate of pay for plumbers rose to a large premium'.

For months the waste was enormous; consumption was up to nineteen million gallons every day or twice the expected usage. And although the waste was gradually reduced, mainly due to new fittings and the diligence of inspectors, the problem remained. This was usually due to people leaving taps running in the belief that this would flush the drains and reduce the pressure on old fittings.

The total cost of the Vartry water scheme, including alterations made during the work or immediately afterwards, was £620,000. A major pioneering project, more work than originally intended was carried out and further enlargement later became necessary. The works and the increased necessary expenditure were authorised in Acts of 1866 and 1874. Spread over a population of 330,000, the final costs worked out at £1 17s 6d (€2.38) per head of population, and compared most favourably with the cost in other cities then enjoying the benefits of new water supply systems. Parke Neville was justifiably able to boast on completion of the work that 'every part of the city is now effectively supplied with water, and the service affords universal satisfaction … and which has proved one of the most successful and effective works of the kind ever executed'.

One temporary difficulty, however, gave rise to some complaints. Old mains and service pipes were amply coated on the inside with a deposit of lime and iron resulting from the canal water previously used. This accumulated to a thickness of about an inch and reduced the capacity of the pipes. The softer Vartry water acted as a solvent, detaching the coating from the pipes. A dirty, muddy deposit was formed, leading to water users accusing the corporation of delivering bog water. Fortunately the annoyance lasted only a few months.

The Vartry River, above the Roundwood dam, has a catchment of 14,000 acres. In the 1860s, when rain gauges were still new and not yet universally trusted, it was estimated that the annual rainfall would be 29.4 inches, of which 14 inches would represent the needs of the waterworks. On these figures, a supply of twelve million gallons per day could be expected. In fact, the annual rainfall yield in the Vartry catchment turned out to be a welcome average of 29 inches over a period of 123 years.

When planning the Vartry scheme, Parke Neville was concerned about the likelihood of difficulties with downstream millers or riparian proprietors. A compensation reservoir shown on the plans laid before parliament was eliminated before the committee stage of the Bill and monetary recompense was given instead to the downstream interests. By this arrangement the corporation became the sole owner of all the water and was protected from any possible litigation.

There were genuine doubts about the adequacy of the Vartry supply and some belated efforts were made by the canal companies to retain a number of industrial users. There was begrudging opposition to accepting a Vartry supply from some other quarters as well, including Bray Town Commissioners. This was a classic case of looking a gift horse in the mouth because the legislation provided water to the township at a fixed price of 2.4 pence, or just over one cent per 1,000 gallons (4.5m^3). The Bray commissioners even dallied with the possibility of getting their water supply from the Sugarloaf Mountain, but this was not pursued. *The Irish Builder* (January 1867) reported that at a meeting of the township commissioners on 17 December 1867 'The noble chairman (the Earl of Meath) … held that it would be of great advantage to Bray to get rid of any connexion with the Vartry Works as a permanent incubus'.

WATER FOR FIREFIGHTING AND INDUSTRY

There were 1,399 fire hydrants, to Bateman and Moore's patent, on the water mains as originally laid. These were installed one hundred yards apart, and this is still the standard spacing. The intention was that no premises would be more than fifty yards from a hydrant. This ready availability of water contrasted starkly with earlier times when the main had to be excavated or the water had to be brought from the nearest watercourse or river. The dread of fire that haunted so many people in a way we would find hard to understand today was now greatly reduced.

In his book, *A Description of the Dublin Corporation Waterworks* (1875), Parke Neville pointed out that in the event of a fire increased pressure could be achieved rapidly to deal with the outbreak. He went on to say that the advent of Vartry water eliminated the need for fire engines:

> Since the Vartry water has been introduced into the City, the necessity for maintaining fire-engines has ceased. In every case of fire which has occurred (and there have been several serious ones), the water thrown from the mains by simply attaching a stand-pipe and hose to the hydrants, has been found sufficient to extinguish the largest fire with a facility and rapidity which no number of steam or hand fire engines could effect.

In his annual report for 1869 the superintendent of the fire brigade wrote:

> During the year, I have been able to dispense with the use of both steam and hand engines, on all occasions of fires within the limits of the city, owing to the high pressure of the Vartry water, working direct from the stand-pipe attached to hydrant on mains. By this means I can get to work a great deal sooner than I otherwise could do.

While the viewpoint and experience just described had its adherents, it did not find long-term favour. In an experiment carried out to test their relative merits, the power from a hydrant exceeded that of a steam pump in some circumstances. Hoses connected directly to hydrants were used for several years but the practice eventually ceased, and there would always be occasions when a fire crew would have to work in an area without a convenient high-pressure water supply. Established under an Act of 1862, Dublin Fire Brigade was funded from the water rate, thus making it subservient to the waterworks committee. When first set up, the brigade had four manual pumps, acquiring its first horse-drawn steam pump in 1864. A second steamer was in service by 1872, four years after the Vartry scheme was completed and three years before Neville's book was published. The next steam pump was purchased in 1893, more than six years after Parke Neville's death. Uneasy relations between the waterworks committee and the fire brigade continued for many years, at times escalating into open hostility.

In fire brigade regulations drawn up by the waterworks committee on 3 February 1893 it was laid down that every member of the committee was a member of the brigade, but was not to interfere with the superintendent or firemen attending a fire.

Prior to the inauguration of the Vartry scheme the charge for water for manufacturing purposes in Dublin was made according to the diameter of the supply pipe without regard to the size of the tapped main or pressure. This changed with the arrival of the new system. The 1861 Waterworks Act described several categories of users and the purposes to which water might be applied. Various charges were set out, especially in relation to horses, the road-going motive power of the day. Steam engines were covered only in the contexts of railways and industry.

Industrial users now had their supplies metered and this initially led to considerable resistance. It was then discovered that waste had been occurring on a vast scale, because consumers had no incentive to economise or to keep their fittings in good order.

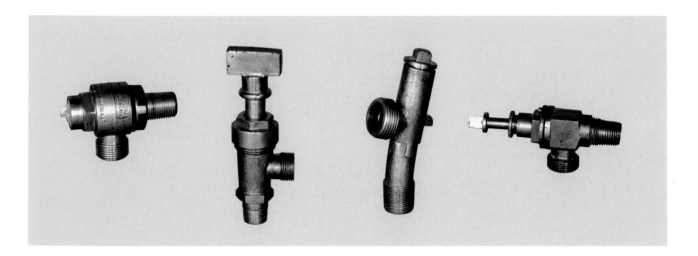

In time, the situation improved and the corporation derived large increases in revenue from metered water. The water was supplied on a sliding scale of charges, all quantities under 500 gallons being charged at 12*d* (one shilling, equal to 6.35 cent). Users of more than 75,000 gallons paid 4*d* (just over 2 cent) per 1,000 gallons.

LIVING IT UP – THE 1892 INSPECTION

Sir John Gray, first chairman of the waterworks committee, gained fame and honour for his sterling public service. Unfortunately some of his successors on the committee came to public notice for very different reasons in a celebrated court case, *Bridgeman v Drury*, in 1894.

The case was taken by a Dublin ratepayer, Bridgeman, against the local government auditor, Drury. The latter had approved the sum of £51 16*s* 8*d* (£51.83 or €65.82) for luncheon expenses, arising from the annual inspection of the Vartry waterworks by the committee in August 1892. Bridgeman sought to have this approval overturned and to have the members of the committee pay their own expenses. He succeeded and the following extract from Judge Peter O'Brien's summing up gives a flavour of what was described as a very liquid lunch.

Now I think it is relevant to refer to the character of this luncheon. I have before me the items in the bill. Amongst the list of wines are two dozen champagne, Ayala, 1885 – a very good brand – at 84s (£4.20) a dozen; one dozen Marcobrunn hock – a very nice hock; one dozen Chateau Margaux – an excellent claret; one dozen fine old Dublin whiskey – the best whiskey that can be got; one case of Ayala; six bottles of Amontillado sherry – a stimulating sherry; and the ninth item is some more fine Dublin whiskey! Then Mr. Lovell supplies the 'dinner' (this was dinner, not a mere luncheon!) including all attendance, at 10s (50p) per head. There is an allowance for brakes; one box of cigars, 100; coachmen's dinner; beer, stout, minerals in siphons, and ice for wine. There is dessert, and there are sandwiches, and an allowance for four glasses broken – a very small number broken under the circumstances. In sober earnestness, what was this luncheon and outing? It seems to me to have been a pic-nic on an expensive scale. By what principle of our common law is it sustainable? By none that I can see … this is a question of providing a sumptuous repast for the members of the Corporation on the Wicklow hills. It is not certainly for the benefit of the Corporation, or of the rate-paying citizens of Dublin, that the members of the Corporation should lunch sumptuously. I asked for statute or for case, but neither was cited. The Solicitor-General in his most able argument – I have always to guard myself against his plausibility –

Brass fittings.

A selection of nineteenth-century brass fittings used by Victorian plumbers.

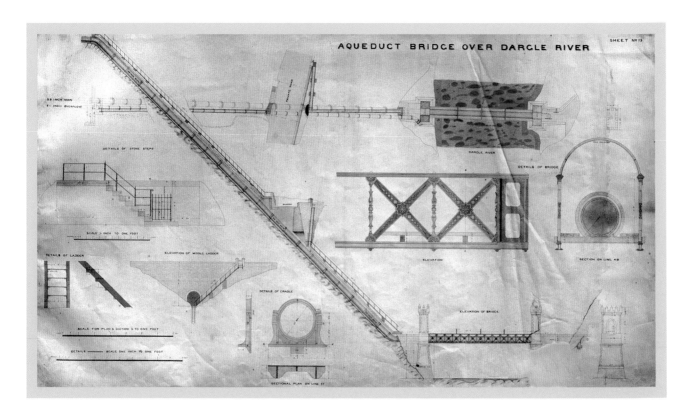

Design for aqueduct and bridge over the Dargle River.

The Dargle Valley, just outside Enniskerry in Co Wicklow, is still a popular beauty-spot, just as it was in the nineteenth century. An aqueduct was designed to bring water across the river, but it was camouflaged by a decorative bridge.

appealed pathetically to common sense; he asked, really with tears in his voice, whether the members of the Corporation should starve; he drew a most gruesome picture; he represented that the members of the Corporation would really traverse the Wicklow hills in a spectral condition, unless they were sustained by lunch … In answer to the pathetic appeal of the Solicitor-General, we do not say that the members of the Corporation are not to lunch. But we do say that they are not to do so at the expense of the citizens of Dublin. They cannot banquet at their expense in the Mansion House and, in our opinion, they cannot lunch at their expense in Wicklow. We agree with the opinion of the Law Adviser of the Corporation – an excellent opinion of a most admirable officer – when he expressed himself to the effect that the payment of the expenses and entertainment of the general body of the Corporation, when inspecting the Vartry Works, could not be legally justified.

The reference to brakes in Judge O'Brien's remarks may need explanation. A brake was a passenger vehicle, usually an open four-wheeler in the days of

horse-drawn transport. It could carry up to eight or ten people and was widely used by shooting parties. The term 'shooting brake' was still current in the 1950s for what is now called an estate car. Such vehicles were available for hire at many railway stations. It is also worth recording that councillors and corporation personnel visiting the Vartry works usually travelled by train to Bray rather than Wicklow, continuing the journey to Roundwood in hired road vehicles.

THE 1893 DROUGHT

An understandable and constant worry for the waterworks committee and staff was a possible failure of the Vartry supply. Twenty-five years passed before such a hiatus occurred, and it was in no way due to any fault in the system. The level of water at Roundwood was meticulously observed and recorded. When originally designed it was intended that the storage reservoir at Roundwood should hold six months' supply. In 1893 there was a severe drought, the rainfall in the Vartry catchment being only 15.22 inches. The water level began to fall on 18 March and during the eight months from April to November the rainfall yield was down to 2.39 inches, leading to a failure of the supply for the only time in its history.

On 11 September 1893 the city engineer reported that with great hesitation the waterworks committee had had to take 'safe and unexceptionable' Grand Canal water from the Fifth Lock works into the distribution system. On 16 October it became necessary to fall back on the supply from the Royal Canal basin at Blessington Street to maintain a severely reduced service. This supply of three million gallons per day was negotiated at a price of ½d per 1,000 gallons from the Midland Great Western Railway, owners of the Royal Canal.

In *The Dublin Fire Brigade* (Dublin City Council, 2004) Tom Geraghty and Trevor Whitehead record that the fire brigade was called in to assist the waterworks during the 1893 drought. In October, less than a month after being commissioned, a Shand Mason 850 gallons per minute pump was used to over-pump water at the Dargle and thus mitigate the supply crisis. To ensure that such a mischance would not happen again, a second reservoir of 1.3 billion gallons capacity was later constructed at Roundwood.

The minutes of the waterworks committee meeting held on 15 June 1894 contains the following: 'Messrs. Merryweather and Sons having expressed their willingness to accept £400 for the steam fire engine loaned by them during the recent drought, and to waive the charge for its hire of £120, the Committee decided to retain it'. More than thirty years later, waterworks engineers, always keen to have sufficient pumping capacity available to cope with any unexpected difficulty, paid £25 (also quoted as £75) for what is thought to have been the fire brigade's last serviceable steam pump.

The 1893 partial water supply failure that threatened to become complete was taken very seriously by Kingstown Township. The drought greatly affected the poor because, unlike the well-to-do,

Bridge over River Dargle. *This charming bridge still spans the Dargle today, with the aqueduct cunningly tucked inside.*

they had no means of storing water conveniently. The township again considered developing its own water supply but desisted when the Local Government Board refused it a provisional order to buy land compulsorily. However, Joseph Berry MICEI, surveyor, reported in that year that Jugge's Well, located near Monkstown Hospital, Pakenham Road, had been improved and pipes laid to Kingstown to provide a reserve supply.

Construction of the second Roundwood reservoir did not commence until 1908 and, owing to contractual difficulties, the outbreak of the Great War and the War of Independence, it was not completed until 1923. This additional reservoir is situated to the north of the original one. Its embankment is longer than that for the first reservoir but the depth of water is less, at a maximum of 44 feet. This newer reservoir has successfully safeguarded Roundwood against the effects of a drought such as happened in 1893.

A further development of the Vartry complex was the construction of four additional filters (Nos 11–14) in 1930–32. In more recent times the following improvements have taken place: the present lime treatment building was constructed in 1986–87; all the sand in the filters was replaced in 1995 and new sand skimming and washing equipment was also installed; the Roundwood-Callowhill tunnel shafts were lined and strengthened in 1996, and in 1999 the Upper Dam was raised and a wave wall constructed to enable the structure to withstand future predictable flood conditions.

Fears that the Vartry supply might fail again at some future time led to a survey being undertaken

to find a supplementary source of water. Lough
Dan, which is only five and a quarter miles from the
Roundwood works, was found to be a suitable
source. The water was considered to be similar to
that of the Vartry – though highly coloured – and it
was envisaged that a conduit could be laid from
Lough Dan to the Vartry works. Using this source
was still an option that appealed to waterworks
engineers in the 1930s. By then, however, because
another source of water – the Liffey – was under
consideration, a supply from Lough Dan was seen
only as a long-term possibility.

THE BASINS AND PRECAUTIONARY CANAL SUPPLIES

The continuing sense of achievement inspired by
the completion of the Vartry scheme and the
beginning of a new era certainly surrounded the
decision made by the waterworks committee on
16 January 1872 to fill in the redundant basin
at James's Street. In *The Grand Canal of Ireland*

(Lilliput Press, 1995) Ruth Delaney records that the
water supply to this basin ceased on 24 June 1869.
However, even after being back-filled, the site
remained undeveloped well into the twentieth
century. Use of Portobello ceased in 1870, but this
basin remained for many years. We have seen how
Blessington Street continued to supply a distillery
and was a vital element in alleviating the worst
effects of the 1893 drought.

Failure to supply industrial water users and
whatever difficulties might arise from a drought
worried Parke Neville. A comparatively minor but
important source of water to serve particular needs
was therefore designed by Neville in 1868. This
small waterworks was built on the Grand Canal at
the Fifth Lock, directly opposite the ESB depot on
Jamestown Road, Inchicore. Well outside the city
boundary at the time of its construction, this works
was primarily intended to supply the Dublin
breweries and distilleries with the same quantity of
water as they had used prior to the introduction of
the Vartry supply. Situated 147 feet above Datum,

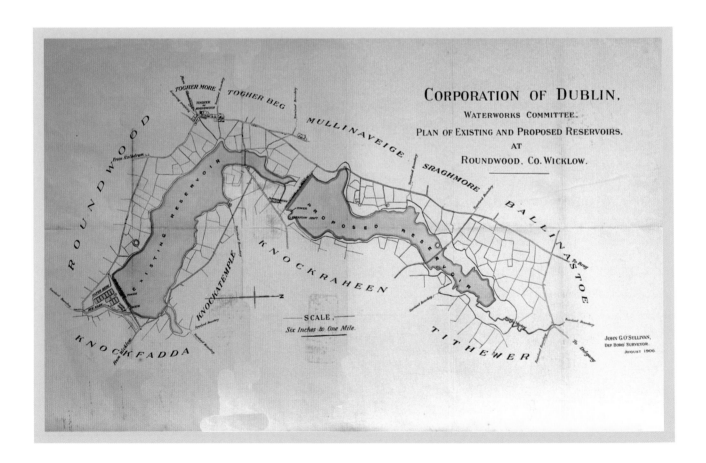

the pressure of water from this works pre-empted any possible litigation against the corporation by industrial users. Known as the Fifth Lock works, it was later connected to the former Rathmines works on the Grand Canal (Chapter 6) which was acquired by the corporation in 1894 during the regime of Spencer Harty, Neville's deputy and successor as city engineer.

On the north side, a small supply was also taken from the Royal Canal at the Eighth Lock, situated beside Reilly's Bridge on the Ratoath Road and about three miles from the city. The installation consisted only of a small intake chamber and a system of screens. The water pipe to the city, laid in 1893, was of cast iron and was 16 inches in diameter. Under an agreement with the Royal Canal Company its contribution to the system was limited to 800,000 gallons per day and it was almost entirely used by distillers.

ROUNDWOOD'S LEGACY AND FUTURE

At the time of writing – Spring 2005 – the average output from the Roundwood plant exceeded the long-term safe yield from the catchment and no further increase in output is therefore possible without an additional source of raw water. As a result, future works will be concerned with ensuring that the scheme can continue to supply water of the highest possible quality. Planned future works include the construction of a new covered reservoir for the treated water and two additional filters (construction commencing in 2004), replacement or refurbishment of the Roundwood-Callowhill tunnel, upgrading the Lower Dam drawoffs and overflow, and a rolling programme of filter reconstruction.

The original structures and much equipment dating from the 1860s continue to serve Dublin's needs. The scheme is still as relevant and enduring in today's context as it was when built, which is a remarkable tribute to those whose vision and achievements it represents. Many of the original drawings and other documents relating to the

design and construction of the Vartry scheme are preserved, some in the city water division's offices at Marrowbone Lane and others in the City Council Archives.

When built, Roundwood was among the most advanced installations of its kind, and among its features was one of the earliest direct current (dc) electricity generators in the country, which for many years supplied all the power requirements of the plant. Plans are well advanced at present to install a new water turbine, which will again make the plant self-sufficient and enable surplus power to be fed to the National Grid.

FOUNTAINS AND HORSE TROUGHS

Wells (pumps and fountains) 'for the use of the poor', as described in earlier chapters, were erected in several parts of the city, and in small courts and streets. Some fountains were free standing, others incorporated into the walls of buildings and some survivors are to be found in the city centre. Long disused, they are highly individual in design and much photographed by visitors. There is one beside the Gate Theatre in Cavendish Row and another in the northern wall of the former Newcomen bank building, now the Rates Office, at the city end of Lord Edward Street.

Waterworks at the Fifth Lock on the Grand Canal. *These were constructed in 1868 to supply water to Dublin's breweries and distilleries.*

Clockwise from top left: Lady Laura Grattan fountain and horse trough; obelisk and fountain at James's Street; fountain near the Dublin Gate Theatre; fountain at the Rates Building, Lord Edward Street.

The fountains shown date from the mid-eighteenth to the late nineteenth century, and provided a critically important supply of water for households which did not have any. The granite trough at Lady Grattan's fountain in St Stephen's Green is still used by horses who provide carriage rides for visitors.

There were numerous horse troughs throughout
the city, but these became redundant as the number
of horses declined, slowly in the 1930s but more
rapidly in the 1950s. A very late addition to the stock
of horse troughs was the one erected in Wapping
Street in 1927 at a cost of £5. Traction engines and
steam lorries could sometimes be seen replenishing
their tanks from the troughs until the last of these
vehicles disappeared in the mid-1950s. By that time,
the provision in the 1861 Waterworks Act requiring
these vehicles to pay for water was almost forgotten.
A service provided under the same Act and still in
operation is the supply of fresh water to ships.

Intermittently Lord Lieutenant of Ireland from
1858 to 1864, the Earl of Carlisle keenly favoured
the provision of drinking fountains throughout
Britain. He supported a similar programme for
Ireland, the cost of each fountain being estimated
at between £15 and £20. Dublin's two attractive
Carlisle fountains are described in *Hoggers, Lords
and Railwaymen* (Custom House Docks Development Authority, 1996). These fountains, which cost
£50 each, were designed by the celebrated architectural partnership of Deane and Woodward. The one
at the corner of Beresford Place and Custom House
Quay, a ten-feet high pillar of limestone, appears in
some photographs taken prior to the building of the
Loop Line railway, the construction of which caused
its demolition around 1887. The other one, at
Parkgate Street, was set into a wall but was blocked
up a long time ago and eventually demolished.
Fortunately, excellent drawings of both these
fountains survive.

The Five Lamps, the imposing landmark that
stands at the junction of Amiens Street and North
Strand Road with Portland Row and Seville Place, is
probably the best known of the surviving fountains.
Its water supply function ceased many years ago,
but the construction of its base shows clearly its
former water supply function.

Between the horse troughs on St Stephen's Green,
opposite the top of Dawson Street, there stands a
well-preserved fountain reminiscent of those
erected through the interest of the Earl of Carlisle.

This one bears the inscription 'Presented to the
Corporation and Citizens of Dublin by Lady Laura
Grattan 1880'.

The Crampton Memorial, a highly distinctive
monument incorporating drinking fountains which
stood at the junction of College Street and D'Olier
Street, was taken down in 1959. Its removal was not,
as widely believed, to facilitate traffic flows, but
because of deterioration of the structure, which was
deemed dangerous.

At the other end of the fountain spectrum were
the many cast-iron pillars, usually about two and a
half feet high, to be found near groups of old
houses or cottages. Most had a spout shaped like a
lion's mouth, a knurled handle to twist for water
and a decorated finial. Some had a bracket on
which to rest the receptacle to be filled. Many of
these fountains were still in situ well into the
1970s but only a few isolated examples now remain.
The *Dublin Builder* believed that if a fountain
'should succeed in detaining one visitor per
diem from entering the alcoholic depot, the philan-
thropic purpose of the promoter shall have been
recompensed'.

In the townships, too, public drinking fountains
and drinking troughs for horses were provided.
In Dun Laoghaire, examples still exist at
Monkstown and near the County Hall. The latter
can be seen at the bottom of Marine Road where
a splendid replacement for the similar vandalised
fountain erected in 1900 in honour of Queen
Victoria now stands

ULYSSES

The Vartry scheme attracted the attention of James
Joyce, who was clearly impressed by major engineering works. In one passage in *Ulysses* Leopold
Bloom ponders on all that lies behind the simple act
of turning on a water tap. Spencer Harty, the city
engineer who succeeded Parke Neville, is one of the
real historical figures identified in Joyce's masterpiece, and the terrible inequalities of contemporary
Dublin life are also cleverly articulated.

Detail of iron fountain on James's Street obelisk.

Cast by T. Kennedy of Kilmarnock, Scotland, the inscription urges the thirsty to 'Keep the Pavement Dry'.

THE PODDLE'S CHANGING STATUS

With the development of the water supply from the canals and later from the Vartry scheme, the City Watercourse was no longer important as a source of drinking water. Andrew Whelan ME, who was divisional engineer in charge of the Grand Canal Drainage Scheme, recorded that the corporation purchased the water rights of the Earl of Meath in 1861 for £6,000. This ensured that nobody except the corporation could abstract water from the Poddle. However, the rights of mill owners still had to be respected and the supply was maintained solely for their benefit. The Earl of Meath retained the actual lands and the river bed and banks where it flowed through his lands, and his right to use the water for operating mills also remained.

A number of mills along the watercourse were abandoned when electric power became available. The waterworks department inherited the responsibility of maintaining a supply from the headworks at Balrothery to the few remaining mills. On closure of these mills and forfeiture of rights the water supply from the Dodder was discontinued and only surface water drainage flowed along the lower stretches of this line.

The Poddle's changing fortunes and standing will recur in later chapters.

5 Draining the City Effectively 1851–1880

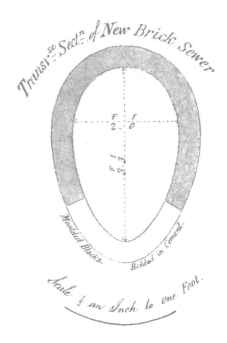

A NEW ERA

By 1849, the Commissioners for Paving and Lighting had constructed more than 35½ miles (57 kilometres) of sewers in Dublin. Between 1851 and 1879, Parke Neville built 65 miles (104km) of new sewers and improved some 30 miles (48km) of the older ones. The minimum improvement of existing sewers consisted of replacing flat earth inverts with dished stone or brick ones, while random rubble sidewalls were superseded by brickwork. Where necessary, sidewalls were also strengthened or replaced, this process and the replacement of inverts being known as underpinning. This work was carried out as the availability of funding would allow. The lengths of older sewers with slab sides or flat soffits (crowns) have long been called shores by drainage division staff. Another feature of some old sewers is the variation in height along particular sections; this is because the work was carried out by various builders at different times.

Most of the new sewers were built of brick and were ovoid in shape. They were designed to carry surface water as well as foul drainage, this arrangement being known as the combined system. Three times the dry weather flow could be carried in rainy conditions, storm and surface water being essential to flush the sewers before the advent of the Vartry water scheme and the more widespread use of domestic water systems.

The brick sewers were of different sizes, the commonest being three feet and three inches high and two feet wide at the shoulder. Known as 'three by twos', these are the smallest and most ubiquitous conduits in approximately 90 miles (144km) of inner city man entry sewers. Lines expected to accommodate larger flows were bigger. Chancery Street is an example, the sewer here, rated as Class 4, having dimensions of three feet nine inches by two feet and six inches. Some circular brick sewers were also built, as for example in Ballybough Road. To cater for streets with more modest flows, considerable lengths of 12-inch diameter pipe sewers were also laid. 'Class 4' is from a long obsolete and not wholly accurate system of categorising sewers according to their size.

'Three by twos' are the smallest man entry sewers on the city drainage system. They were also the most economical to build and account for the greater part of the sewer mileage. In August 1859, when £8,000 had been spent on sewers since the city engineer had taken over responsibility for this work, concern was expressed about the safety of men working in these conduits. An observer who witnessed a sewers employee experiencing difficulty while travelling through a three by two in High Street – 'nearly as paralysed as in a coffin' – suggested that the minimum internal height should be increased to four feet. This suggestion was not taken up.

When a contract for sewer works was awarded, it was standard practice for both Parke Neville and the contractor to sign a copy of the drawing relating to the project. Two or more streets were often covered in one contract and these were usually shown on a single sheet. Nearly four hundred of the drawings survive, most of them on cartridge paper and delicately tinted. The usual format consists of a location map, longitudinal and cross-sections and an enumeration, or list, of items. The oldest extant example in the city drainage division shows the proposed sewers for Church Street, Cornmarket and Thomas Street and is dated April 1852. Seventeen years later, the first stage of Parke Neville's drainage programme, covering the city centre, was completed. In that year of 1869 he produced a comprehensive map (which survives) showing the drainage network as it existed at the time.

SUPERVISING CONTRACTORS AND WORKERS

Sewer work was strictly supervised by Parke Neville and his assistants. Most of the contractors were honest and competent, but difficulties inevitably arose from time to time. None was more aggravating than the trouble created by John Stanfield, a contractor who in 1879 submitted the lowest – and successful – tender for the construction of more than five miles of brick sewers. The contract also covered the underpinning of almost four miles of old sewers and the laying of more than seven miles of pipes. The work was found to be badly and carelessly carried out, there was trouble with creditors and more than a hint of dishonesty. At the end of a painful process, Stanfield sought release from his obligations in July

1881 and much of the contract was remedied or completed by the corporation's own staff.

Very little is known of the individual workers who constructed the drainage system, but the standard of craftsmanship found by the inspectors, who minutely examined the conduits a century after they were laid, was exemplary. Until well into the twentieth century, bricklayers and most other tradesmen served seven-year apprenticeships, the highest standards of workmanship and personal behaviour being demanded of the young men. The very restrictive rules governing apprentices included prohibitions on gambling and visiting hostelries or theatres. Fornication or getting married without the master's permission were among the other pleasures forbidden by the indenture.

The first Ordnance Survey Town Maps on a scale of 1:1056 (88 feet to one inch), published in 1847, had shown underground sewer and water lines as they existed at the time of survey. It would obviously be impossible to continue showing this level of detail in later editions as the networks expanded and changed continuously. In any case, as the services were underground, their omission actually enhanced the superb surface detail shown on the maps.

Somewhat later, sets of 88-inch maps (1864 edition) were acquired and the sewer details meticulously marked on. An element of colour coding was employed, broad blue bands indicating the areas

Detail of drainage contract, 1859.

With signatures of City Engineer Parke Neville and William Bonsall, Chairman Main Drainage Committee.

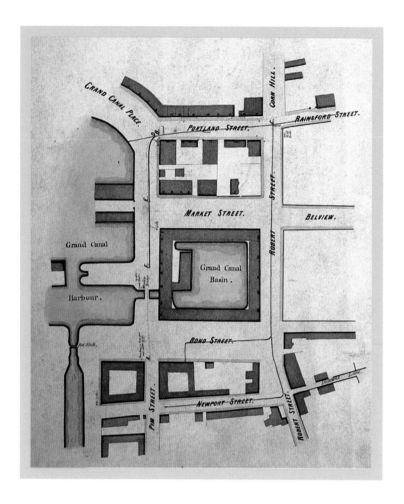

Plan of new drainage system in vicinity of Grand Canal Basin, 1859.

This densely built-up area, with its rich mix of industry and working-class housing, was urgently in need of a modern drainage system.

occupied by the expanding tram track layout. These sheets and the succeeding 1887 edition record the years in which most of the sewers in the city centre were laid down or underpinned.

Among the streets provided with new sewers was the infamous Braithwaite Street referred to in Rev James Whitelaw's 1798 survey. Michael Derham, contractor, signed the documents covering Braithwaite and five other streets in the same area on 25 October 1867 and carried out the work within a short time.

Plunkett Street, twice surveyed by Rev Whitelaw in 1798, already had a sewer, laid by the Commissioners for Paving, when Parke Neville included its underpinning in a contract covering four streets on 12 April 1878. The work was executed in the following year and Plunkett Street later became part of the Dublin Artisans Dwelling

Company's housing estate. The length of this now pleasant thoroughfare, which had two right angle bends, today has different names for its three sections: Thomas Davis Street, John Dillon Street and Dillon Place South.

The copious flows essential to the successful operation of a water carriage sewer system became available on completion of the Vartry supply scheme in 1868. This complemented and enhanced the efficacy of the sewer network, and by 1878, Parke Neville was able to claim that few cities had a more efficient system of sewers than Dublin. Two years later, the sewer network was virtually complete, leaving only the long desired main drainage project, fully described in Chapter 7, to be tackled.

In its relationship to drainage the 1878 Public Health (Ireland) Act is outstanding among the several measures enacted in this field. It covered the powers and duties of sanitary authorities in relation to sewerage and sewage disposal, the construction of buildings, water closets, scavenging, cleansing and water supply. Its 294 sections also covered offensive trades, unsound meat, provisions, and prevention of infectious diseases; mortuaries and burial grounds. Parts of this Act are still on the statute book, providing much of the legislative framework within which sewer authorities have operated ever since its enactment. Greatly strengthening the Corporation's powers to ensure that drainage systems were properly utilised, minimum standards were now laid down.

In existing premises, at least one mandatory water tap and WC had to be provided and connected to the sewer system. Sizeable numbers of defaulters were regularly brought before the courts. 'Abatement of nuisance' was the phrase generally employed to describe the desired result. From time to time essential improvements were frustrated by the machinations of councillors and other vested interests that also happened to be substantial property owners. Nevertheless it is recorded that in one year 15,000 notices were served and 800 defaulters were brought to court.

With the availability of the Vartry supply more and more new houses boasted water storage tanks, WCs and varying further levels of water usage. These, and the compulsory connection of existing premises, continually increased the demand for drainage. Additionally, from the 1880s onwards the provision of new housing by the corporation and organisations such as the Dublin Artisans Dwelling Company and, later, the Iveagh Trust rendered the need to extend the system all the more urgent.

In some places, conservative attitudes to what was known as indoor plumbing took a long time to change, and one example will illustrate this. Upper St Brigid's Road in Drumcondra has substantial houses built in the 1890s but with water laid on at ground floor level only. The bathroom was located off the kitchen and contained the bath and wash hand basin. The WC was in a separate outbuilding to the rear and one house of which the writer has personal knowledge retained this arrangement more than seventy years after it was built.

Since that house on St Brigid's Road was new, drainage and plumbing artefacts, their definition, meaning and even pronunciation have all changed. The somewhat crude predecessor of the kitchen sink fitted in that house was a heavy vitreous unit known as a trough, but the word was pronounced trow. This usage is one of the innumerable nuances of meaning and pronunciation applied to everyday items in the Dublin of a century ago that have been ignored by folklore collectors.

RIVER POLLUTION

The downside of the drainage programme was that every sewer emptied into the nearest river. The River Poddle, once the source of Dublin's water supply, but for years a notorious channel for waste, now effectively became part of the foul drainage system. A contemporary report described it as 'an immense sewer, putrefying the streets under which it passed'. It and the equally obnoxious Camac became major contributors to the terrible and constantly worsening state of the Liffey.

Industrial pollution, a problem first tackled in 1718 (Chapter 1), worsened in the more industrialised nineteenth century. Destined to persist and grow for another century, it was yet one further ingredient in the whole filthy mess. Allowing cesspools to be connected to sewers that were originally intended to carry only storm water to the Liffey was a problem that became progressively worse with the construction of more sewers and the development of the waterborne disposal system.

Transferring pollution from the streets to the Liffey led to increasingly vociferous criticism. The river had been reasonably clean in the closing years of the eighteenth century but, as each new sewer was laid, growing volumes of effluent were discharged to the Liffey. Following her visit in 1814, Anne Plumptre wrote favourably about Dublin in her *Narrative* but had this to say about the Liffey:

> Instead of being an ornament to the town, as a river ought to be, it is really rather a revolting sight. From what cause this may proceed I know not; but it should seem that it must be from some very great mismanagement of some kind. Are no pains ever bestowed in cleaning it? Or do the sewers of the town run into, and thus contaminate, it? I know not whether either of these causes may have any share in the evil, but I know that the magistrates of the town would do well to exert their influence in having the cause thoroughly investigated, and proper remedies applied. It is generally expected that a tide river should be sweet and pure; that the constant ebb and flow should keep it free from impurities; at any rate it should seem as if the cause might with ease be ascertained, and the effect remedied…

By 1832, complaints were being articulated more frequently and stridently about the ever-growing nuisance, but nothing was done. In 1853, Parke Neville noted that the matter discharged into the Liffey 'renders its bed foul, and, at low water, excessively disagreeable to the inhabitants of the Quays and to the public generally passing over or by the bridges, from the noxious inhalations which rise from it, particularly in hot weather'.

**Plan of new
drainage system in
vicinity of Gloucester
Diamond, 1859.**
*The Gloucester
Diamond was at the
centre of Georgian
houses which had degen-
erated into tenements
by the mid-nineteenth
century and were rife
with disease. The new
drainage system was
basic to public health.*

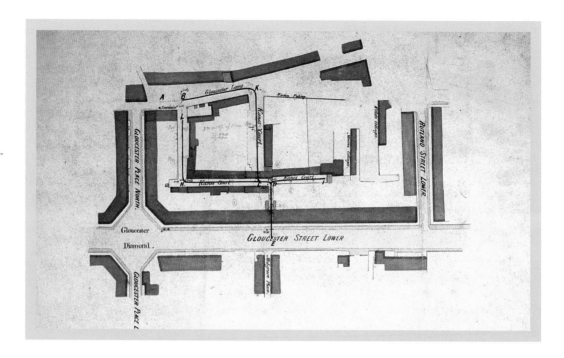

PLANNING TO CLEANSE THE LIFFEY

Parke Neville became convinced, as early as 1853, of the indispensability of interceptor sewers, described in Chapter 3, to end the pollution of the Liffey. Neville carefully considered their benefits before interceptor sewers became an integral part of his proposals for the drainage of the city and the purification of the Liffey. As time passed, what was at first a desirable advantage became an increasingly vital necessity.

Neville produced a map of Dublin in 1853 'showing lines of proposed intercepting sewers north and south of the River Liffey to prevent the sewerage of the City discharging as at present into the River – Also high level sewers to relieve the low districts'. An interceptor along each line of quays was the principal feature, with separate outfalls at East Wall and Ringsend. However, he recommended that a final decision should be deferred until a scheme under consideration in London for cleaning the Thames came to fruition. In any event, a shortage of finance prevented his proposals from being implemented for many years, while the pollution got steadily worse. In an era when

standards of hygiene were low generally and filth abounded, there had been tolerance of conditions that were now being increasingly challenged.

In 1865 the distinguished physician and city councillor Dr (later Sir) Dominic Corrigan (1802–1880) espoused the cause of tackling river pollution. He too proposed laying along the quays interceptor sewers that were to combine and discharge to the sea at Poolbeg. Parke Neville largely concurred in an 1865 report but suggested a single outfall at East Wall, which at that time was on the shoreline.

Messrs Barrington and Jeffers, entrepreneurs who later became involved in Dublin's earliest horse tramways, saw commercial possibilities in sewage. In 1865 they put forward a £225,000 scheme to pump sewage from a proposed North Bull outfall to a covered reservoir high enough to service the entire area envisaged in their scheme. This consisted of 1,460 acres of land to be reclaimed at Baldoyle, Malahide and what is now the Bull Island. Pipes were to convey the sewage to these locations, which would be fertilised. The income, added to the sale of sewage for use as manure, would produce a dividend of 6%, the profit to be divided between the entrepreneurs, the corporation and the townships.

Utilising the Liffey as a main sewer, although the only obvious option available in the earlier years of the city's drainage system, was at best an objectionable makeshift. It now threatened to become permanent and, in his anxiety to purge the worsening pollution of the river in the absence of intercepting sewers, Parke Neville did not oppose the Barrington and Jeffers scheme, which never went ahead. While this form of sewage disposal had its adherents, Dr Corrigan and Viscount St Lawrence, Earl of Howth, were among its most determined opponents. The viscount wrote a forceful booklet on the subject, which was published by Joseph Dollard of Dame Street and addressed to the lord mayor.

As the increasing volumes of sewage made purification ever more difficult and expensive to achieve, various proposals to pave, flush or cover the Liffey were all found to be impractical. In Parke Neville's modified version of Dr Corrigan's 1865 interceptor sewers proposal, the South Quays interceptor sewer was to join the North Quays line to East Wall via a cast iron siphon under the Liffey at Carlisle (O'Connell) Bridge. A tidal storage basin to retain the flow at flood tide was envisaged at East Wall. Sir Joseph Bazalgette, who created the Central London main drainage system and its accompanying amenities (Chapter 3), was a consultant to Dublin Corporation. In 1866, he suggested further changes, with a pumping station at Annesley Bridge and an outfall sewer along Clontarf Road and the Bull Wall. This scheme was yet another of several important projects that failed to proceed due to a lack of funds.

In 1868, Neville reported that the Liffey had 54 sewer outfalls downstream of Islandbridge, 32 on the south side and 22 on the north side. One of the latter was the River Bradogue, discharging at Upper Ormond Quay and for many years part of the sewer network. Among the 32 outfalls on the south side, the Camac caused gross contamination from just upstream of Kingsbridge (Heuston Bridge). Deteriorating further at each succeeding outfall, the condition of the river became almost indescribable east of Capel Street Bridge (then Essex, now Grattan Bridge), where the Poddle joined it at Wellington Quay. Except for the tributary rivers, most of the outfalls had flap valves to prevent tidal surcharging (backflow into) of the sewers.

During the years of planning for interceptor sewers along the quays, there were differences of opinion about where these conduits should be laid. Some proponents of the scheme believed that the new sewers should be laid on the bed of the river, immediately outside the quay walls, but this idea was eventually dropped. Both Parke Neville and Joseph Bazalgette, who visited Dublin in September 1866, firmly believed in laying the sewers under the carriageways of the quays and this was in fact what was done, many years later (Chapter 7).

In 1868 the corporation advertised for advice from competent parties about eliminating pollution from the Liffey. It was decided to seek an Exchequer loan to carry out the work, the application being backed up by a memorial to the lord lieutenant from a group of influential citizens. In the quaint phraseology of the time, this prayed that the Privy Council would make an order requiring the corporation to take measures for the purification of the Liffey.

The situation in London in 1858, when MPs at Westminster had to isolate themselves from the stench of the Thames, found its parallel in Dublin a decade later. Overwhelmed by the smell from the Liffey, the judges in the Four Courts threatened to move to some more salubrious location, the threat being taken seriously. Meanwhile, Bazalgette and Neville's recommendations for a main drainage scheme were adopted by the corporation on 11 June 1869 and were described in the first report of the corporation's main drainage committee on 2 September 1870, chaired by Sir John Gray.

The committee received a comprehensive account of a deputation that had gone to London in July, when Sir John was accompanied by Lord Mayor Edward Purdon, Councillor Norwood, Councillor Sir William Carroll, the town clerk and city engineer. The deputation lobbied intensively,

Pollution entering the Liffey from the Camac, 1950s.

A perennial problem, the white-coloured water is the discharge of effluent from the Camac. Today, this has been eliminated by culverting this tributary of the Liffey.

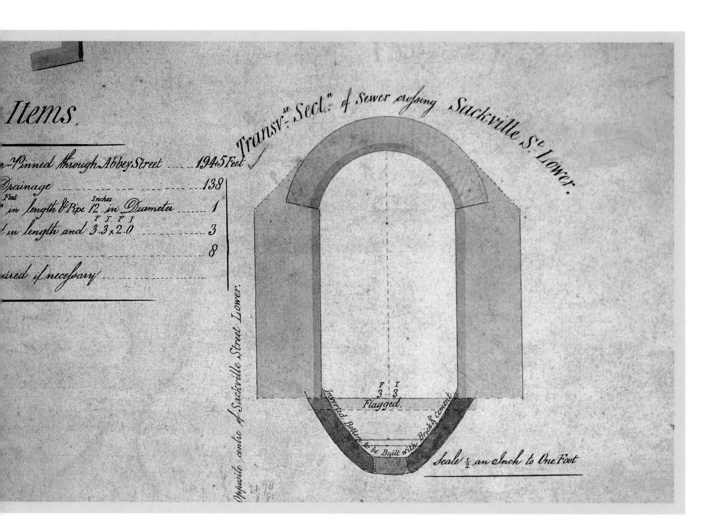

Items.

—Pinned through Abbey Street .... 1945 Feet ✓

Drainage 138

Feet
in length & Pipe 12 Inches in Diameter 1

t in length and 3·3 × 2·0 3

.... 8

ired if necessary ....

Transv.ᵉ Sect.ⁿ of Sewer crossing Sackville Sᵗ Lower.

Opposite centre of Sackville Street Lower.

*F I
3 3
Flagged.*

Inverted Bottom to be Built with Bricks & cement

Scale ½ an Inch to One Foot

**Transverse section of
sewer crossing Lower
Sackville Street, 1864.**
*The new Dublin
sewers were triumphs
of engineering and the
carefully-executed
working drawings were
works of art in their
own right.*

secured financial provision for the main drainage
project and promoted legislation to reach an
outcome similar to that being achieved in London.
While they were in London, the Dublin deputation
visited several of that city's new drainage
installations and agreed consultancy terms with
Joseph Bazalgette.

The main drainage scheme was approved by
the corporation at its meeting on 17 October 1870.
A £350,000 Exchequer loan was available and the
Dublin Main Drainage and Purification of Liffey
Act 1871 authorised the necessary work. There was
an attempt by unnamed parties in Dublin to defeat
the Bill 'on imperial economic grounds', but the Bill
became an Act that should have led to rapid action.

FINANCIAL OBSTACLES

The 1871 Act was a most comprehensive measure,
and was intended to deal with drainage well beyond
the city boundary. It included the townships of
Rathmines, Pembroke, New Kilmainham and
Clontarf, but omitted Drumcondra, which had not
yet been constituted. Unfortunately, the plans
remained unfulfilled because the lowest tender
came in at £775,054, more than twice the approved
expenditure. Forty years would pass before all the
areas covered by the 1871 Act were to enjoy the
benefits of a main drainage system. In the
meantime the corporation granted a concession to
Barrington and Jeffers, on 6 May 1871, to remove
sewage an process it as a fertiliser.

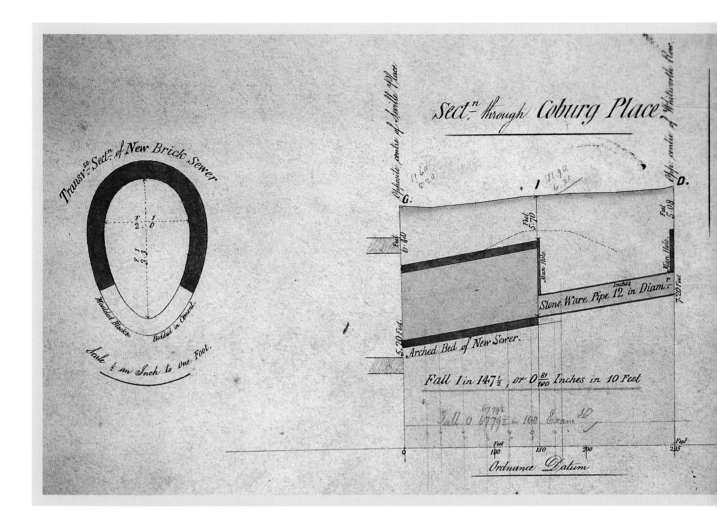

Transverse section of new brick sewer at Coburg Place, 1876.

The line of the sewer is carefully measured against the Ordnance Datum to show the fall required to conduct soil away successfully.

Parke Neville's further revised 1873 scheme also fell, mainly due to unresolved financial difficulties and disagreements outside his area of direct responsibility. Complicated political games on various levels continued to be played out, effectively blocking progress. Similar circumstances thwarted various other progressive Neville projects, several of which were only brought to fruition years after his death. Meanwhile, the higher than expected costs quoted or experienced in the 1870s were ascribed to dearer materials and a disturbed labour market.

Somewhat lower tenders obtained in 1874 still exceeded the corporation's borrowing powers and although these were extended, the Treasury declined to authorise an advance of £500,000 because of doubts surrounding the adequacy of the city rate.

It is noteworthy that the cost of living index, usually related to a base of 100 in 1914, stood at 120 in 1872. With a few minor blips, costs fell continuously in the forty years prior to the Great War of 1914–1918.

Ireland in general and Dublin in particular suffered a severe blow in April 1875 with the death of Sir John Gray. A supporter of every movement that benefited the people, whether urban or rural, he was universally mourned and the subject of eulogies even from those who differed from him but recognised his humanity, vision, tenacity and tact. The main drainage committee and the corporation in general took some time to recover from the loss of his rich talents.

While the 1870s and 1880s were disastrous for people in rural Ireland, the business and profession-

**Transverse sections
of sewers in Hardwicke
Street, 1876.**

*Sewers were still being
constructed of brick,
which allowed their
characteristic ovoid
shape to be developed.*

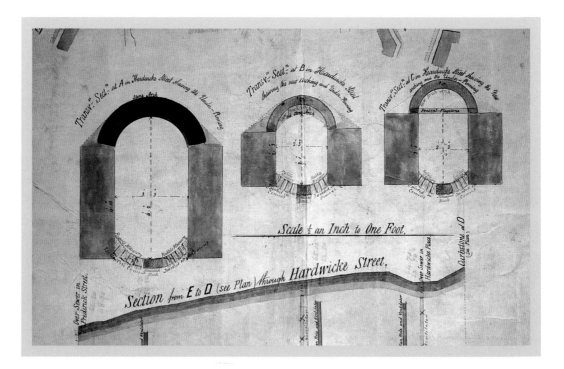

al classes in Dublin enjoyed considerable prosperity
during those decades. And, despite serious anomalies
including rampant communal poverty, poor public
health and the dire state of its municipal finances,
Dublin was at that time regarded as a commercially
affluent city.

The legal and financial obstacles to the construction of the main drainage scheme were not resolved
until the last years of the century.

THE LOCAL GOVERNMENT BOARD

Until the last year of the nineteenth century, local
government outside the cities and large towns of
Ireland was largely in the hands of Grand Juries
(See also Chapter 8). Responsible for a narrow
range of services, these elite oligarchies became
more irrelevant and ineffective as public services
developed and electoral registers expanded. In 1831
the Board of Works was established to carry out or
facilitate major works of public benefit. The Board
was based in the Custom House and, from its
inception, had a strong engineering background.

To further assist in the provision and

supervision of essential local services, the Local
Government Board for Ireland was established in
1872, and it too had its headquarters in the Custom
House. It took over some functions of the Board of
Works and was the predecessor of today's
Department of the Environment, Heritage and
Local Government. It was hoped, somewhat naively,
that the Board would assist local authorities in
obtaining approval and funding for essential works.
But, although it could claim numerous successes,
the Board caused many disappointments through-
out its existence.

The Local Government Board was frequently
accused of putting the interests of its political
masters in London before the needs of local communities in Ireland. The amount of information
amassed by the Board and its associated bodies, and
its grip on local authorities, has been cited as one of
the reasons for the destruction of the Custom
House in 1921. Some of the many historical figures
connected with the Custom House are comprehensively described by Joseph Robins in *Custom House
People* (Institute of Public Administration, 1993).

RATHMINES AND PEMBROKE DRAINAGE

The first main drainage scheme to be completed in the Dublin area was that of the wealthy Rathmines and Pembroke townships, established in 1847 and 1863 respectively. The two townships, which had been included in the corporation's 1871 proposals, became severely frustrated by the subsequent lack of progress and the increasing pollution of the River Dodder. So they joined together to provide their own main drainage scheme, the necessary Bill being promoted in Parliament in November 1876. Parke Neville, who firmly believed in the unified system for the city and townships envisaged in the 1871 Main Drainage and Liffey Purification Act, unsuccessfully opposed the Rathmines and Pembroke (often abbreviated to R&P) scheme.

In 1877 the area of Rathmines Township was 1,518 acres and the population was estimated at 24,000 (the Milltown district, comprising 185 acres, was not added until 1880). Pembroke Township covered 1,592 acres and its population was reckoned to be somewhat more than 25,000. The Rathmines and Pembroke drainage system was designed to cater for an area of 3,295 acres, only half of which was developed at that time, when the combined population of the two townships was 50,000. Rathmines and Pembroke covered an area equal to about 90% of Dublin Corporation's extent, and had a population density that was approximately a fifth of that in the city.

The Rathmines and Pembroke Drainage Bill received the royal assent on 12 July 1877 and work began at Pigeonhouse Road early in July 1878. A high-level sewer was built along the course of the Swan River (largely culverted in 1867) from Harold's Cross via Rathmines, Ranelagh, Wellington Place and Ballsbridge. The Swan had some minuscule tributaries, which also became part of the Rathmines foul sewer system. From Ballsbridge the trunk sewer followed the Dodder to just northwest of Londonbridge (Bath Avenue) where it crossed under the river by siphon beside another Rathmines and Pembroke sewer coming from the Pembroke Road and Shelbourne Road areas.

Siphons on drainage systems and other pipelines operate on the principle of a pipe or other conduit descending to go under an obstacle such as a river or a railway line, and ascending again at the other side to continue at a reasonable depth and gradient. The exit from the ascending (downstream) leg is lower than the entrance at the descending

The Rathmines Drainage Scheme.

Built at the turn of the twentieth century by the Rathmines and Pembroke Main Drainage Board, to service Dublin's south-eastern suburbs.

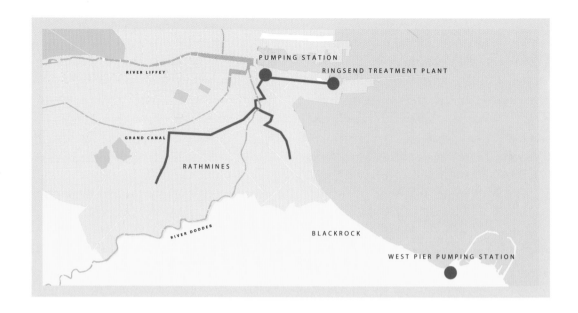

(upstream) side, thus maintaining the flow.

A third, low-level, sewer was laid beside the railway from Sydney Parade to Lansdowne Railway Bridge, continuing along the east bank of the Dodder to the Londonbridge Road pumping station. This pumping station raised the sewer flow to a high level culvert into which the sewers that siphoned under the river also flowed. From Londonbridge Road, this high-level culvert ran to Whitebanks on the South Wall. Sewage was stored in the culvert during the flood tide and allowed to discharge only in the first hours of the ebb tide, when the flow was seaward. The culvert began at 5 feet in diameter, enlarging downstream to 6 feet at a flatter gradient, and was carried in an embankment 1,902-feet long across what was then Ringsend Strand to Pigeonhouse Road. The Strand was where Ringsend Park and Irishtown Stadium are today.

The Rathmines and Pembroke sea outfall at Whitebanks on the South Wall operated for over one hundred years. The effluent was stored in the culvert from Ringsend and discharged to the ebb tide through valves located in a stone building at Whitebanks. In later years a man travelled from the corporation's Ringsend pumping station to operate the valves at each turn of the tide. For several years prior to the diversion of the Rathmines and Pembroke sewer to the new treatment works in 1986 the brothers Kevin and Vincent Costello shared this duty.

Built by P. J. Pile, Londonbridge Road pumping station was the first installation of its kind in the Dublin area. It had two wet wells or sumps, each having a pair of beam plunger pumps; the individual pumps were capable of discharging 550 cubic feet per minute. Each pair of pumps was driven by a separate steam engine of the horizontal high-pressure surface condensing type. There were three boilers, one sufficient for each engine and working at a pressure of 65 lbs per square inch. Victor Coates & Co of Lagan Foundry, Belfast, was the contractor for the mechanical installation. The original pumping equipment continued to work until 1953, when it was replaced by vertical spindle mixed flow centrifugal pumps, driven by diesel engines.

Small buildings were erected on both banks of the river at Londonbridge Road to afford access to the siphons. Adjacent to the one on the western (city) side of the river was the local morgue. For safety and convenience, the coroner's instruments were kept in the pumping station, and drainage staff provided assistance for the morgue, especially at night. This arrangement continued into the 1960s, and corporation employees called upon to assist at post-mortem examinations were paid seven shillings and sixpence (equivalent to 47.5 cent) for their work. One of the two siphon houses was refurbished in 2000, the other in 2002.

Engineers Richard Hassard and A. W. Tyrrell designed and supervised the construction of the Rathmines and Pembroke main drainage project, for which the principal contractor was J. W. Stanford. The total cost of the scheme was approximately £105,000, and the system came into operation in 1881, managed by a joint board of eleven members. Five came from each township, the eleventh being appointed by the Local Government Board for Ireland. A comprehensive description of the system was given to the Institute of Engineers on 1 December 1881 in a paper delivered by Henry T. Crook, who was the first resident engineer on the project. His successor was F. P. Dixon and the entire scheme came under the aegis of Henry Johnston, the Rathmines Township Engineer.

Both the War Office and the Port and Docks Board exercised their authority over the R&P programme by insisting on expensive extra work. The military authorities required a wall to be built to carry the sewer round the guardhouse at the east gate of the Pigeonhouse Fort, more fully described in Chapter 7. They also wanted a wharf and additional work to prevent access to the fort. In contrast, the work carried out at the behest of the Port and Docks Board, while expensive, actually enhanced the usefulness of the South Bull Wall.

To serve new residential development and cleanse the River Dodder (which experienced similar problems to the Liffey, albeit on a smaller scale) the Rathmines and Pembroke townships constructed the first Dodder Valley sewer in the mid-1880s. Commencing at Orwell Road, this interceptor sewer still follows the river valley on the north side, except for a short section between Dartry Cottages and the Milltown Weir, where it is on the south bank. On re-crossing to the north side, the line continues along the riverbank, part of Milltown Road and the riverbank again, to Vergemount. Here it crosses under the river to Beaver Row, continuing via Anglesea Road and Beatty's Avenue, where it finally crosses the Dodder to join the main R&P line at Estate Cottages, behind Shelbourne Road. At Beatty's Avenue, the original river crossing, which was by means of a pipe on piers, known as the 'boiler', was replaced by a siphon in 2000.

Exterior of Londonbridge Road pumping station.

Built by contractor P.J. Pile for the Rathmines and Pembroke Main Drainage Board, this was the first installation of its kind in the Dublin area.

Londonbridge Road pumping station, interior. *Victor Coates & Co of the Lagan Foundry, Belfast, was the contractor for the mechanical installation here.*

DRAINAGE IN KINGSTOWN AND BLACKROCK

During the long gestation period of the Dublin Main Drainage Scheme, a similar pollution problem was festering in what were then Kingstown and its neighbouring townships of Blackrock, Dalkey and Ballybrack-Killiney.

In his history of Dun Laoghaire water and drainage, Matt O'Brien recalls the conditions of Kingstown's poor that provoked Charles Haliday, a noted humanitarian, to publicise the situation in 1844. He described the Kingstown tenements, which housed large families in one- or two-roomed hovels without toilets, light or air. Haliday decried the fact that landlords were not obliged to meet certain standards in the dwellings they let. He also deplored the fact that the railway had cut off access to the sea for ordinary people, while the rich such as Lord

Cloncurry insisted that the railway company build bridges and private baths for their own use. As a result of Haliday's pressure, public baths were eventually built at the back of the West Pier and at Salthill. In 1863, the Ballast Board gave the Kingstown Township permission to make a bathing place at the Forty Foot, in front of the battery and in the cove.

The priorities of the Kingstown commissioners did not include the provision of a sewer system. Water closets would have been unusual and the norm would have been latrines or pail closets, the contents of which were removed regularly as night-soil. As late as 1872, it was reported that out of 41,820 feet of streets and roads which should have drainage, only 15,000 feet had sewers that actually worked; a sewer was not laid in George's Street until 1872. The population of Kingstown was given

by the 1871 census as 17,528 people.

With the advent of the Vartry water supply in the late 1860s, the provision of foul drainage systems became a priority for Kingstown and its satellite townships. Hitherto the limited quantities of waste-water used for washing and cooking would have been disposed of in cesspits or local sewers if these were available. These sewers were originally laid to remove surface water from the streets and discharged to streams or directly to the foreshore. With the arrival of copious mains water and the increasing use of water closets, the sewers and streams carried growing quantities of foul matter.

The consequent pollution of the beaches from Booterstown to Sandycove, which led to foul smells and threatened diseases, caused rented property to lie vacant and the cessation of building along the coastline. Problems were also caused for the seawater baths at locations such as the West Pier and Sandycove. In the overcrowded tenements of York Road and Glasthule, the lack of proper drainage must have had serious repercussions for the health of the inhabitants.

In Glasthule the situation was especially dire and cholera sheds were erected on the West Pier for fear of an imminent outbreak. It was only under such threat that the Town Commissioners undertook a sewerage scheme that included the 'West Pier Project' at a cost of £15,000. A thousand-foot outfall was extended seawards behind the West Pier in 1877, and three years later a Sandycove outfall was proposed.

Concern about these matters caused the town commissioners of Kingstown and Blackrock to enter into a signed and sealed agreement in 1882 to develop a joint drainage scheme, which the

Londonbridge Road pumping station, interior. *Each pair of pumps was driven by a separate steam engine and the original pumping equipment continued to work until 1953.*

Kingstown commissioners failed to carry out. In 1888, the Blackrock commissioners again expressed their willingness to join in and contribute towards another drainage scheme proposed by W. G. Strype CE for the drainage of the two townships. Kingstown did not respond and Blackrock despaired of being able to do anything in regard to a joint scheme that would eliminate the discharges to the foreshore through several box culverts. However, on hearing that Kingstown had a scheme in view, Blackrock commissioners once more indicated their willingness to co-operate.

Kingstown received a report dated 30 January 1891 from James Price MICE and Shirley A. Going CE which proposed lifting the Kingstown and Blackrock sewage by pumping into a high-level interceptor sewer at the West Pier. This in turn would discharge into a tank sewer along the Glasthule seafront and would empty into the sea at Bulloch.

In September 1891 the Kingstown commissioners agreed to have W. G. Strype explain a new joint scheme that he had prepared for the drainage of Kingstown and Blackrock. This appears to have been commissioned by Blackrock and included a sea outfall at the West Pier. Kingstown made no decision on this proposal and, later in the year, refused to meet a deputation from Blackrock or to support the Strype proposal. This joint scheme envisaged constructing a series of interceptor sewers along the coast from Booterstown to the West Pier where it would discharge through a holding tank and sea outfall. The holding tank and outfall would also facilitate the off-shore disposal of sewage from Kingstown.

It appears that both Kingstown and Blackrock residents desired to have their sewage discharged as far away as possible from their own beaches. While the NIMBY (Not in my Back Yard) syndrome may have had to wait until the second half of the twentieth century to be named, it was already alive and well in the late nineteenth century townships!

Monkstown Ward (Blackrock) residents objected to the proposal to route of the pipeline through

their area and were as determined as Kingstown to oppose the discharge of sewage from Blackrock at the West Pier, where the existing outflow was already very offensive. Independently, Blackrock sought by a special Act of Parliament to enter Kingstown to construct its proposed sewage works. At a special meeting of the Kingstown commissioners held on 26 November 1891 astonishment was expressed at the action of the Blackrock commissioners to coerce Kingstown into a joint scheme.

Early in 1892 the Kingstown commissioners appointed a special committee to manage its opposition to the Blackrock and Kingstown Main Drainage Inprovement Bill and a resolution to oppose the scheme was carried unanimously. The House of Lords rejected the Bill in March of that year despite the efforts of the Earl of Pembroke to have it reconsidered. Pembroke had a personal interest in the proposal as he presumably wished to see the Blackrock sewage discharged as far away as possible from the Sandymount and Merrion foreshores.

At the same time, the Kingstown No. 1 Committee, which dealt with drainage and expressed regret at the exclusion of its members from the special committee, received from E. C. Hart a 'Preliminary Report on the sewage of the Township of Kingstown' which quoted the population as being approximately 18,600 at the time and went on to point out that owing to the lack of strong currents the sewage remained in the vicinity of the shore and predicted that, unless remedial measures were taken, the town would cease to be a favourite health resort and the permanent residents would suffer ill-health and loss of income.

Hart suggested chemical combustion of the organic constituents of sewage before discharge to the sea and listed the existing points of discharge:

a) Bulloch Pier, serving the whole area south of the railway line to Dalkey and east of Albert Road, population 1,025

b) twenty independent sewers scattered along the shore for a distance of a mile and serving about 575 persons

c) the very offensive Glasthule sewer, serving a
population of 3,000

d) the West Pier outfall, also deemed very
offensive and serving a population of 14,000.

In 1893 the townships of Blackrock and Kingstown
obtained an Act that enabled them to carry out a
joint main drainage scheme. This consisted of intercepting the several coastal discharges in the areas of
the two authorities and bringing all the sewage to a
large holding tank near the West Pier. This operated
in a similar manner to the Rathmines and Pembroke
installation at the South Wall, only discharging
into the sea at ebb tide. It was in operation by 1894
and continued to work for nearly a century.
Sewage from the Monkstown area and, later, from
Sallynoggin, discharged through the West Pier tank,
as did outflows from the Newtownpark and
Stillorgan areas of County Dublin through the
Albany (Avenue) sewer.

Foul drainage from the Glasthule area appears to
have discharged to the Glasthule River, which rose
in the upper Glenageary area and discharged to
Scotsman's Bay. The stream was eventually covered
and in time became part of the combined system of
the area, carrying both foul and surface water.
Drainage from the central area of Kingstown was
intercepted by an ovoid brick sewer, known as the
Board of Works Culvert, which extended from the
People's Park along the Metals and Crofton Road to
the West Pier.

DALKEY, BALLYBRACK AND KILLINEY

The original foul drainage from the township of
Dalkey (established in 1863 and having a population of 2,584 by 1871) discharged directly to the sea
through small outfalls. Many of the sewers in the
area were combined box culverts constructed of
masonry covered with slabs of rock. Dalkey became
an Urban District in 1899.

Killiney and Ballybrack Township was established
in 1866 and had a population of 2,290 in 1871.
Much of the original housing development relied
on septic tank or cesspool drainage. The Urban

District Council that took over from the Commissioners in 1899 purchased a horse-drawn Merryweather vacuum tanker to clear the tanks and pools
in this area. This vehicle, which is preserved in the
Transport Museum in Howth, bears witness to the
severity of the hills in the Killiney area in its
unusual yoking arrangement. This consists of a
separate pair of shafts for each of the two horses
used to draw the tanker, in which the vacuum was
created by a separate pump.

RATHMINES WATER:
THE GRAND CANAL SCHEME

As recorded in Chapter 4, all the townships in the
Dublin area, with one exception, were provided
with Vartry water. We have seen how the Kingstown
Water Company derived statutory advantage from
the 1861 Water Act, Dublin Corporation being
forced to carry out work in the township.

While the practice of trying to squeeze the
maximum out of Dublin Corporation was indulged
in by all the townships, it plumbed the depths of
cynicism when performed by Rathmines. This
township, that always sought bargains and exhibited
serious paranoia whenever it had to deal with
Dublin Corporation, lurched from one crisis to
another in the matter of water supply. From the
township's establishment in 1847, its commissioners
were acutely aware of the need to have a more
sophisticated supply than could be obtained from
wells. In 1845, two years before the township came
into being, there had been a proposal to supply the
Rathmines area with water from the corporation
basin at Portobello, but this was not pursued on the
grounds of cost.

When Dublin Corporation promoted its Water
Bill, the Rathmines Township could have availed of
a supply as one of the extra municipal areas. It not
only opted out, but endeavoured by various and
usually unethical methods to undermine the corporation's negotiations with the other townships. Its
reasons were, first, a fear of corporation pipes in its
territory and, later, of city water rate collectors

Vaulted brick reservoirs near the Eighth Lock, at Gallanstown. *Constructed by the Rathmines Township to draw water from the Grand Canal, and a superb feat of engineering, this system was already obsolete when it came into operation in 1863.*

operating in the township. Several rounds of negotiations took place, but all proved abortive. Then, in 1863 and against all logic or considerations of health, Rathmines established a supply system that took water from the Grand Canal.

Water for Rathmines was extracted from the canal upstream of the Eighth Lock at Gallanstown, near Clondalkin, at a level of 178 feet above Poolbeg Datum. Here, on a site of just under two acres, the township constructed a compact filtration plant with covered clear water tanks capable of dealing with two million gallons per day. The complex, designed in 1862, originally contained one reservoir and three filter tanks, and was thought to be the first of its kind in Ireland. Three more filter tanks and a second vaulted brick reservoir were added later. A settling pond was added early in the twentieth century.

A 15-inch pipe conveyed the water from Gallanstown for over two and a quarter miles, at which point it flowed into two pipes, 12 inches and 9 inches in diameter, to the township boundary. From here, an urban network distributed the water

to users' premises. Unless householders had excessive numbers of water closets or baths, usage was paid for in the standard water rate. However, there was an extra charge for supplying stables, and ownership of a horse and carriage was a status symbol of the time. A premises with up to five horses paid 3s (19c) annually for each beast, owners of five or more being charged 4s (25.4c) for each animal.

Unfortunately the Rathmines water system was both obsolete and a potential public health hazard even as it came into operation on 23 July 1863. Furthermore the supply was often intermittent and a pumping station had to be built at Harold's Cross, with a water tower in Rathgar to serve the higher parts of that district. Séamus Ó Maitiú records that two engines pumped all night at Harold's Cross to supply Rathgar through a 9-inch main, entailing additional expenditure that raised the cost of the waterworks to £29,000.

Fully described in Chapter 3 of *Dublin's Suburban Towns*, the Rathmines canal water saga was one of recalcitrance and repeated reluctance to avail of a Vartry supply, even with the goodwill of a negotiator as diplomatic and skilled as Sir John Gray. Indeed E. J. Bourke's 1960 report tells of the spite exhibited on a grand scale by the vindictive Frederick Stokes, chairman of the Rathmines commissioners. When Sir John Gray suggested a charge of 6d per 1,000 gallons from the Pembroke Commissioners for Vartry water, Stokes offered them a canal supply for 4d. Years later he stated in evidence that he would have given it for 2d to close the corporation out and admitted that there was not enough water available to supply Pembroke when he made his offer.

BOHERNABREENA WATERWORKS

The success of the Vartry project and the fact that their neighbours in Dublin enjoyed an abundant supply of pure soft water from 1868 onwards greatly unsettled the residents of Rathmines. The Town Commissioners therefore decided to seek something better than the meagre supply of intensely hard water of indifferent quality reaching them from the canal.

The Rathmines commissioners again sought a supply from the Vartry scheme in 1880. Failing to agree terms with Dublin Corporation, they decided to establish a modern water supply system of their own. They engaged Richard Hassard to advise them and promoted a Bill in parliament to obtain the necessary powers. This was unsuccessfully opposed by Dublin Corporation – a most fortunate failure in the light of developments that at that time lay far in the future.

In retrospect corporation opposition to the Dodder scheme is puzzling because Parke Neville had earlier proposed a reservoir at Glenasmole and a service reservoir at Kimmage. Situated three miles from the city centre, the Kimmage reservoir would have been at a level of 170 feet above Datum and capable of holding 380 million gallons. It would also have been capable of meeting the needs of the township.

When the Rathmines Bill passed into law in 1880 Richard Hassard, who could take justifiable pride in having conceived the scheme for the Vartry, drew up detailed designs for the Bohernabreena water supply project. The scheme came into operation in 1887, and was capable of delivering three million gallons of water per day. By that time the population of the township had increased to 30,000.

The former Rathmines Township waterworks lies in the valley of Glenasmole, the last primordial Gaeltacht area in County Dublin. In this remote place, Irish was the spoken language well into the twentieth century. Through this isolated and lonely valley flows the often turbulent River Dodder, together with its tributaries, the Cot and the Slade Brooks. Amazingly, the Bohernabreena reservoirs are a mere nine miles from the General Post Office in Dublin city centre and only seven from Rathmines.

To compensate the many mill owners on the Dodder for the reduction in river flow due to the water abstraction a second reservoir was constructed just below the waterworks reservoir. From the lower reservoir compensation water could be released to maintain an adequate flow in the river during dry periods to permit continued operation of the mills. The upper or clear water reservoir contained 360 million gallons, with its top water level 578 feet above Ordnance Datum. The lower or mill owners' compensation reservoir had a capacity of 156 million gallons, its top water level being 495 feet above Datum. This reservoir had catchwaters, gauge basin and duplicate measuring flumes for preferential supply to mill owners.

Bohernabreena Works, as the complex became known, lies at the foot of Kippure Mountain (2,473 feet or 753 metres high). The gathering ground consists of an area of 4,340 acres (1,756 hectares), partly granite, partly granite covered with peat, but principally metamorphic and Silurian formations. It was from the latter that the clear water was collected into the upper reservoir for drinking purposes. The peaty water from the granite areas was channelled around the upper reservoir and routed through the lower reservoir. The bypass was partly in a canal and partly through a line of 27-inch diameter piping. It was possible to divert some of the river water into the upper reservoir, if this was required to maintain the supply.

Very heavy flash floods affect the valley periodically and there have been several landslips, and a peculiarity of the catchment is that the water flows off the slopes very quickly. The overflow weirs were therefore made 200 feet in length to deal with the excess water. On 25 August 1905 the highest rainfall recorded up to that time occurred. In the space of 27 hours, 6.23 inches were recorded, with 5 inches falling in 9 hours. On that occasion 4 feet of water was measured passing over the 200-foot waste weir of the lower reservoir. The dam crest level is 6 feet above the overflow weir level.

Water for Rathmines could be drawn off from the upper reservoir at different levels. After passing through a gauge basin it was carried through four and a half miles of 15-inch pipes, with two relief pits en route, to slow sand filter beds at Ballyboden. It then passed to an adjacent open service reservoir with a capacity of 12 million gallons, about two and three-quarter miles from the township. This reservoir was an impoundment contained in an earthen embankment at 327 feet above Ordnance Datum and 175 feet above the highest point in the township. From Ballyboden, the water passed through copper wire fine screens and was delivered to Rathmines by two pipelines, 18 inches and 12 inches in diameter.

As recorded earlier, the same team as had been responsible for the drainage project – Richard Hassard and Arthur W. Tyrrell – designed the Rathmines water supply system. The resident engineers who supervised construction were, successively, Henry Crook and F. P. Dixon. The main contractors were Falkiner and Stanford of Dublin, whose representative on site was E. J. Jackson. Seven hundred men are said to have been employed on the project. Arthur Tyrrell comprehensively described the works in a paper read to the Institution of Mechanical Engineers in London on 25 October 1888.

During the discussion that followed Tyrrell's paper it was stated that 1886 had been very wet but 1887, the year in which the Rathmines system came into operation, was the driest recorded until that time in the catchment area. The drought lasted for 161 days from 23 May until 31 October, but when it ended there was still enough water in the Bohernabreena reservoirs to maintain the supply for a further 51 days.

Michael Moynihan, city engineer from 1927 to 1936, read a paper entitled 'The Water Supply of Greater Dublin' to the Institution of Municipal and County Engineers on 5 May 1932. In it he recalled that the former Rathmines Grand Canal Works was purchased by the corporation in 1893, formal possession being effected on 20 January 1894. A settling basin of 2.5 million gallons capacity was built in 1925 as well as a covered clear water tank that could hold 4 million gallons. A 15-inch diameter cast iron pipe was laid to deliver water to the city and in 1932 the Grand Canal Works could supply 4 million gallons to the two systems, presumably those of

Dublin and the former Rathmines Township. Consumption from this source was 1.4 million gallons per day in 1932.

The former Rathmines Grand Canal Works was later connected to the smaller 1868 Corporation Works at the Fifth Lock (Chapter 4). Reverting to the beginnings of the Bohernabreena scheme, it is retrospectively strange that little notice was taken of the comprehensive report about Dodder flooding and the embryonic millers' reservoir proposed in 1844 by the distinguished engineer Robert Mallet (1810–1881). Such provision was made in the scheme adopted nearly forty years later and Parke Neville, city engineer, had also considered the Dodder as a possible source for Dublin when examining various schemes in the 1850s. Neville's outline proposals also made provision for the mill owners along the Dodder, whom he regarded as a potentially expensive source of litigation, which they did in fact turn out to be – causing Rathmines Township considerable embarrassment and cost.

The alarming possibility of serious injury being inflicted on people relying on public water supplies was considered by the corporation's waterworks committee on 31 August 1893. It was discovered that poison had been put into the River Dodder in an attempt to catch fish, but this apparently was an isolated incident and did not arise again.

WATER AND DRAINAGE IN DRUMCONDRA, CLONTARF AND KILMAINHAM

Rathmines (established in 1847) and Pembroke (1863) were regarded as the senior, more upmarket and best endowed of the five townships immediately outside the city boundary; Rathmines actually accomplished three boundary extensions up to 1880 (Chapter 4). Of the other three, Clontarf (incorporated in 1869) considered itself superior to New Kilmainham (1868) and Drumcondra (1878) which were probably the least influential of the townships. The three junior townships, never as powerful as their two southern rivals, had modest drainage systems. They all obtained water from the Vartry

RATHMINES WATERWORKS.10549.W.L.

system and were generally more susceptible to a take-over by Dublin Corporation than either Rathmines or Pembroke.

In 1876 when the North Dublin Union was still the rural sanitary authority for the area preliminary plans for draining Drumcondra and Glasnevin were prepared by a consulting engineer, P. F. Leonard. Among the many nuisances cited in his report was Clonliffe Road, where open channels or ditches conveyed the filthy contents of house and yard drains alongside the public road to discharge to the River Tolka. He described the Tolka as 'gathering a miscellaneous mass of abominations along its whole course'.

In April 1880 Leonard produced a detailed drainage scheme for Drumcondra, which had been established in 1878 as a township that also incorpo-

rated Glasnevin and Clonliffe. The resulting network of seven main sewers readily facilitated the development of the township until well into the twentieth century. The areas served included Botanic Avenue, Botanic Road, Ballymun Road and Washerwoman's Hill, Whitworth Road, and Drumcondra Road Upper and Lower.

The sewers from these districts all flowed via Richmond Road and Clonliffe Road to what were euphemistically described as clarifying tanks located on the south bank of the Tolka, west of Ballybough Bridge and opposite Richmond Avenue.

The Richmond Road sewer was originally intended to continue via what is now Annesley Bridge Road to the bridge over the Tolka. The Clonliffe Road sewer was to have been extended via Poplar Row to the same point, at which a

Rathmines Township's reservoir at Bohernabreena.
At the foot of Kippure Mountain, these waterworks were on the river Dodder. Designed by Richard Hassard, the scheme came into operation in 1887.

pumping station was to send the combined flows along East Wall Road. The outfall sewer in East Wall Road would have traversed Dublin Corporation territory to a sea outfall at a place called the Smoothing Iron (Chapter 8). A corporation sewer already discharged at this location and the city engineer objected to the Drumcondra proposal, which was not constructed as originally planned. It should be reiterated here that Parke Neville's main drainage proposals that failed to secure finance in the early 1870s also included Rathmines, Pembroke, Drumcondra and Clontarf.

Instead, the Drumcondra tanks at Ballybough discharged directly into the Tolka on the ebb tide, contributing to what was probably the most objectionable nuisance in North Dublin. Downstream from the Ballybough outfall the pollution was intensified by the effluent from a vitriol or chemical factory at Poplar Row. Where Fairview Park is today was a tidal sloblands created by the construction of the railway embankment in 1844. The Tolka flowed through this, entering the open sea at the east side of the embankment through the Middle Arch, also known as the Third Arch. Until work on the Port tunnel began in recent years, the crown of this arch was visible just above ground level and below the west wall of the DART depot.

The ebb and flow of the tide constantly reinvigorated the filth and stench of the malodorous sloblands. Plans for its reclamation by dumping, drawn up by Parke Neville in 1873, were eventually implemented during the years 1907–1930, following which process Fairview Park was laid out and progressively developed. The fill material was municipal waste conveyed to the site in special trains of tramway wagons from the destructor (incinerator) at the Stanley Street cleansing depot. Rubble from buildings destroyed during the 1916 Rising was also deposited in Fairview.

Straddling the railway line, Clontarf – incorporated under a Township Act of 1869 – relied exclusively on discharges to the foreshore for its drainage.

New Kilmainham Township lay to the south-west of the city. Its commissioners took office in 1854 under the Towns Improvement Act and the township was incorporated under an Act of 1868. Most sewers in New Kilmainham flowed to the Camac, already grossly polluted by industrial effluent from several paper mills along its course upstream of the township. The polluted waters of the Camac were almost wholly responsible for the sulphurous stench of the Liffey that persisted for nearly a hundred years. The closure of the paper mills, coupled with the diversion of other polluting flows into the new trunk sewers of the Greater Dublin Drainage Scheme (Chapter 12) finally brought water quality in the Liffey to an acceptable state.

Although in existence since 1796, many years before the township came into existence, Kilmainham Jail enjoyed two sources of water in the early nineteenth century. In addition to a conventional river supply, it also had a second, more unusual arrangement involving a well that was 70 feet (21 metres) deep. Working for two hours at a time, pairs of convicts operated a wheel pump to maintain the water requirements of the jail.

New Kilmainham, Clontarf and Drumcondra failed to achieve the rate of growth, generate the quantity of municipal income or develop the services necessary to ensure their long-term viability as independent urban districts. As will be seen in Chapter 8 they did not survive as autonomous entities following the 1901 Dublin Corporation boundary extension, when they became part of the city.

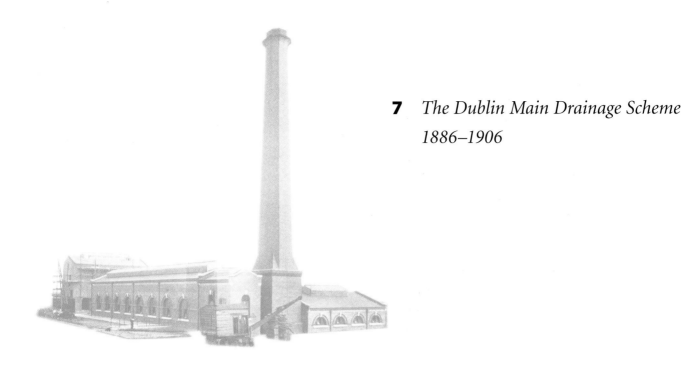

7 *The Dublin Main Drainage Scheme*
1886–1906

The saga of Parke Neville's attempts to have the
Liffey purified by laying interceptor sewers along
the quays is unfolded in Chapters 3 and 5. During
the 1870s, as the need for action became ever more
urgent, several alternative proposals involving dams,
weirs and flushing reservoirs were made, as had
been the case during the previous decade. They
were all found to be impractical and were decisively
rejected by Bindon Blood Stoney, the Port and
Docks Board's distinguished engineer, who at that
time had responsibility for the river, its walls and
bed as far inland as Chapelizod.

More than twenty-five years after Parke Neville's
1853 proposals to clean the Liffey it looked at long
last as if his plans for this most necessary project
would finally go ahead following the appointment
of a Royal Commission in 1879 to 'inquire into the
sewerage and drainage of the City of Dublin'. The
commissioner was Sir Robert Rawlinson, Chief
Engineering Inspector of the Local Government
Board in England. His task was to bring forward
proposals for the ever more sorely needed Dublin
main drainage programme. He was assisted by Dr
Frederick Xavier McCabe, an inspector with the

Local Government Board for Ireland. Both he and
Sir Robert were referred to in Queen Victoria's
Order of Appointment as 'trusty and well-beloved'.

Five schemes were considered by the commission,
most of them coinciding on the broad features of
providing interceptor sewers. Parke Neville's
proposals, which closely followed his 1853
proposals, were the ones finally recommended by
the commission. Its comprehensive *Report on the
Sewerage and Drainage of the City of Dublin* was
published in 1880 by Alex Thom & Company, but
not acted on for more than another ten years.

The report dealt very thoroughly with every
aspect of housing, health, water, drainage, paving
and cleansing. It traced the history of each of these
subjects in a Dublin context and highlighted, firmly
but courteously, the corporation's shortcomings and
the efforts of its hard-working officials to cope with
many difficulties that were not of their own making.

Old sewers with earthen inverts, described in
Chapter 2, which had by now all been replaced
or underpinned and given brick or stone floors,
came in for particular stricture. Another subject of
criticism was the dearth of ventilators on the
sewers, which had given rise to numerous complaints from citizens assailed by the stench from

Spencer Harty, Dublin City Engineer.

Responsible for designing the Main Drainage Scheme, Harty was one of only two officials to receive the Freedom of the City, the other being Sir Charles Cameron, Chief Medical Officer.

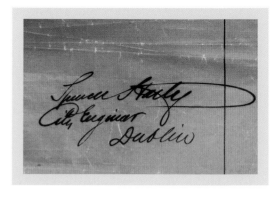

inadequately vented lines. All the sewers discharged to the Liffey, where the outfalls were protected by tidal flaps. Behind these, sewage built up during high tides, creating a highly obnoxious stench. The commission recommended the installation of additional ventilators to achieve a total of twenty per mile. It also suggested manholes with side entrances and flushing arrangements, and 1,000 gullies.

Many very useful facts about the city as it existed in 1879 abound in the report, with several sets of statistics. It noted that the area of the city between the North and South Circular Roads was 1,264acres (511.5 hectares), with 23,000 houses and 120 miles of streets.

A particularly apposite observation related to the glaring contrast the commission saw between the city and the townships. Middle-class and affluent people lived in the townships, contributing little if anything to municipal taxes, while many poorer people went to work in the townships but came back each night to live in the impoverished city.

SPENCER HARTY SUCCEEDS PARKE NEVILLE

After the Rawlinson commission, Parke Neville continued to work as diligently as ever on the many parts of his remit. In addition to water and drainage, roads (including new streets such as Lord Edward Street), paving, lighting, cleansing and the building of a municipal abattoir kept him very busy. On 30 October 1886, recently returned from a working holiday in Britain, he died in his home at Pembroke Road, aged seventy-four years. He had served with distinction as city engineer for more than thirty-five years but, through the inertia and parsimony of others, several of his progressive and necessary civic improvement schemes were not carried out until twenty or more years after his death. Many well-deserved tributes were paid to Parke Neville, but the most enduring one is the introduction or improvement of the many public services we enjoy today; his record in water and drainage alone render any further comment superfluous.

One of eighteen applicants for the corporation's most senior engineering position was Spencer Harty (1838–1923). Harty had been with the corporation since 1860, when he assisted with the preparation of plans for the Vartry water scheme. Described at that time as a draughtsman, he was in fact a fully qualified civil engineer, possibly gaining postgraduate experience. Parke Neville's most trusted assistant, Harty was formally elected by the city council as borough surveyor and waterworks engineer on 14 March 1887. A notable aspect of the election was that fourteen of the eighteen candidates had addresses outside the city of Dublin and none of these applicants received a single vote.

INNER CITY LIFE AROUND 1900

The many new or improved public services introduced in the last half of the nineteenth century greatly enhanced the lifestyles of the expanding middle classes, whose standard of living improved constantly. The fortunes of the poor, however, did not improve perceptibly with the approach of the twentieth century. Conscientious officials like Spenser Harty and Sir Charles Cameron made strenuous efforts to alleviate their lot, as did the Iveagh Trust and numerous charities. But thousands of these unfortunate people still lived in conditions little better than those castigated in the previous hundred years by the Rev James Whitelaw, Mother Mary Aikenhead and Dr Thomas Willis (1789–1881). These great humanitarians would

have readily empathised with the poor who still formed the bottom layer of the class system that dominated people's lives and would continue to do so for many more years.

Frenchwoman Anne Marie de Bovet, quoted in Diarmaid O Muirithe's *A Seat behind the Coachman*, recorded her impressions of Dublin in the 1890s. She described the city as

> a conglomeration of poor quarters, whose misery overflows on to the doorsteps of the rich .... but to see the abject squalor of Dublin in its very depths one only has to walk along St. Patrick's, and particularly the street which joins the two cathedrals – a street consisting of two rows of tumble-down, mouldy-looking houses, reeking of dirt, and oozing with the accumulated filth of many generations .... The streets are connected by a network of stinking little alleys and infected courts .... What one sees in the interiors makes one sick and sad at the same time. One day the sanitary officers found in a large room eighteen human beings, huddled together asleep on the floor, whose only furniture was their bundles and a few bits of dirty straw. In the next room were lodged twelve, seven of whom were ill with typhoid fever.

Iveagh Buildings.

Built in the style of seventeenth-century Dutch Billies, and funded by the Guinness Family, this fine example of social housing was constructed in the early twentieth century to replace some of Dublin's worst slums.

De Bovet described in detail the appalling clothes the people wore, their efforts to get work, their begging, and the terrible, rotten food they ate. And she marvelled at their good temper, sociability and even politeness that survived such degradation. She told of pretty girls who were far from being ashamed of their rags and were proud of being looked at; of cheeky children; and of mothers smiling gratefully in return for a glance at their babies.

Through the efforts of the Iveagh Trust and scrupulous corporation officers like Sir Charles Cameron, the shame of the area around Patrick Street was to be largely terminated in the opening years of the twentieth century. But extensive slum areas and many very poor people remained, and over sixty more years would pass before the last tenements would be cleared. Meanwhile, however, the city was about to receive a great amenity, properly funded at last. The Dublin main drainage project would complement the Vartry water scheme, improve public health, enhance the environment, and encourage civic progress.

IMPLEMENTING THE MAIN DRAINAGE SCHEME

Spencer Harty pushed ahead resolutely with Parke Neville's drainage proposals. In 1891 the corporation engaged George Chatterton – Sir Joseph Bazalgette's consultancy colleague and successor – as adviser for the long-frustrated main drainage project that was at last assured of implementation. Before coming to a conclusion, Chatterton re-examined the previous schemes put forward by others. He rejected the earlier outfall locations proposed by Corrigan,

Bazalgette and Neville, but most other features of his scheme, especially the riverside interceptors, were almost identical to those Parke Neville had first visualised thirty-eight years earlier.

The Dublin Main Drainage Scheme was intended to cater for a population of 400,000 people and for several districts that lay outside the city boundary prior to 1901. The main features of the scheme in the city centre were the interceptor sewers along the North and South Quays, taking the flow from most of the outfalls to the Liffey (22 on the North Quays, 32 on the South Quays). However, the Poddle and Camac rivers could not be taken into the interceptors and still polluted the Liffey. While the Poddle improved over time as foul matter was diverted from it, the Camac continued to poison the Liffey for another three quarters of a century.

At Ringsend a large pumping station was planned to lift and deliver sewage to the treatment and outfall works at the Pigeonhouse, with sludge discharge in the open sea. Following a local government inquiry held in February 1892, the necessary provisional order to acquire any lands required for the scheme was obtained.

A major acquisition, essential to the drainage programme, was the Pigeonhouse Fort and Harbour, where the outfall works was to be sited. This place is of great historical importance, the title of the fort being corrupted from the name of the Pidgeon family. The Pidgeons operated a hotel and catering business on the site in the eighteenth century, adjacent to the berths for ships plying between Dublin and ports in England and Wales.

In 1813 when the government feared a French invasion, the War Office bought the fort from the

The Main Drainage Scheme. *Diagram showing interceptors as built in 1906 and as extended to the Ringsend Treatment Plant in the early twenty-first century.*

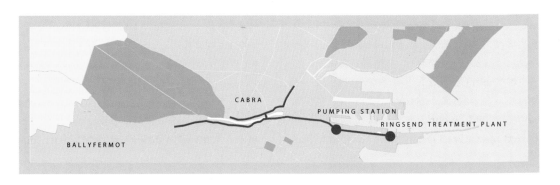

BALLYFERMOT

CABRA

PUMPING STATION

RINGSEND TREATMENT PLANT

then Harbour Commissioners for £100,183 and developed it for defensive purposes. Ninety years later the War Office engaged in protracted and acrimonious exchanges with the corporation, which needed immediate possession. A second local government inquiry became necessary, holding up progress by nearly four years until 1895. Eventually the corporation purchased the fort for £65,000.

INTERCEPTORS, LIFFEY SIPHON AND RINGSEND TUNNEL

Some preparatory drainage work was carried out at Parkgate Street in the autumn of 1895, the long-delayed main programme finally starting in 1896. In March of that year contracts were entered into with H. & J. Martin for the construction of seven and a half miles of intercepting sewers along the quays and in the city centre. A building strike delayed this segment of the work, which was completed in 1900. The entire project took ten years to carry out, the year of completion giving the scheme its title of 'The 1906 Main Drainage Scheme'.

Reflecting the differences in catchment, population density and any future development it was intended to serve when it was designed, the North Quays interceptor is smaller than its counterpart south of the river. Starting in Parkgate Street as a pipe sewer 18 inches in diameter, the North Quays line changes to a circular brick culvert three feet in diameter at the Esplanade, enlarging to 3 feet 9 inches at Ellis Quay.

Horse tram services on the North Quays from Parkgate Street to O'Connell Bridge were suspended while the sewer was being laid and the tramway was reconstructed for the imminent change to electric traction. Later the same procedure was followed on the South Quays. Progress drawings in the city drainage archive show completion dates for various sections of these and other associated sewers.

The South Quays interceptor begins at the junction of South Circular Road and Hospital Lane, just south of Islandbridge (Sarah's Bridge), as a box culvert measuring 3 feet 9 inches (1,143mm) high

by 2 feet 6 inches (762mm) wide. From the eastern end of Hospital Lane it turns north and then east to follow the Liffey to Heuston (Kingsbridge) Station. Here it changes to a circular brick structure, with a diameter of 3 feet 3 inches; this increases to 4 feet 6 inches at Wood Quay. A painting by Walter Osborne in the National Gallery of Ireland shows what is believed to be construction work on this interceptor on Wood Quay.

The interceptor along the South Quays was described in 1906 as having three important branches. The first, which enters at Heuston Station, brings in sewage from Kilmainham. At Winetavern Street the second main tributary from the south city joins the interceptor. Because this flows from Nicholas Street under the high ridge at the eastern end of High Street, two manholes in Winetavern Street outside Christchurch Cathedral have the deepest conventional shafts in the city centre, measuring more than 30 feet 7 inches (9.3m).

The third tributary, coming in on Wellington Quay, was virtually an interceptor for the Poddle, which at that time carried a great volume of sewage. Happily the river later recovered as the foul matter was diverted from it over the years.

From Eden Quay, opposite Marlborough Street, the North Quays interceptor passes under the Liffey in a siphon 3 feet 4 inches (1m) in diameter, joining

Outfall Works at Ringsend, under construction.
The Dublin building firm of H. & J. Martin were the contractors for the project and this rare photograph shows the mammoth foundations for the Outfall Works.

The Four Courts by Walter Osborne.

This painting by the distinguished nineteenth-century Irish artist shows city council workers re-laying a sewer along the quays in the foreground.

its South Quays counterpart on Burgh Quay. This work was carried out by the firm of H. & J. Martin, which was recommended for the contract on 7 December 1900.

When the sewers that previously discharged to the Liffey were connected to the new interceptors, overflows were provided at the original outfall points along the quays. This arrangement allowed the highly diluted excess flows to discharge to the river in wet weather. Weir boards, the height of which could be adjusted as required, set the water levels at which the overflows came into operation. This arrangement was still operational in 2005.

The local sewers along the quays, which discharged to the Liffey through the chambers at the existing outfalls, now entered the interceptors. To avoid a multitude of unnecessary connections to the interceptors, these sewers were extended, renewed and re-laid as required. They still serve buildings along the quays and are known as rider sewers. A device encountered on the drainage systems of basements in the city centre, particularly along the quays, is the widely misunderstood anti-flooding trap. Its purpose is simple – to prevent the ingress of water into basements that are lower than the water level in the Liffey at high tide when there is a

danger of surcharging (backflow) in the sewer serving the premises. If this happens, anxious occupiers sometimes call in plumbers, who are often unfamiliar with the principle of the anti-flooding trap.

The trap works on the same principle as the domestic ballcock, closing the drain as soon as the water backs up. For a short time, this also restricts or stops discharges to the sewer, creating a temporarily blockage. Unfortunately, injudiciously using a rod or other implement in these circumstances can damage the ball or knock it out of shape, with unfortunate results. In recent years, the mandatory installation of pumps to keep basements clear has eliminated the need for anti-flooding traps. However, although less widespread than formerly, they can still be encountered in older buildings and have to be treated with respect.

A tragedy occurred at Burgh Quay on 6 May 1905 when the main drainage scheme was under construction. Two men working underground were overcome by town gas that had entered the sewer. Despite heroic rescue efforts, one of the workers, John Fleming, died. So too did one of the rescuers, the young Constable Patrick Sheahan from College Street Police Station. The splendid memorial that stands at the junction of Burgh Quay and Hawkins Street commemorates Patrick Sheahan's bravery.

At Hawkins Street the combined flows from the two riverside interceptors go over a weir at the head of an 8-feet (2.43m) diameter tunnel. From Hawkins Street this tunnel runs via Townsend Street, Hanover Street, Ringsend Road, Ringsend Park and Pigeonhouse Road to the main pumping station. In Ringsend, a Greathead Shield, then a new concept in tunnel boring, was used to achieve progress of seven feet per day through made-up ground consisting largely of rubble and loose filling. The tunnel was driven in compressed air and, because of the relatively small depth of cover and the loose fill, the Liffey was said to boil like a cauldron. Much of the land in this area had been reclaimed from the sea from the second decade of the eighteenth century onwards.

RINGSEND PUMPING STATION

The firm of H. & J. Martin was also the contractor for the buildings at Ringsend pumping station, which operated for seventy-nine years until 1985. Here the sewage was screened – a process that removes rags and other potentially damaging matter from the sewage before it reaches the pumps. The pumps lifted the flow 23 feet to a high-level 8-feet diameter tunnel leading to the outfall works.

At Ringsend pumping station the original equipment consisted of four Lancashire boilers supplied by Stewarts of Glasgow. They worked at a pressure of 140lbs per square inch, supplying four vertical triple expansion direct acting engines. These drove centrifugal pumps, each capable of raising twenty million gallons of sewage in twenty-four hours. Gwynnes supplied the engines and pumps. Three pumps were capable of dealing with the maximum wet weather flow, the fourth being in reserve, and space was left for two more sets.

Bennis mechanical stokers and a Green's Economiser also formed part of the equipment, and two 7-inch pumps supplied sewage to the milk of

Grafton Street.

Road re-instatement by city council workers at the corner of Grafton Street and St Stephen's Green. Paving setts to be replaced can be seen along with tram-rails in the foreground.

**Main Pumping
Station, exterior.**

*The new Pumping
Station was opened
with due ceremony in
1906 and transformed
the health and life-
expectancy for genera-
tions of Dubliners.*

lime mixers, part of a system intended to speed up
the treatment process. These centrifugal Worthington
pumps were driven by vertical compound direct
acting engines. They were duplicate sets, the duty
pump sending sewage to the milk of lime mixers.

Replacement of the steam plant by electricity
began at Ringsend in 1923. Despite some unavoid-
able delays this was completed in 1924 and the
entire steam plant was offered for sale in 1925. In
1932 the Ringsend installation consisted of two
Worthington and three Cochrane 22-inch centrifugal pumps, all coupled direct to Oerlikon motors.
Each of these pumps was capable of lifting eighteen
million gallons per day through 24 feet.

THE OUTFALL WORKS:
SLUDGE DISPOSAL

From the main pumping station, the 8-feet
diameter conduit, already described, delivered the
sewage to the precipitation tanks, 1km (0.68 of a
mile) east of the main station and located on
reclaimed foreshore beside the Pigeonhouse
Harbour. Each of the eighteen rectangular tanks had
a capacity of 6.5 million gallons.

The treatment process involved the precipitation
of the sewage solids by the addition of lime as the
sewage left the pumping station. The eighteen tanks
operated as sequencing batch reactors. The tanks
were allowed to fill by opening penstocks in the
inlet channel and when the sewage had settled, the

clarified liquid was drawn off by floating arm drawoffs into the outlet channel, which discharged to the adjoining Liffey at all stages of the tide. When a sufficient depth of sludge had accumulated in a tank, it was manually squeegeed from the flat tank floors to the central sludge culvert and thence to the sludge lift – not an enviable task! The sludge lift consisted of buckets, which raised the sludge to an elevated holding tank, to discharge to the sludge ship berthed alongside. It is noteworthy that the new treatment works commissioned in 2002 also processes sewage on a batch basis.

Described as novel when the main drainage project was commissioned, the system appears to have been unduly complicated. This led to its being examined in detail in 1914 and again in 1915. Simple sedimentation was found to improve the effluent and the abolition of the lime plant resulted in considerable savings in both labour and materials. After some years' disuse the plant was sold off in 1920 and the building in which it was housed was used for other purposes. The operation of the settlement tanks was modified to allow sewage to pass continuously through the tanks and over the peripheral walls. Sludge was removed manually as before. Despite their shortcomings as primary settling tanks they did manage to remove a surprising percentage of the suspended sewage solids.

The sludge was shipped out to sea in the sludge vessel TSS *Shamrock* (more fully described in Chapter 15) and discharged in the deep and fast current northeast of the Baily Lighthouse. Under the corporation's provisional order the discharge area was defined as being 'outside the Port and Bay of Dublin, not less than six miles distant from Poolbeg Lighthouse and North of a line drawn due east from the Baily Lighthouse'.

The main drainage scheme, which cost £508,000, was executed in the closing years of Spencer Harty's regime as city engineer. He was made a Freeman of Dublin on 2 September 1907 and also became a Justice of the Peace. He retired in 1910 and was succeeded as city engineer by John G. O'Sullivan.

Main Pumping Station, interior.
The original equipment consisted of four Lancashire boilers supplied by Stewarts of Glasgow, which worked at a pressure of 140 lbs per square inch.

First employed by the corporation in 1890 and latterly deputy borough surveyor, O'Sullivan was elected on 2 May 1910.

Spencer Harty's son George followed in his father's steps as a civil engineer and joined the staff of the main drainage scheme in 1897. He subsequently became engineer in charge of the sewers and main drainage department, where he served until the late 1920s.

Construction of the main drainage system coincided with two other major developments in the city's infrastructure. The corporation had provided a municipal electricity service from 1892 onwards, the original generating station at Fleet Street being supplemented (and later superseded) by the much larger Pigeonhouse plant in 1903. All distribution lines were underground, necessitating considerable excavation work but avoiding the erection of unsightly overhead wiring networks. The power was produced by direct current generators, a dc supply serving the centre of the city until the 1950s.

TSS Shamrock.

The residue or sludge from the Main Drainage System was shipped out to sea in this vessel and discharged northeast of the Baily Lighthouse.

During 1898–1900 all the tramways inside the city boundary were electrified, the former horse system being considerably expanded. In several streets with restricted road space, side-entry sewer manholes were constructed, the access shafts being located on or beside footpaths. This arrangement obviated potential traffic congestion and hazards like open manholes between the tram rails. During construction of the South Quays interceptor a subsidence occurred at O'Connell Bridge in the summer of 1898, disrupting tramway traffic for some weeks.

Construction of the main drainage scheme was one of the positive factors that alleviated Dublin's chronic unemployment problem between 1895 and 1906. A more enduring benefit was the creation of some permanent jobs when the system came into operation. At that time labourers were paid between fifteen and eighteen shillings (€0.95–€1.14) per week, while a skilled fitter could earn up to £1 7s (€1.71). However, widespread poverty and abom-

inable housing conditions remained, as is clearly evidenced in the many photographs taken in the city during the first quarter of the twentieth century.

A notable ceremony took place at Ringsend on Monday 24 September 1906 when Alderman William Cotton, Chairman of the Improvements Committee, formally declared the main drainage scheme complete. An attractive and informative souvenir handbook was produced to mark the event. The commemorative plaque marking the 1906 ceremony was relocated to the new main pumping station in 1985 (Chapter 12).

EXTENDING THE MAIN DRAINAGE SYSTEM

Following the extension of the city boundary, detailed main drainage proposals for Drumcondra, Clontarf and New Kilmainham were implemented over a number of years (Chapter 8). North Lotts and areas east of Butt Bridge were also tackled. The

Builders of Main Pumping Station and TSS Shamrock.

Top row, left to right: James Martin, managing director of building contractor H. & J. Martin Ltd; George Chatterton, consultant engineer; H.H. Hellins, resident engineer in charge of works; bottom row, left to right: John Smellie and Walter Scott, builders of TSS Shamrock.

provisional order granted to the corporation for the main drainage system on 9 May 1892 specifically precluded construction of an interceptor sewer on the South Quays east of Hawkins Street.

Meanwhile, in April 1901, the sewers department reported that it had only two tumbling carts and would need two more to cover the extended city area. Two extra carts were therefore ordered from Potter and Company, coach builders, for £37 10s (€47.62) each.

THE 1901 CITY BOUNDARY

While the main drainage scheme was under construction, sweeping changes took place in local administration throughout Ireland. Under the 1898 Local Government Act county councils replaced grand juries and many townships became urban district councils. The extinction of the elitist and unrepresentative grand juries and the transfer of powers to democratically elected councils vested considerable power in ordinary people, to whom the new councils were answerable. But, by extension, placing all the functions previously exercised by other bodies under the aegis of the new councils further widened the powers of supervision and the trend towards centralised control achieved by the Local Government Board and jealously guarded by its successors.

The five townships adjoining the Dublin City boundary achieved urban district council status in 1898. Rathmines and Pembroke were by far the wealthiest and most influential of the five and had several own-account public services, including water (Rathmines), drainage (a joint service), electricity and fire brigade (separate undertakings). As far as could be seen at the time, both urban districts had reasonably bright futures.

Clontarf, Drumcondra and New Kilmainham did not own any facilities remotely comparable to those of Rathmines and Pembroke. They had primitive drainage systems, discharging directly to rivers or the seashore. Their water came from the corporation's Vartry supply and none of them had its own electricity service. The rate of development in the three urban districts had also been slower than hoped for, their populations remained disappointingly low and there were therefore serious question marks over their long-term viability.

To increase the municipal income and provide a land bank for sorely needed housing development, Dublin Corporation had long been anxious to enlarge the municipal area. These objectives were partly accomplished when the corporation's 1900 Bill passed into law. On 15 January 1901 the urban districts of Clontarf, Drumcondra and New Kilmainham were incorporated into the city, as was an area adjoining the South Wall and east of Ringsend. Dublin Corporation would have liked to annexe Rathmines and Pembroke but both urban districts commanded sufficient clout to retain their independence. Rathmines was especially hostile to the concept of any association with Dublin Corporation.

Apart from their built-up areas, Clontarf, Drumcondra and New Kilmainham had extensive tracts of land that would eventually be used for the municipal housing Dublin Corporation clearly had to provide. And so the boundary extension, which also encompassed Cabra, Donnycarney and other former county council districts on the north side, more than doubled the municipal area from 3,733 to 7,894 acres.

AN ENLARGED DRAINAGE NETWORK

As soon as the main drainage system became operational the corporation set about extending the sewer network. Districts hitherto unsatisfactorily served and as much as possible of the added areas were connected to the main drainage system. Sewage was also accepted from the neighbouring rural district councils (RDCs) which had come into existence in 1899. In several instances the new RDCs inherited drainage situations akin to those excoriated by Rev James Whitelaw a hundred years previously. Three of the five rural district councils created within County Dublin in 1898 were contiguous to the city boundary. These were North Dublin RDC, South Dublin RDC and Celbridge No. 2 RDC. The various areas served, the drainage solutions adopted and the sequence of events are outlined in later chapters.

None of the rural district councils was overburdened with funding and naturally sought to solve every problem as economically as possible. Not every council was convinced of the benefits of a sewer system, especially in less populated areas, and the use of cesspools therefore continued well into the twentieth century.

A new, expanded edition of the 1:1056 Ordnance Sheets, covering the extended city area, was published in 1907–09. The drainage network was marked up on a set purchased by the city sewers and main drainage department. These sheets were updated regularly and, together with a few more modern maps from the 1928 edition, are still consulted regularly by drainage staff.

REVIEWING SIX MODERNISING DECADES: 1850–1910

Although Dublin still had appalling problems of slums, social deprivation, poverty and ill-health, the first decade of the twentieth century saw it emerge as an infrastructurally modern city. The work needed to achieve this had begun with Parke Neville's drainage programme (1852–1880). Construction of the Vartry water scheme (1861–1868), which also facilitated the establishment of the municipal fire brigade in 1862, enhanced people's lives even further. Commissioning of the main drainage scheme in 1906 completed this first segment of modernisation.

During the last quarter of the nineteenth century the corporation greatly upgraded the paving of the city streets. It also established an efficient municipal electricity service, which rapidly outgrew its first (1892) generating station at Fleet Street. This was augmented and later replaced by the larger and more modern Pigeonhouse plant, opened in 1903. By 1901 the Dublin United Tramways Company's electrified system was the envy of other cities and widely emulated. The city had a company-owned gas supply from the 1820s and telephones since 1882. Ireland's first undersea telegraph cable, connecting Dublin with Holyhead, had been in situ since 1852.

Another invaluable resource was the harbour, which had been developed spectacularly during the second half of the nineteenth century by the Port and Docks Board. This was a modern facility in 1900 and still growing. The Dublin Fire Brigade was about to build three new stations following an 1897 report from the chief officer, and was also seeking a site for a new headquarters. The areas added to the city in 1901 increased the municipal income and made available within the corporation boundary the land on which to build great numbers of sorely needed houses.

THE PORT OF DUBLIN

A most important factor in the development of modern Dublin and of our economy has been the Port of Dublin. A brief outline of its history, every facet of which is intimately tied into that of the city, is worth recording.

In the Norse era, ships sailed up the Liffey as far as Wood Quay. During the eighteenth century the centre of the city began to move eastwards. Construction of the South, then the North and East Walls and Gandon's Custom House, all contributed to this process, as did the reclamation of land in the North and South Lotts areas. The Corporation for Preserving and Improving the Port of Dublin (the Ballast Board), established in 1786, gave way to the Port and Docks Board in 1867. The history of the port is fully described in H. A. Gilligan's *History of the Port of Dublin* (Gill & Macmillan, 1988)

Sewers on the North, South and East Wall roadways were laid by the corporation, while drainage of the former transit sheds on the campshires was carried out by the Port and Docks Board, and several foul discharges to the river were carried out by private companies or individuals. The drainage network within the present port area was connected to the city system and co-operation between the port and city authorities has worked satisfactorily over the years.

EARLY TWENTIETH-CENTURY SOCIAL CONDITIONS

Despite its modern infrastructure and the availability of land for house building, the lower strata of Dublin's class-ridden population continued to suffer extreme deprivation well into the twentieth century. It was against this background that the solvency of the taxpayers and the plight of the poor were differentiated by James Joyce in his description of the waterworks. In *Divided City: Portrait of Dublin in 1913* (O'Brien Educational, 1978) the Curriculum Development Unit of the City of Dublin Vocational Education Committee set out more graphically the appalling conditions in which the city's poor barely existed in that terrible period of industrial and social unrest

So rigorous was the insulation of every class from the one above or below it that the higher people climbed on the social ladder, the more out of touch they became with the cruel realities of life for those less well off then themselves. Until the terrible events of the 1913 industrial strife most of those at the top of the social pyramid were ignorant, either through genuine innocence or because they simply did not want to know, about the injustice and social brutality perpetrated on the general service class, as the people at the bottom of the social order were called.

Section 3 (8) of the provisional order of 9 May 1892 relating to the main drainage scheme described exactly how the establishment of the period viewed working people. It reads as follows:

> The expression 'labouring class' includes mechanics, artisans, labourers and others working for wages, hawkers, costermongers, persons not working for wages but working at some trade or handicraft without employing others except members of their own family, and persons other than domestic servants whose income does not exceed thirty shillings a week, and the families of any of such persons who may reside with them.

Endemic unemployment ensured that there were always more people than jobs, making workers fearful for their continued employment if they did not please their bosses. There was moreover a widespread bias in favour of workers from a rural background, who arrived in considerable numbers and were regarded by many employers as being physically and morally superior to Dubliners. The absence of heavy industry resulted in large numbers of unskilled workers – much of the available work was casual and the wages were often below subsistence level. The vast majority of workers were unorganised, allowing for wholesale exploitation and the many scandals so authentically described in James Plunkett's *Strumpet City*.

The Dodder Walk, near Rathmines.

A meandering path follows the line of the river Dodder down to the sea and is still enjoyed by modern Dubliners, just as here during the 1920s.

IMPROVING THE LOT OF THE WORKERS

In the circumstances just described it was inevitable that working people would make efforts to better their lives as soon as they could organise effectively. Craft unions, which had their origins in old guilds, had existed for a long time when the 1871 Trade Union Act recognised the rights of workers to organise and negotiate improvements in wages and conditions.

Because of the great numbers of individuals involved and the casual nature of so much employment, organising general workers was more difficult than in the case of tradesmen. Efforts at organising unskilled workers were especially difficult throughout the 1880s and 1890s and the recession that lasted from 1884 to 1887, when employment dropped, was a setback. Nevertheless the Dublin Trades Council was established in 1886 and the United Corporation Workmen of Dublin Trade Union was formed in 1890. This became the Irish Municipal Employees' Trade Union in 1918. The story of this Union is told in Sean Redmond's history, published in 1983.

Redmond relates how, leading up to the turn of the twentieth century:

Corporation labourers were badly paid and their working conditions were deplorable. Councillors had a vested interest in keeping pay levels low. Many were businessmen themselves, and the rate paid by the Corporation was not permitted to raise pay generally .... on December 15th 1902 the Lord Mayor read a memorial from the men who had been paid off through lack of work. They prayed the Council 'to relieve their destitution' by starting work.

City engineer Spencer Harty reported 'that destitution amongst these unfortunate people at the present time is appalling' and said that relief road work could be provided for three or four weeks. Meanwhile the men's union sought to raise the social status of the members and to advance their interests in every possible way. Legislative provision for compensating injured workers had been made in 1897 and the Factories and Workshops Act of 1901 was extended to cover work sites. A 1905 Act of Edward VII enabled the Corporation of the City of Dublin 'to grant Pensions or other

Superannuation Allowances to Artisans, Workmen, Labourers and Servants in their service, in certain cases'. The first government social welfare scheme was introduced in 1908 and, in time, all the various measures were improved and extended.

The 1901 Factories and Workshops Act was one of many British statutes extended by the Dáil in 1922 to cover a special need. This measure was eventually replaced by the Factories and Workshops Act of 1955 and the enforcement of safety in workplaces eventually became the responsibility of the Health and Safety Authority.

In 1914 the poverty line was estimated at £2. This was also known as subsistence level, below which no working person could subsist. A widespread practice among employers was to pay their workers slightly above the subsistence level, and this practice continued for many years. Many workers, however, were paid much less. In 1916 junior sailors on the sludge vessel TSS *Shamrock* were paid as little as the equivalent of £1.35 per week, while the maximum of the scale for the First Mate was £2.50.

VERY SERIOUS PROBLEMS

Despite the best efforts of the corporation's officers, public health and housing remained high on the list of scandals. Killer diseases included typhus, measles, whooping cough and tuberculosis (consumption). Infant mortality was shocking, prompting Sir Charles Cameron to state that 'infants perish from want of sufficient food'. Poor and inadequate diet, a lack of sanitation, criminality and prostitution were among the many other elements in the depressing kaleidoscope of woes. Drunkenness was a serious problem, and an especially obnoxious practice was the widespread payment of wages in public houses, leading to a whole catalogue of abuses.

The hitherto barely acknowledged disgrace of slum housing exploded into prominence on the evening of 2 September 1913, when two tenement houses in Church Street collapsed. Seven people were killed, several others were injured and there was widespread fear that further collapses would

occur. A committee of inquiry was set up and reported that 87,305 people – more than one in five of the population – lived in tenement houses in what is now called the inner city. Eighty per cent of tenement families were crowded into only a single room and committee members visited 'one house that we found to be occupied by 98 persons, another by 74 and a third by 73'. In the Church Street tragedy there were 46 members of 11 families in the two houses that collapsed. It also transpired that at that time five aldermen and eleven city councillors were themselves owners of tenements.

Among the more palatable descriptions given by witnesses to the committee were the following:

> … one room measuring about ten feet square, with a small closet off it: contains absolutely no furniture. The family of nine (seven children) sleep on the floor, on which there is not enough straw for a cat, and no covering of any kind whatever.
>
> ……
>
> In some tenement rooms the bedstead is not to be seen in its usual place in the corner, but in its stead there is spread on the floor a mysterious and repellent assortment of rags, which few inquirers have had the hardihood to investigate and which is believed to serve as a bed.

The foregoing could have been written by Rev James Whitelaw in 1798, by Mother Mary Aikenhead in 1833 or by Thomas Willis in 1845. At last, after 1913, some improvements came, although delayed by the Great War and the dramatic events of 1916–1923. These changes, which included the infrastructural advances described in this and later chapters, took a long time to implement.

In 1899 when the city had an assumed population of 260,000 the population density was seventy persons to every acre. Twenty-five years later the 1924 Dublin Civic Survey stated that 'it has been found in cities elsewhere that density is clearly the factor most consistently conducive to high mortality, and a tendency can be traced to a rise in death-rates corresponding to an increased density of population when this figure exceeds 50 per acre,

and a real and serious mortality when the figure reaches 100'.

CLONTARF MAIN DRAINAGE

A main drainage scheme for Clontarf, provided for in the Chatterton proposals of 1895, was begun in 1906. From a point some 148 yards west of the Nanniken Bridge at St Anne's an intercepting sewer nearly two miles long was laid along the coast road to the city side of Clontarf Railway Bridge. The Clontarf scheme was designed by Michael Buckley, an assistant to Spencer Harty in the early years of the twentieth century who was himself destined to become city engineer.

The unavoidably very flat line proposed for Clontarf was to utilise ejectors, which are effectively pumps operated by compressed air and set to operate when a predetermined level of material accumulates in the sumps or tanks. When the scheme was being designed there was no similar installation anywhere in Ireland, so Buckley was despatched to Britain to study existing systems there.

Meticulous design work produced a system that worked satisfactorily for fifty years. The first station on the Clontarf sewer was at Dollymount and had two ejectors, each of 50 gallons capacity, and capable of lifting the sewage 12.9 feet. The second station, at Vernon Avenue, also had two ejectors, but of 350 gallons capacity each. The lift here was 12 feet.

Air for the ejectors was supplied via underground pipes from a compressor in the main ejector station at Clontarf, which adjoins the more modern 1950s building. This station had four ejectors, all of 550 gallons capacity. Two of these lifted the sewage 15 feet to flow to the high level sewer at Fairview, opposite the junction of Annesley Bridge Road with Fairview Strand. This sewer also drained the upper portions of this district and proceeded through a siphon under the River Tolka and on via North Strand Road towards the city centre. Meanwhile back in Clontarf station the second pair of ejectors was used for storm pumping into the sea.

Certain equipment and practices, perfectly acceptable when Clontarf was being drained, would not be tolerated a hundred years later. For example on several Clontarf sewers with necessarily flat gradients, including the interceptor from Nanniken Bridge, the heading (first) manholes were built as flushing chambers. These had water taps just below road level and lever controlled penstocks (gates) on the outgoing sewer. Opening the penstock when the chamber was full cleared the pipeline in a spectacular fashion.

Some of the Clontarf flushing chambers dated back to the laying of local sewers during the regime of the township commissioners. As more exacting standards were adopted, water connections in sewer manholes lost favour on health grounds and the building of flushing chambers was discontinued. With the passage of time they were made completely redundant when lorry-mounted jetting machines capable of unblocking virtually any sewer became available.

Another procedure widely practised, especially in Clontarf, was the unrecorded piping of ditches and land drains that, years later, are exposed from time to time in the course of building operations. In his presidential address to the Institution of Civil Engineers in November 1953 Harry Nicholls praised the Clontarf Drainage Scheme, but revealed that the lengthy compressed air main was troublesome and had to be almost entirely renewed in its last years of service.

DRUMCONDRA-EDEN QUAY DRAINAGE, 1910–1926

In 1910 the drainage of Drumcondra, which hitherto discharged to the Tolka at Ballybough Bridge (as described in Chapter 6), was diverted to the North Strand sewer via Poplar Row and Annesley Place, eliminating a nuisance once described as rivalling that of the Liffey prior to 1906.

The North Strand sewer runs in a siphon beneath the railway and Royal Canal at Newcomen Bridge, continuing along Amiens Street, Store Street, Lower Abbey Street and Marlborough Street. At Eden

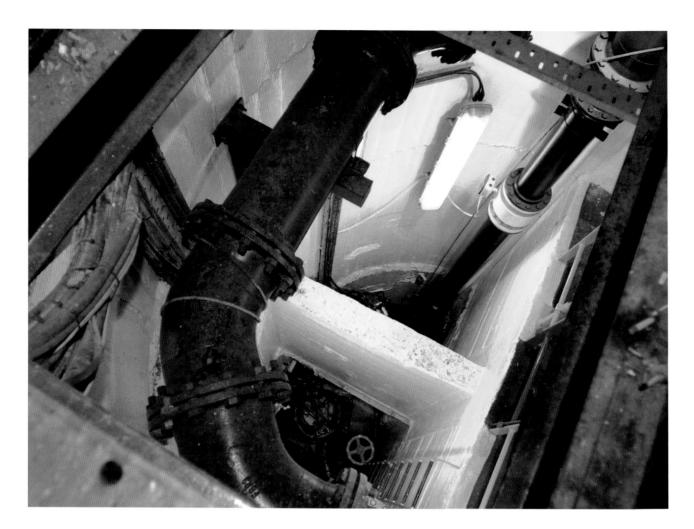

Original pipes at East Road Pumping Station.

East Road pumping station, the oldest in the city council system, is shown on contract drawings signed by Parke Neville and John Cunningham in May 1882.

Quay it joins the North Quays interceptor at the descending leg of the Liffey siphon to Burgh Quay. In the Eden Quay chamber, penstocks (renewed in 1974) can be closed to block the flows to the siphon, facilitating maintenance or generating a flushing flow.

In 1926 the first Tolka Valley sewer was laid from Drumcondra Road (Millmount Avenue), through the grounds of Clonliffe College and Donnelly's Orchard (now the Orchard Road residential district) to Clonliffe Road and Poplar Row. This 27-inch diameter conduit relieved the Richmond Road sewer, taking the drainage from Botanic Avenue, Upper Drumcondra and Glasnevin. It also catered for the new housing development of more than 500 houses at Drishogue (Walsh Road and

Ferguson Road) and opened the Ballymun Road area for building.

The Drumcondra housing development was but one of the many large suburban housing estates built by the corporation as it tackled its massive slum clearance programme from the 1920s onwards. To cater for these estates, water and drainage services had to be in position before building began. While difficulties occasionally arose, the waterworks and sewers departments managed to cater for all these developments in good time, connecting – and often laying down local networks to connect – with the existing water mains and sewers.

Suitably extended, the Vartry water system coped until the 1940s, while the original main drainage system had no increase in capacity until 1958. The drainage arrangements made for various development areas are described in later chapters.

DRAINING NORTH LOTTS

North Lotts is an obsolete general description of the area bounded by Amiens Street, North Strand Road, East Wall Road and North Wall Quay. This very flat, low-lying and formerly tidal district, referred to earlier in this chapter, was largely reclaimed in the eighteenth century. Its real importance began with the completion of the Royal Canal in the second decade of the nineteenth century.

From the 1840s onwards the significance of North Lotts grew apace with the continuous expansion of the railway system and Dublin Port, together with more intensive industrialisation. Considerable house building, mainly for artisans and trades people, also took place in the East Wall, North Strand and Ballybough areas.

Construction of the Royal Canal in the closing years of the eighteenth century divided North Lotts into two future drainage areas, north and south of the waterway. Part of the northern section drained through a culvert and ditch into the sea at the Smoothing Iron, a large flat stone adjacent to what is now the junction of East Wall Road and Tolka Quay.

Another portion of North Lotts drained to a barrel culvert 4 feet in diameter, known as the Cunningham sewer after the contractor who laid it. This work began in 1882 when much of the local drainage system was altered to suit railway construction and new canal works at Spencer Dock, which led to flooding and surcharging (overpowering) of the sewers. Sewage was pumped from East Road through a high-level sewer along Fish Street (now Castleforbes Road), finally discharging into the Liffey. Areas of the North Lotts district lying south of the Royal Canal, which were not connected to the 1906 main drainage scheme, also continued to discharge into the Liffey.

From the late nineteenth century onwards all new development in the North Lotts district had to fit in with the numerous railways in the area. Several unco-ordinated and unconnected developments characterised the district well into the twentieth century. All of this occurred before town planning or even the first building bylaws came into operation in 1904. For more than a century, further progress has been hampered by difficulties in reconciling existing road patterns, housing, industry and the railway yards that dominate so much of the area. Large tracts of land, awkward in shape and difficult to access, remained undeveloped in 2005.

Similar problems affected drainage and the result was that several sewers ended up either in or crossing private property. It should be explained that a sewer is a publicly owned and maintained line that cannot legally be built over and must always be accessible to the drainage authority. A drain however is in private ownership and not as severely circumscribed. Sanitary authorities strive if at all possible to avoid location of sewers in private property. Rationalising the local foul and surface water sewers around East Wall consequently absorbed much time and effort.

While problems caused by a lack of co-ordination have since arisen in other places, they have rarely been as difficult as those around the East Wall area. Perusal of the drainage maps for the Fairview, North Strand and East Wall districts shows how complicated a network can become for reasons of history or a lack of overall planning. In this instance the information became so difficult to interpret on frequently revised Ordnance Sheets that a diagrammatic colour coded drawing, known to drainage personnel as the 'underground map', was produced by C. L. Sweeney in 1958.

East Road pumping station, the oldest on the city council system, is shown on contract drawings signed by Parke Neville and John Cunningham on 17 May 1882. These documents also set out details of the Cunningham Sewer and the outfall at Fish Street (Castleforbes Road). This was the only pumped outfall in Dublin city until 1906, all the others being gravity discharges. The pumping stations at East Road and Fish Street were both

Cole's Lane near
Henry Street, 1913.

*Open-air markets
like this survive in the
vicinity of Henry
Street to this day.*

steam-driven and were reported as being satisfactory
in Parke Neville's reports of the 1880s.

While the 1906 main drainage scheme largely
cleansed the Liffey west of Butt Bridge, untreated
sewage from the North Lotts area continued to
pollute the river further downstream. In 1912 a
detailed drainage programme was drawn up for the
entire Lotts area, the growing requirements of which
had up to then been dealt with on an ad hoc basis.

Two additional pumping stations were planned.
The first, at Castleforbes Road, would send sewage
from that district back to East Road, eliminating a
discharge into the Liffey. East Road station was
intended to pump back to the North Strand sewer
at Newcomen Bridge, leaving the Cunningham and
ditch lines exclusively for storm water. The second
new station, at Mayor Street, was to divert sewage
then emptying into the Liffey at Commons Street
back to Amiens Street and onwards to the Eden
Quay siphon.

TRAUMATIC TIMES 1913–1923

Only part of the North Lotts drainage programme,
that of laying the pipelines, was carried out before
the Great War halted the programme in 1914. Later
the 1916 Rising, the War of Independence and the
Civil War all delayed progress further, each occurrence proving more traumatic than the previous
one. The citizens of Dublin lived through one terror
after another and the lives of those who provided
essential public services, including water and
drainage, were under constant threat, while the
city's economy and social life also suffered severely.

Various shortages made the maintenance of
public services increasingly difficult as the Great
War dragged on. An instance was the availability of
coal, vital to power Ringsend pumping station. The
supply came under the aegis of a coal controller,
who tried to ensure that the fuel was shared fairly
between the various essential services. Shortages
continued after the Armistice and in 1919 some 423
tons of coal intended for the sewers and main

drainage department had to be diverted to the Ringsend power station of the Dublin United Tramways Company. The shipment was later replaced, but the incident serves to mark one of the many problems faced by the public services in those difficult times.

Between 1916 and 1923 anybody working in the various public services was at high risk, especially if working a night shift whenever a curfew operated. People could be summarily arrested and detained by the police, army or the Black and Tans. Most of those detained were simply innocent workers going about their legitimate business. Immediately after the 1916 Rising ('Rebellion' in the language of the time) the corporation adopted a policy of granting leave of absence with pay to arrested

men for the period of their detention without trial and conviction.

On 16 May 1916 the authorities were reported to have made an admission: 'It is possible that persons may have been inadvertently arrested who had no connection whatever with the rebellion or with the movement which fomented it'. Later, during the War of Independence, arrests became more frequent. Among the municipal employees whose detentions were reported to the corporation during the last quarter of 1921 were Michael McClure, arrested on 2 October, Richard Ward (messenger) on 3 December, and Assistant Foreman Mason and Peter Fearon of the sewers and main drainage department on 6 December.

In a special report George Harty, the engineer in charge of the sewers and main drainage department, stated that on 8 March 1921 he was taken under duress from his residence to his office by crown forces in an armoured car. He was compelled to disclose information regarding certain of the Ordnance Sheets and plans showing the River Poddle and sewer arrangements in the vicinity of Dublin Castle. His office was thoroughly searched and certain of the plans and maps taken, a receipt for which was given. On the following day he was forced to accompany a military officer through portion of the Poddle. Harty also revealed that

Auxiliaries or Black and Tans visited Clontarf pumping station on the night of 16 March, when they prized open map drawers and four of the staff lockers and examined the contents.

Another highly unwelcome development that coincided with the North Lotts programme was the unprecedented escalation of costs. In the early part of the twentieth century costs fell, 1914 becoming the benchmark year with a base of 100 for a cost of living index. Following the outbreak of the Great War the figure soared, reaching 123 in 1915 and a peak of 249 in 1920.

The index fell back in subsequent years, dropping to 174 in 1929, but this had a detrimental effect on industrial relations when employers began to claw back from workers the temporary pay increases awarded in the years 1914–1918. A fitful equilibrium was achieved during the 1930s, but any remaining certainties that had not been swept away between 1914 and 1924 were gradually eroded and destined for almost total oblivion from 1939 onwards as inflation accelerated.

RESUMING MAJOR WORKS: INFLATION AND COSTS

When work on the North Lotts drainage programme eventually resumed under a new political regime in 1927, modifications were made to the original plans. Electrically driven centrifugal pumps were substituted for the ejector equipment previously proposed at East Road and the station was arranged to pump via a rising main that went to Ringsend through the then new Liffey tunnel, described below.

Pumping direct from East Road to Ringsend was an early initiative to ease pressure on the North Strand Road sewer and the city centre system. The East Road, Castleforbes Road and Mayor Street installations all consisted of automatically controlled Oerlikon electric motors driving Mather and Platt centrifugal pumps. Planned during the regime of John G. O'Sullivan, who was city engineer from 1910 to 1913, the North Lotts scheme was completed during the stewardship of his successor Michael Buckley, who held office until 1927.

As noted earlier, pollution of the Liffey east of Butt Bridge, although lessened by the 1906 main drainage scheme, remained a problem until the North Lotts programme was completed. But even then, numerous outfalls to the river, many from individual industrial and business premises, continued to operate and took several years to eliminate.

A legacy of the improvement works carried out on both sides of the river in this area is a number of sewers that originally flowed into the Liffey but now execute a U turn just short of the quays and go back to the nearest line into which they could most easily discharge. There were eight such south side reversals on City Quay and Sir John Rogerson's Quay, as against four along the North Wall.

The Breviate or quarterly reports compiled by the city engineer sometimes went beyond strictly technical matters, affording glimpses of wider contemporary attitudes and events. The traditional and still prevalent attitude of severity towards petty criminals who damaged or stole from public facilities was well illustrated in the Breviate presented on 12 February 1930. The police had arrested a man who had robbed the slot lock in a public convenience. He was sentenced to two months with hard labour and fined five shillings for being in illegal possession of a false key.

THE LIFFEY TUNNEL

For ninety-nine years after its opening in 1879 Butt Bridge was the most easterly Liffey crossing, except by ferry. To preserve the navigability of the river, a tunnel near the mouth of the Liffey was long seen as a desirable alternative to a bridge and there was a proposal for a railway tunnel as early as 1864. In 1921, two months before the signing of the Treaty, a plan for a Liffey tunnel was sent to the Ministry for Transport in London for approval. While this made no further progress for political reasons, a smaller tunnel was built later. The genesis, design

and construction of this tunnel was described to the Institute of Engineers on 6 May 1929 by Harry Nicholls, who was resident engineer on the project and later became engineer in charge of the sewers and main drainage department.

The corporation had first considered the tunnel project in 1918 in connection with the supply of electric power from the Pigeonhouse generating station to industries in the North Wall area. Cables were laid on the bed of the Liffey as an interim measure but by 1923 the provision of a tunnel had become an urgent necessity. There was also the problem of extending and improving the water supply to serve the expanding north-eastern suburbs and further planned development. A tunnel crossing of the Liffey offered considerable engineering and economic advantages for the projects outlined.

In 1925, following widespread consultations, the city commissioners (who had replaced the elected councillors in the previous year) concluded that the building of a tunnel to accommodate water mains and electric cables could no longer be deferred. A contract was accordingly offered to Sir Robert McAlpine & Sons (Ireland) Ltd in 1926 and work began on 18 August of that year.

Originally conceived as a river crossing for pedestrians the Liffey tunnel was finished solely as a utilities conduit. It initially accommodated electricity cables from the Pigeonhouse generating station and a water main 24 inches in diameter, with both services carried through the tunnel on benching. The 15-inch diameter rising main (pressure sewer) from East Road to Ringsend also traversed the tunnel. Finished in March 1928, the Liffey tunnel is 831 feet long and 7 feet in diameter. The South Shaft, 107 feet deep, is at Thorncastle Street, with its northern counterpart, 111 feet and 5 inches in depth, located at the former Harbourmaster's Office at North Wall.

A physician, Dr F. J. O'Donnell, was a member of the management team that supervised the construction of the tunnel. This was because a compressed air working environment was used, with air locks at either end of the tunnel. The men

Terenure Road, showing Rathfarnham Rectory.

View of Terenure, early twentieth century. *South Dublin Rural District Council was the sanitary authority for Terenure, a Victorian suburb of Dublin which was linked to the city centre by the tramway system.*

employed on the contract were continuously monitored. Dr O'Donnell was an important speaker at Harry Nicholls's presentation to the Engineers' Institute. He described how twenty-five of the seventy men passed for work in the tunnel suffered from the 'bends'. This is the condition suffered by divers and others who return too quickly from a compressed air environment to a normal atmosphere. Divers who surface too quickly without going through a decompression chamber can suffer serious consequences. In the case of the Liffey tunnel Dr O'Donnell noted that men working from the south shaft were more susceptible to the condition than their colleagues operating from the north end.

CABRA, ASHTOWN AND CHAPELIZOD

The drainage of Cabra was tackled in 1911 with sewers along both the Old and New Cabra Roads. The New Cabra Road sewer flowed via Charleville Road to the existing North Circular Road line. Later extensions brought in Navan Road and the Ashtown district, part of which went to the main

drainage system at Parkgate Street.

Drainage plans for Chapelizod were held up owing to the events of the 1913–1924 period, but Chapelizod North was connected to the city system in 1928, followed by Chapelizod South in 1937. A feature of these schemes was the building of two pumping stations on the north bank of the Liffey. The first is near the Chapelizod gate of the Phoenix Park, the second immediately west of Sarah's Bridge (Islandbridge). From this station the sewer goes under the river to Hospital Lane where it connects to the head of the South Quays interceptor.

DRAINING KILMAINHAM, OLD AND NEW

Old Kilmainham, the portion of this district inside the pre-1901 city boundary and east of South Circular Road, was drained in stages between 1862 and 1877. Sewers serving Brookfield Road, South Circular Road and Old Kilmainham discharged to the Camac at Mount Brown. As part of the 1906 scheme a sewer 3 feet (36 inches) in diameter was laid beside the Camac to St John's Road and connected to the South Quays interceptor in front of Kingsbridge (Heuston) Station. This sewer takes in other lines that previously discharged into the Camac at Bow Bridge.

DRAINAGE OF CRUMLIN, TERENURE, RATHFARNHAM AND DUNDRUM

The drainage of the Crumlin area was tackled in 1925–1926 with two sewers in Dark Lane (now Sundrive Road) and Crumlin Road. These join at Herberton Lane (Herberton Road) and tunnel under both branches of the Grand Canal (one of which is now closed) before turning northeast towards the grounds of St James's Hospital. A tunnel under the hospital complex takes the line to Mount Brown where it joins existing sewers. Although subsequently built over along much of its length this sewer, like most of those described in this volume, still operates. The village of Crumlin was drained in 1929 by a sewer laid to the Inchicore system at Blackhorse Bridge.

South Dublin RDC was the sanitary authority for Terenure, part of Rathfarnham, Whitechurch, Tallaght, Clondalkin and Palmerstown, while Rathdown No. 1 RDC was responsible for Rathfarnham (part), Whitechurch and Tallaght.

The Terenure sewer, a metal pipe for some of its length and completed in 1911 from Kimmage Road to Dean Street, has some manhole shafts that began 12 inches below the road surface. This arrangement, common on sewers laid more than twenty years previously, precluded unauthorised access or connections.

The outlying district of Dundrum (Rathdown RDC) was taken into the main drainage system through an interceptor sewer laid along the south and east banks of the Dodder in 1911 and connecting with the Ringsend tunnel (known as the 'eight-foot') at Fitzwilliam Quay. Rathfarnham was linked to the Dundrum sewer in 1913.

Prior to the great housing schemes carried out around Crumlin in the 1930s the village was separated from the built-up area of Dublin by intervening undeveloped land. Much of this land would be developed as residential estates around Crumlin and other previously separate villages over the next fifty years. An exception however were the large tracts of institutional land, particularly those owned by religious orders, which did not fall to developers until the 1970s or later. Examples from each side of the city are the Christian Brothers' land at Artane and that of the Carmelite monastery at Ranelagh.

9 *Working in a Changed Political Landscape 1930–1940*

3 BOUNDARY EXTENSIONS: 1930, 1941 AND 1942

The Local Government (Dublin) Act of 1930 brought about momentous changes, including a massive city boundary extension. Effective from 30 September 1930 the urban districts of Rathmines and Pembroke were incorporated into the city. Also taken in were the Bull Island, Raheny, Beaumont, Cabra and Phoenix Park on the north side, Chapelizod to the west and Rathfarnham on the south side. Around the same time the rate of suburban development, almost at a standstill between 1914 and 1923, picked up.

At the time of the 1930 boundary extension Dun Laoghaire Borough Corporation also came into being. Kingstown Urban District Council, which had replaced the town commissioners in 1898, changed its name to Dun Laoghaire in 1920. To the north of Dun Laoghaire was Blackrock UDC and to the south the UDCs of Dalkey and Killiney & Ballybrack, all established in 1898. These four authorities were now amalgamated to form Dun Laoghaire Borough. The Rural District Councils in the Dublin area were merged with Dublin County Council in 1930.

The first of two further boundary extensions took place in 1941 when part of Crumlin was transferred from the county council area to that of the corporation. Howth, the history of whose water and drainage services are described later in this chapter, came into the city area in 1942, together with Sutton. However, some of the north side villages for which the corporation provided drainage before World War Two – for example Finglas, Santry and Coolock – remained in the county council area until 1953.

MANAGEMENT AND ADMINISTRATION

Following the establishment of the Irish Free State, civil administration passed to new or reorganised government departments. The functions of the erstwhile Local Government Board now rested with the Department of Local Government and Public Health, ancestor of the Department of the Environment, Heritage and Local Government. Officials in both central and local government, who had performed their tasks conscientiously under the old regime, continued to serve the new state loyally and efficiently for many years. The youngest were aged about twenty when the state was established and they set the standards by which it existed and was

Gerald J. Sherlock, first Dublin City Manager.

The concept of the city manager was introduced from America to Dublin in 1930. This portrait, from Dublin City Gallery, the Hugh Lane, is by Sarah Cecelia Harrison.

governed for more than half a century. Most of them had retired by the late 1960s.

In the 1920s, existing administrative structures were adapted to the needs of the time and new ones were created where necessary, but in some instances prevailing circumstances called for more drastic measures. Local government in the Dublin area was in obvious need of major change. The composition and behaviour of the city council were regarded as unsatisfactory by the government; it therefore

abolished the corporation in 1924. The functions of the councillors were transferred to three stipendiary commissioners until 1930 when a new milieu was ushered in.

The 1930 boundary changes coincided with the introduction to Dublin of the local authority management system that is now universal. This American concept had been successfully brought to Ireland the previous year in Cork. The first Dublin city manager was Gerald J. Sherlock (1876–1942) who had begun his distinguished career as a junior clerk in the city engineer's department in April 1894. He was progressively promoted to greater responsibilities, becoming waterworks superintendent in January 1910 and town clerk in 1927. This most senior statutory officer's authority included administrative, staff and legal functions. It was amalgamated with the post of city manager in 1930.

The incorporation of Rathmines and Pembroke into the city expanded the remit of both the waterworks and the sewers and the main drainage department considerably. It also presented an opportunity for Michael Moynihan, city engineer from 1927 to 1936, to reorganise the several departments under his control. Some schemes planned during Moynihan's tenure of office were carried out under the aegis of his successor Norman Chance, who held the office from 1937 to 1950. There was also a new city manager in 1937 when after a short interregnum P. J. Hernon was appointed to the post which he held until 1955. During the early 1950s the city manager also became responsible for Dublin County and Dun Laoghaire, assistant managers being appointed to look after particular areas and functions.

THE DIFFICULT 1930s

All business and public works in the 1930s took place within the brittle financial environment of a world recession, our own 'economic war' and the worsening threat of a fresh European conflict. Nevertheless much was accomplished in that period of extreme austerity and a culture antipathetic to cities in general and the former seat of foreign power in particular. What was achieved reflects great credit on those who worked hard to improve Dublin and its infrastructure long before the capital was accorded its rightful place in the national consciousness.

Following the boundary extension, the Rathmines waterworks at Ballyboden was modernised. Its maximum output was increased to 18,000m³/day (4 million gallons) by the provision of a second raw water main, and a physico-chemical treatment process replaced the slow sand filters. These changes improved the appearance and quality of the finished water, to which chlorine was now added to ensure disinfection. Rapid gravity filters replaced the slow sand type and in 1931–1932 additional slow sand filter beds (Nos 11–14) were built at Roundwood to increase output.

The large estates of both public and private housing built in the years leading up to World War Two were all served by the 1906 main drainage scheme. Among the large corporation estates developed between 1925 and 1940 were Marino, Drumcondra (the Walsh Road area), Ellenfield, Larkhill, Donnycarney, Cabra East, Kimmage, Crumlin and Drimnagh.

An estate at Killester that came into the city following the 1930 boundary extension well illustrates how a previously relaxed drainage regime could create problems in later times. This was the Soldiers' and Sailors' Land Trust development comprising Demesne, Middle Third and Abbeyfield. Largely built in the first half of the 1920s, the sewers in this estate were laid at the backs of the houses. This led to hardship when householders sought permission to construct domestic extensions.

A pipe draining a single property is defined in law as 'a single private drain'. It is part of the property and the owner is liable for its maintenance. Where a pipe serves more than one property it is known as a 'combined drain' and those properties served by it are jointly liable for its maintenance. The number of properties on a combined drain is normally about six, at which stage the drain is connected to a 'sewer'. There is no set limit to the number of houses on a combined drain however and should a developer choose not to have the drainage system of an estate taken in charge by the local authority the entire system could be regarded as a combined drain. A 'sewer' is defined in the Public Health Act as being vested in the sanitary authority and there is therefore no such thing as a 'private sewer'.

The Malahide Road sewer drained the older parts of the Donnycarney housing estate from its beginnings in the early 1930s. A new main (the Clonturk Valley Sewer) was laid in 1937 to cater for Whitehall and allow for the further development of Donnycarney. This sewer begins to the west of Swords Road at Larkhill and follows the course of the Wad River to Donnycarney (Scurloges) Bridge where it joins an existing line on Malahide Road. Although the Wad River was culverted long ago, the parapets of the bridge on Malahide Road remain, showing a rebuilding date of 1896 below the Donnycarney title. Artane and Coolock were also drained in 1938 by an extension of the Malahide Road sewer northwards from Donnycarney.

The Clonturk Valley, Artane and Coolock sewers facilitated considerable house building along and adjacent to Malahide Road. This resulted in progressively more serious overloading of the drainage network throughout the 1940s and 1950s and would not be ameliorated until the North Dublin system (Chapter 11) came into operation in the late 1950s. In 1937 Raheny was connected to the existing Howth Road sewer near Ballyhoy Bridge, allowing for building in that area.

Ballyhoy is one of several townlands whose names the corporation endeavoured to preserve in a built-up environment. In this case the townland of Ballyhoy gave its name to the bridge over the culverted Nanniken River where it flows under the Howth Road, about fifty metres on the Killester side of its junction with All Saints Road. East of Ballyhoy Bridge the Nanniken continues as an open stream and amenity through St Anne's Park before discharging into the sea at Dollymount.

THE SECOND WORLD WAR YEARS

Plans to extend and improve the drainage system had to be severely curtailed during the years 1939–1945 when World War Two progressively increased the isolation of the state. Finance was severely limited and materials were almost impossible to source. In that miserable era, quaintly described in official circles as 'The Emergency', most public services in the state were maintained by the ingenuity, dedication and determination of those who managed and worked in them. Old and often obsolete material such as disused piping was routinely recovered and re-used, 'make do and mend' being a widely used exhortation of the period.

Stretching to the limit the meagre resources available during the war the corporation carried out infrastructure schemes that would expedite badly needed new housing developments as soon as circumstances improved. An example was the provision of drainage for the future suburb of Ballyfermot. Here a trunk sewer to join the Liffey Valley line was planned in 1941 and laid shortly afterwards. The road network in the eastern end of Ballyfermot was constructed long before houses were built. In this instance services laid down a decade earlier enabled development to continue until additional drainage capacity became necessary in the mid-1950s.

Finglas was drained in 1941 but the contours between the village and existing sewers presented problems. From the southern end of Main Street the sewer struck off in a south-easterly direction through the present-day Glenhill Estate, which in 1941 was still open country. It then touched the sites of the future Griffith and Tolka Estates to reach Old Finglas Road which it followed to connect with the former Drumcondra Township sewer at Glasnevin.

DEVELOPMENT OUTSIDE THE CITY: DRAINAGE AGREEMENTS

For nearly a hundred years the corporation accepted effluent from adjoining local authorities for treatment and discharge at Ringsend, the quantities and areas served being covered by a series of drainage agreements. The Dublin Board of Public Health, which was responsible for draining various places adjacent to the northern boundary of the city, provides an example: several drainage districts under its control were connected to corporation sewers between 1937 and 1953, and the first formal drainage agreement was drawn up in 1943.

Old Howth Village · Howth

View of Old Howth Village.
The fishing port of Howth became an increasingly attractive residential area during the second half of the nineteenth century.

In the years following World War Two effluent from increasingly large and more numerous developments outside the municipal boundary had to be taken into the city sewer system. Mount Merrion, Lucan, Palmerstown, Blanchardstown, Castleknock and Portmarnock were catered for by 1950. These were very extensive areas and the new sewers caused overloading of the existing network in several instances. A series of drainage agreements was concluded with Dublin County Council, setting out more precisely the areas served and the quantities that would be accepted.

HOWTH WATER

Only nine miles from the General Post Office and served by rail as early as 1846, Howth became an increasingly attractive residential area during the second half of the nineteenth century – for anybody who could afford to live there. From 1900 onwards, trams and trains competed for passengers, both locally and between the peninsula and Dublin. Season tickets at extraordinarily favourable rates were offered to anybody building or buying a house in the area. This boosted the growth of residential development and fuelled demands to establish an urban district council, which did not happen for several years. Meanwhile the increasing population and growing allure of Howth as a tourist destination made the provision of modern water and drainage systems an urgent necessity.

Prior to the establishment of the new local authorities set up by the 1898 Local Government Act the sanitary authority for Howth was the North Dublin Union. On 24 January 1867 the civil engineer Arthur Cousins submitted a comprehensive report to the Union on water and drainage in Howth. No effective action followed. An original copy of the Cousins report, together with much subsequent material, is preserved in the archives of the Howth Estate. There was another, highly critical report by a Dr Stafford in 1894 but this too was largely ignored. Only work on an ad hoc basis seems to have been undertaken until the early years of the twentieth century, when action could no longer be delayed. This took place within the remit of the North Dublin Rural District Council,

Dublin City Council Survey Staff, 1930s.

Back row, left to right: J.F. Gogarty, J. Brennan, C.J. Kavanagh, M.J. Greene, L. Kavanagh, G.H. Clifton, J. Griffin. Front row, left to right: R.M. Young, E.J. Bourke, N.A. Chance (City Engineer), D.K. Ryan, J.H. Reade.

established under the provisions of the 1898 Local Government Act.

A small pond or reservoir had been created by a Mr Macdougall at Balkill (Knocknabohill) to supply his own house and those of his tenants. Under powers conferred by the Howth Waterworks Order 1904 the rural district council acquired some six acres at this location and constructed a reservoir that incorporated Macdougall's pond. At the public inquiry into the Howth water scheme held in March 1904 by P. C. Cowan, chief engineering inspector of the Local Government Board, detailed calculations were provided by Richard Hassard. He was the very experienced engineer who had been closely involved

in similar work for both the Vartry and Bohernabreena waterworks schemes.

Hassard put the catchment area for water at 255 acres and calculated the expected yield at more than 104,000 gallons per day. Assuming a population of 1,000 people in Howth and a daily usage of 20 gallons per head, the design provided for 300 days' storage. The reservoir was located on the Howth Estate, on one of the present golf courses. Under the arrangements made, the Castle and its farm were entitled to 7,000 gallons of water every day, free of charge.

Following its establishment as an urban district in 1917 Howth negotiated a mains water supply from the corporation. A 12-inch main was laid to serve the peninsula in 1923 and this was metered at Killester. When a water supply was laid on to serve the new Soldiers' and Sailors' Land Trust Estate at Demesne, Middle Third and Abbeyfield (Killester) in the 1920s, this connection was found to lie beyond the Howth meter. The meter was moved outwards in 1927, and a financial adjustment was also made with the Howth UDC.

A new 24-inch water main was laid from Stillorgan to the city and continued through the new Liffey tunnel in 1927, easing considerably the water pressure and volume problems in the north east of the city. The problems this main was intended to eliminate were prominently proclaimed by the presence of a water tower at Abbeyfield in Killester. This structure has long since disappeared, as have some others in areas that had problems of supply and pressure in earlier times.

DRAINING HOWTH

Virtually none of the drainage work recommended by Arthur Cousins in 1876 had been carried out by the turn of the twentieth century when the population of Howth was growing rapidly. The only sewers or public drains in the town were those originally laid down to convey surface water, and some foul matter was diverted into these. Already serious health hazards were compounded at discharge points, particularly around the harbour. Cesspools were widely used but the sandy soil made them especially obnoxious and several houses drained directly on to the beaches. As with the water supply, urgent action was imperative.

In a notice published on 17 August 1904 the North Dublin Rural District Council invited engineers to take part in a competition that would identify the best means of finally solving the peninsula's escalating drainage problem. The various proposals were considered and interested parties and objectors were examined at a public inquiry held on 9-10 February 1905. The inspector was the same P. C. Cowan who had conducted the

Howth Water Inquiry the previous year and the venue was again the boardroom of the North Dublin Union Workhouse at North Brunswick Street.

One of the witnesses who appeared before the inquiry was the sanitary sub-officer for Howth, Ms Margaret Rickard. Female officials were virtually unknown in public bodies in 1905 but by the time of the inquiry Ms Rickard had been nearly four years in her post and was therefore quite experienced. Among the various diseases prevalent at the time, diphtheria was a major concern for Margaret Rickard. Her answers under cross-examination were clear and concise and when the inspector thanked her at the conclusion of her evidence, he expressed his satisfaction at seeing her in the position she occupied. Sir Charles Cameron, the city medical officer, was an early advocate of appointing women in the health service, believing that they had a far clearer appreciation of hygiene and its importance than most men of that era.

The winner of the Howth drainage competition was P. H. McCarthy, founder of an engineering consultancy that still bears his name. McCarthy, whose winner's prize was twenty guineas (£21), was closely examined at the inquiry. He proposed to deal with the drainage of the peninsula in three parts, the most important of which was the section serving the town and the area up to the top of what is now Thormanby Road. This would be on a partially separate system, but excluded road drainage which would allow excessive grit to enter the system. The main section of the work was undertaken in 1909 when an interceptor sewer 12 inches in diameter was laid westwards from Balscadden Road along Harbour Road. To compensate for its very flat gradient it had two large flushing tanks, one near its head and the other about half way along its length. A second sewer laid north and eastwards from Corr Bridge also formed part of the Howth main drainage system.

The flushing tanks were each of 1,000 gallons capacity. The one nearest the head of the sewer was arranged to flush every three hours. Fed from springs, the intermediate tank was set to have two flushes per day. Opposite the gates of Howth Castle the sewer turned across the main road into a sewage works located between the present Techrete factory and the North Dublin Drainage Screen House.

Howth sewage works consisted of a series of grit chambers, septic tanks and storage chambers. These discharged via an 18-inch diameter pipe to an outfall at the end of the West Pier which operated only at ebb tide. The Howth 12-inch sewer was connected to the North Dublin system (fully described in Chapter 12) as soon as this became operational, but most of the old tanks still exist under the western end of the Techrete site.

O'Connor & Martin were the contractors for the Howth Drainage Scheme and works, the total cost of which was £7,155 (€9,086). The system was intended to cater for an ultimate population of 3,600 people and was more than adequate for the needs of its time. P. H. McCarthy read a paper to the Institute of Engineers on 4 March 1918 in which he gave details of the Howth system.

Sutton had a more primitive drainage system with two sea outfalls which, like the Howth installation, continued to function as originally designed for more than fifty years. Apart from individual houses, mostly constituting ribbon development, virtually no large-scale building took place on the Howth peninsula before the 1950s, by which time work on the North Dublin Drainage Scheme (Chapter 12) was well under way.

Howth achieved urban district status in 1917 and was taken into the city area on 24 August 1942. With the city boundary changes that accompanied the first stage of the Dublin local government re-organisation in 1986, Howth reverted to being part of the Dublin County Council area. Finally, when the new local authorities were created in 1994, the peninsula came under the control of Fingal County Council.

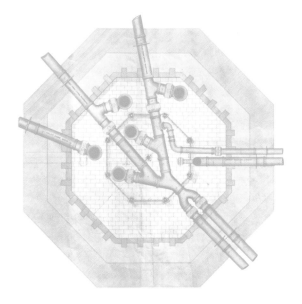

THE LIFFEY'S POTENTIAL

Arguably Dublin's greatest natural asset, the River Liffey rises in the Sally Gap near Kippure and Tonduff in the Wicklow mountains. It flows in a great loop for more than seventy miles before entering Dublin Bay and is tidal from Islandbridge eastwards. This reach of the Liffey suffered increasingly from pollution throughout the nineteenth century and, despite the improvements brought about by the 1906 main drainage scheme, the river continued as a receptacle for much foul matter. The condition of the Liffey east of Butt Bridge remained extremely poor until the North Lotts drainage programme (Chapter 8) became operational in the 1920s. Even after that the river was still afflicted by pollution – principally from the Camac – until the closing years of the twentieth century.

The sudden increase in river depth downstream of Butt Bridge, due to dredging, formed a trap where a large depth of organic matter accumulated. During the warmer months, anaerobic activity in this sludge mass was accompanied by the evolution of large quantities of sulphide gases to the extent that the river seemed to boil. The rising bubbles brought masses of sludge to the surface and envi-ronmental conditions along the quays by the Custom House were sickening. Despite the stench that was almost literally on its doorstep, the Department of Local Government, then responsible for water pollution, was in no apparent hurry to solve the problem!

Several proposals, most notably the Coyford and Cloghleagh Schemes, had been put forward in the nineteenth century to use the Liffey as a source of water, but none of these came to fruition at that time. Before the corporation chose steam power to generate electricity in the early 1890s the possibilities of a hydro-electric station at Islandbridge were examined and rejected. Again in 1920 the corpora-tion looked at the Liffey as a possible source of power rather than as one of water supply.

In the years immediately after Independence there was considerable friction between respective proponents of the Shannon or the Liffey as the location for the great hydro-electric station that would energise a countrywide electricity network. The option chosen was Ardnacrusha, where work began in 1925 and was taken over in 1927 by the newly established Electricity Supply Board (ESB).

The ESB was granted a statutory monopoly and proceeded to acquire existing electricity undertakings

Valve room at Roundwood (right) with scenic view of reservoir (below). *Roundwood remained the principal reservoir for Dublin but the city's expanding population meant that additional supplies of fresh water had to be found.*

throughout the state, including that of Dublin Corporation. There was some resistance to the compulsory acquisition of local electricity undertakings by the ESB, resulting for example in relations between it and the corporation becoming somewhat strained. And while it saw the Liffey as a future source of hydro-electricity the ESB preferred to leave this resource undeveloped until existing generating capacity was nearing full utilisation.

The year 1935 was a critical one for the Vartry system when for the first time demand exceeded supply. Because of this and the constantly growing use of water the corporation proceeded with a scheme to produce an extra one million gallons per day from the Bohernabreena catchment. This consisted of laying a pipe from Bohernabreena to the Stillorgan reservoirs at a cost of £25,000. This extra quantity from a new source enabled the increased requirements of the former townships

and the extra-municipal districts to be met.

The corporation then proceeded with a temporary pumping scheme from the Grand Canal which produced an average of 300,000 gallons per day. This enabled it to relieve the critical supply situation in the south-western part of County Dublin adjoining the city boundary and in the housing development area of Drimnagh.

THE POLLAPHUCA SCHEME

During the same period Dublin Corporation was investigating possible sources of additional water to serve the expanding city. Great housing estates were planned to replace the festering slum tenements in the inner city and private building was also taking off after being in the doldrums for nearly twenty years. Michael Moynihan, city engineer, in a paper read to the Institution of Engineers in 1933, first

mooted the proposal for a major new waterworks on the Liffey at Pollaphuca. Having overcome the bureaucratic obstacles that such projects must endure, the corporation and the ESB reached an agreement on the development of the Liffey at Pollaphuca (also spelt Poulaphouca). The name Pollaphuca derives from Irish: literally the hole or lair of the puca, a mythical horse-like and malevolent creature that in ancient times was believed to inhabit the gorge through which the Liffey flows at this place.

The Liffey Reservoir Act 1936 empowered the Electricity Supply Board to carry out the works required to harness the river for power generation and water supply. It provided for a financial contribution by Dublin Corporation in return for which it would have the right to abstract up to 20 million gallons daily (90,000 m³/day) at all times, equivalent to about 10% of the Liffey's average annual flow.

The ESB was limited in the level to which the water could be drawn down to protect the supply of water to the corporation.

When the corporation's requirements began to approach the 20 million limit a revised agreement was negotiated with the ESB whereby the corporation could draw greater quantities, compensating the ESB on an ongoing basis for the loss of generation potential. While the ultimate yield of the reservoir would be of the order of 200 million gallons daily, environmental considerations limit the abstraction to about 70 million gallons daily. The current (2005) development of the waterworks is based on this rate of abstraction. Precise records of how much water was processed every day from the beginning of Ballymore Eustace Works are preserved there.

The harnessing of the river was accomplished by the erection of a mass concrete dam at Pollaphuca,

Scenic view of Pollaphuca Reservoir. *Pollaphuca is one of the largest lakes in the Irish Republic and has the largest surface area of any impounding reservoir in the European Isles.*

on which work began in 1938. This is described in
the commemorative book edited by Liam Kenny, *50
Years on the Liffey* (ESB, 1994), as of gravity design –
relying on its own weight to resist the water forces
pressing on it. The King's River, a major tributary of
the Liffey, flows directly into the reservoir. The
reservoir created at Pollaphuca contained 37 billion
gallons of water with a top level of 615 feet above
Poolbeg Ordnance Datum. It is some 5,000 acres
(2,023 hectares) in extent, has an average depth of
23 feet (seven metres), maximum 96 feet (29 metres).
It is one of the largest lakes in the Irish Republic
and has the largest surface area of any impounding
reservoir in these islands. Kielder Water (Glasgow)
has more storage volume, at 44 billion gallons, but
with nearly double the average depth has only half
the surface area.

Pollaphuca ESB Works has a capacity of 30
megawatts from two 15 Mw generators, the first
installed in 1944, the second in 1947. It is the
first of the three Liffey stations, the mile-long
stretch of water downstream of Pollaphuca driving
the 4 Megawatt turbo-alternator at Golden Falls.
The third Liffey installation is at Leixlip, 35 miles
downstream of Golden Falls. Leixlip, which is
another major source of water, is described later
in this chapter.

SOCIAL AND ENVIRONMENTAL

A price beyond monetary cost has to be paid
for most human progress and the Pollaphuca
scheme is an outstanding example. In Chapter 6
of their *History of the ESB* (Gill and Macmillan,
1985) Maurice Manning and Moore McDowell
state this reality:

> A sad aspect of the Liffey scheme, and one not often
> remembered, is that it involved drowning a valley in
> the foothills of the Dublin Mountains, where the
> beautiful Pollaphuca reservoir now provides a recre-
> ation area to the west of the city. A small community
> had to be uprooted and a little of the pattern of Irish
> rural life was lost, but not totally, for in the early
> summer of 1939 an effort was made to preserve for

posterity some record of the lifestyle of the area. The
initiative was taken by Professor Eoin MacNeill, who
quickly got the support of Mr de Valera. With their
backing, a group of people, mainly academics,
attempted to put on paper a description of the folk
culture, farming methods and landholdings of the
valley. One of the records of this collection is now
preserved in the Irish Folklore Collection in University
College, Dublin.

Tom Kinirons and Tony Mahon of Ballymore
Eustace waterworks succinctly summarised the
social, financial and environmental aspects of the
Pollaphuca scheme. They pointed out that people
who bought or inherited land in the area during the
1920s saw it fall in value in the following depressed
decade. Land for the hydro-electric scheme was
acquired compulsorily at the lower prices prevailing
in the 1930s, often leaving expensive mortgages
taken out ten years earlier to be paid off. There were
also several instances of half a holding being
acquired, leaving the remainder uneconomic.

Some people were understandably very reluctant
to leave their homes when the time came to flood
the valley and there is at least one account of a
stubborn resident who had to be rescued by boat
just as the water was rising in his kitchen. More
distress was caused by the inundation of Killough
Bog, a commonage from which local people had
taken turf over the years. There was also the deeply
sensitive matter of Burgage cemetery, from which
the bodies were reverently removed and re-interred
at a higher location above the flood line.

During the building of the Pollaphuca scheme
about 250 construction workers were employed on
the project. In addition the ESB's operations
required 300 men. This level of employment contributed greatly to the economy of a depressed area
in difficult times and afterwards the whole
Pollaphuca complex that supplied both water and
electricity created welcome and permanent skilled
employment in the area.

So attractive was the gorge at Pollaphuca that in
1895 the steam tramway connecting Terenure with
Blessington was extended to a point just short of

POULAPHUCA FALL. Co. WICKLOW. 2531. W. L.

Bridge over the falls at Pollaphuca.

The name Pollaphuca comes from Irish and means 'the lair of the puca', a mythical horse-like creature that was believed to live in this part of the Liffey valley.

**Ballymore Eustace
Treatment Plant.**

*Constructed in the late
1930s to treat water
from Pollaphuca,
the plant at Ballymore
Eustace in county
Kildare increased
Dublin's water-supply
by one-quarter.*

Alexander Nimmo's splendid Gothic bridge. Catering largely for tourists and day-trippers the Pollaphuca extension succumbed to bus competition in 1928 and tourist traffic was negligible during the dismal years that followed. However with the creation of the reservoir that became popularly known as the Blessington Lakes a whole range of waterborne sports and other activities developed. Pollaphuca came to attract people in numbers that the steam tramway company would not have deemed possible and what was originally intended as part of a public utility is now also a wonderful environmental and leisure resource.

The ESB is responsible for the management of the reservoir and monitors the various activities that take place there. These include boating (maximum 4 hp engines), fishing, windsurfing, shooting and rowing, but swimming is specifically banned. A user's consultative committee chaired by an ESB

official meets twice a year to deal with any problems that might arise. Litter, pollution, shoreline fencing, tree felling and lakeside development are among the subjects that have received attention.

FROM POLLAPHUCA
TO BALLYMORE EUSTACE

The two waterworks intakes from the Pollaphuca reservoir were laid before the dam was constructed in 1938. Known as the upper and lower intakes, they conveyed the water under the Blessington to Baltinglass road and are respectively 4 and 5 feet in diameter. They enter the hexagonal Valve House on the north side of the road where the water is screened to remove debris. Sluice gates control the intakes, only one of which is in use at any time. From the Valve House the water is conveyed through twin 36-inch (900mm) steel mains to a

new treatment works at Ballymore Eustace, about a mile from Pollaphuca.

The reservoir water is of moderately high colour and physico-chemical treatment was provided. After the addition of alum as a coagulant, the water passed through twin horizontal flow settlement tanks for clarification. The settled water then passed through rapid-gravity filters and was finally disinfected with chlorine. After retention in contact tanks for a short period the treated water was then conveyed through a 900mm cast iron main to the head chamber of an aqueduct constructed to bring the supply to the city.

The settlement tanks were poorly designed. Cross walls interfered with the sedimentation process and the arrangements for sludge removal were woefully inadequate. The plant was designed to process 23,000 m^3/day and appears to have operated flat out from the start. The water, which almost immediately increased Dublin's supply by a quarter, was delivered through an ovoid mass-concrete aqueduct 12 miles (19.3km) long to a small reservoir at Saggart and then through a 33-inch steel pipeline to a nineteen million-gallon (86m^3) service reservoir at Cookstown, near the present Tallaght town centre. Luckily the corporation had the foresight to procure the steel reinforcement for the project before supplies became unavailable during World War Two. From Cookstown the supply was taken to the west city and across the Liffey via Cabra to Griffith Avenue, reinforcing the trunk main network in the west and north city areas. This work was completed in 1944.

By 1950 the plant was being run at twice its rated capacity, with dire results for treated water quality. A second stage of the treatment plant was constructed in 1953 to cope with the increasing demand. Inexplicably the new plant was a duplicate of the first, with all its shortcomings. On completion it was already on overload, and was producing 86m^3/day of poor quality water by 1975 when the next plant expansion was achieved.

In the early 1950s a new 600mm main was laid from Saggart for a distance of 11 miles to bring surplus Liffey water to the Ballyboden and Stillorgan reservoirs as required; the three supply systems were now linked.

By 1967, with production at Ballymore Eustace reaching 18 million gallons per day, it was impossible to produce water of satisfactory quality from these works. It was decided to expand the capacity of the works to 30 million gallons per day by increasing the number of filters from 10 to 15. At the same time all the filters were converted to sand anthracite media to double the filtration rate. A standby generator was installed to take over power supply instantaneously in the event of an ESB breakdown or strike. However the key deficiency in the works, namely the clarification stage, was not addressed and therefore no increase in plant efficiency resulted, although water quality saw a modest, if temporary, improvement.

Filter Beds at Ballymore Eustace.

The reservoir water was of moderately high colour and physico-chemical treatment was provided for it, along with the addition of alum as a coagulant.

Diagram of water-
works at Leixlip
(opposite). *These
waterworks provide a
supply to Blanchards-
town, north county
Dublin and parts
of county Kildare.*

THE CLOGHLEAGH SCHEME

In the late 1960s, Dublin County Council examined
the possibility of obtaining a water supply from
the Upper Liffey at Cloghleagh to cater for the
higher reaches of the south county from Saggart
to Sandyford. This was in effect a revival of the
Ballysmuttan scheme considered a century earlier as
an alternative to the Vartry (Chapter 4). A scheme
was developed for a reservoir at Cloghleagh Bridge
with a yield of 22,000m³/day. After treatment the
supply was to be pumped to a reservoir on the
Crooksling ridge and from there to service reservoirs
at Woodtown (above Ballyboden) and Sandyford.

To cater for immediate requirements the reservoirs at Woodtown and Sandyford and a linking
pipeline were constructed. The initial supply was
provided by a pumping plant and rising main from
Ballyboden waterworks to Woodtown reservoir.
The intention was that the rising main would
function as a gravity service main on completion
of the Cloghleagh scheme.

During the gestation of the new town development plans in the 1970–1972 period it became
apparent that the Cloghleagh project would be
totally inadequate in output. At that stage it was
decided to source the required supply from the
Ballymore-Eustace plant. A detailed 1960s report
about the Cloghleagh project by Michael Dee,
the county engineer, is preserved in the city waterworks archives.

STRATEGIC PLANNING

A number of key decisions were made at this time
on which the evolution of the water supply system
of the metropolitan area was subsequently founded:
- Blanchardstown new town, north Dublin county,
  the north-eastern area of the city and north
  Kildare county would be supplied from Leixlip
- the Vartry supply would be devoted to all the
  future requirements of Wicklow town and the
  coastal belt northwards to Stillorgan. It was
  assumed that this area would ultimately

absorb the entire supply and that there would
be no input to Stillorgan Reservoir
- the Ballymore Eustace supply would be
  developed to supply south Kildare, the new
  towns of Tallaght and Lucan-Clondalkin,
  and the remainder of the city
- a supply from Ballymore Eustace would
  replace the Vartry input to Stillorgan Reservoir
- in the long term the Liffey would be supplemented by another source or sources, such as
  groundwater.

The completion of the draft development plan
for Dublin county in 1971 greatly facilitated the
orderly planning and provision of water and
drainage services in the new towns and throughout
the county. It was now possible to plan in advance
a complete distribution system for very large areas
and to arrange for putting it in place piecemeal
to serve immediate requirements. The advent of
computer-aided design (CAD) and suitable software
was of great assistance at this time.

Water for north Kildare county is also supplied
from Ballymore Eustace, but not to Blessington and
neighbouring villages in Co Wicklow, which have
their own sources – mainly from springs and
ground water. The protection of ground water in
the entire Pollaphuca catchment area is of great
importance and very strict regulations are enforced
to ensure that there is no contamination. The
Ballymore Eustace plant has its own laboratory
where water quality is monitored constantly.

EXPANSION OF THE WATER
SUPPLY SYSTEM

With the maturation of the development plans in
the early 1970s and the upsurge in building activity
it became evident that major expansion of all infrastructural services was urgently required, not only
to provide for the future but to remove existing
inadequacies. The Dublin water supply was now
seriously deficient in both quality and quantity.
Pressures in the city mains were kept to a minimum,
with frequent complaints from the more elevated

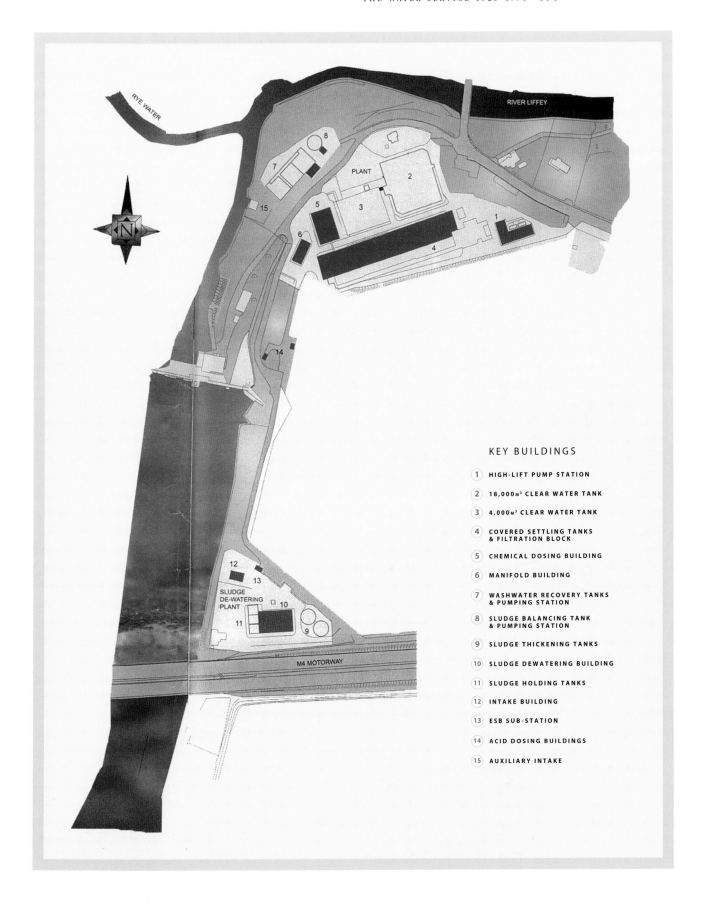

RYE WATER

RIVER LIFFEY

PLANT

SLUDGE
DE-WATERING
PLANT

M4 MOTORWAY

KEY BUILDINGS

1 HIGH-LIFT PUMP STATION

2 18,000M³ CLEAR WATER TANK

3 4,000M³ CLEAR WATER TANK

4 COVERED SETTLING TANKS
   & FILTRATION BLOCK

5 CHEMICAL DOSING BUILDING

6 MANIFOLD BUILDING

7 WASHWATER RECOVERY TANKS
   & PUMPING STATION

8 SLUDGE BALANCING TANK
   & PUMPING STATION

9 SLUDGE THICKENING TANKS

10 SLUDGE DEWATERING BUILDING

11 SLUDGE HOLDING TANKS

12 INTAKE BUILDING

13 ESB SUB-STATION

14 ACID DOSING BUILDINGS

15 AUXILIARY INTAKE

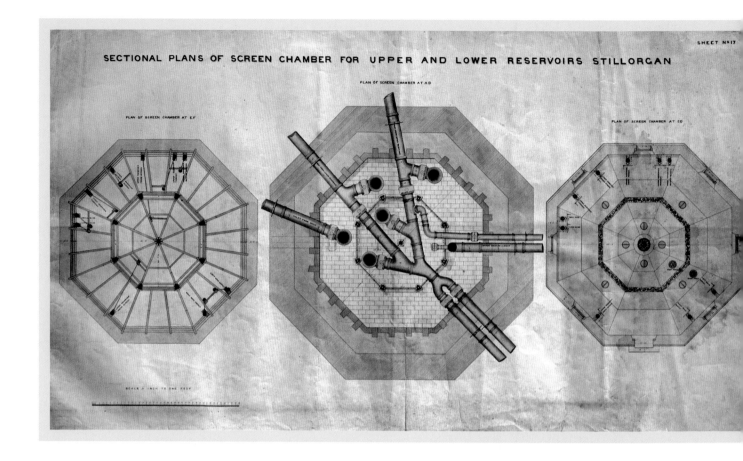

SECTIONAL PLANS OF SCREEN CHAMBER FOR UPPER AND LOWER RESERVOIRS STILLORGAN

Plans for Stillorgan Reservoir System.

The reservoirs at Stillorgan in county Dublin were originally built as part of the Vartry Scheme and feature distinctive octagonal screen houses.

areas, particularly in the north city fringes.

The supply from Ballymore Eustace and Ballyboden had high levels of aluminium from inefficient settlement carried over into the supply. This resulted in deposition of alum floc in the water distribution system, giving rise to frequent complaints when the muddy deposits were disturbed and issued through the consumers' taps. Treated water stored in uncovered reservoirs at Stillorgan and Ballyboden was routinely subject to serious contamination from aerial fallout and particularly from the large flocks of seagulls that rested there after foraging on the nearby tip-heads. Thirty years later in 2005 this is still a problem, although plans are at an advanced stage to remedy the situation.

Resulting from the long lead-in time to have new works completed and the unprecedented rate of development in the 1970s and later, the supply deficit was not made good, even when it had been

doubled in a relatively short time. At that period there was a lack of commitment by the state to provide sufficient funds to the Dublin local authorities for water and sewerage works. This was in contrast to the huge investments made in telecommunications and the natural gas network. Dublin, with one third of the population of the state, might have expected to receive a corresponding proportion of the capital funds available for investment in water supply and sewerage – it usually obtained barely half that amount.

Reasonably accurate estimates could now be made of the scale of the work needed to remedy the situation in water supply and sewerage and plans could be formulated to remedy the deficiencies and provide the capacity for ongoing development. In water supply terms the needs were essentially the expansion of the treatment plants at Ballymore Eustace and Leixlip, new trunk mains to deliver the additional supplies to the growing metropolis, and the provision of distribution systems in the new towns.

WATER TREATMENT

The most urgent requirement at the Ballymore Eustace works was clarifier capacity. This was addressed in 1975 with the construction of a new 135,000m³/day clarifier and associated works under a 'design and construct' contract. The novel design proposed for this clarifier was proved by the construction of a full-scale pilot unit which performed in excess of requirements.

The bottleneck had now been moved to the filtration section. Six new filters were constructed and the existing units refurbished to bring the overall plant capacity up to 180,000m³/day, which exceeded the capacity of the aqueduct to Dublin.

The famous Pale, the outer defences of the English-ruled territory surrounding Dublin at the end of the fifteenth century, ran through the site of the Ballymore Eustace treatment works. A plaque in the grounds of the works marks part of the route and gives accurate information about a feature of our history that is frequently misinterpreted.

THE NORTH REGIONAL SCHEME

For many years Dublin County Council was anxious to improve and extend water supplies to the towns, villages and rural population in the north county area. These included areas such as Swords, Rush, Donabate, Skerries and Balbriggan which had obsolete local systems that were in need of replacement. This was accomplished in yet another collaboration with the ESB – the North Regional Scheme. The 1964 Sanitary Services Act provided a legal and financial basis for Dublin County Council to obtain water from the ESB's Leixlip dam for its scheme

From Golden Falls the Liffey flows for about 35 miles through County Kildare to Leixlip, which is some 12 miles from Dublin. During the construction

of the Leixlip dam and 4 Megawatt generating station by the ESB, provision was made for the county council's requirements. A dam, similar in construction to those at Pollaphuca and Golden Falls, impounds water in a reservoir about 100 acres (40 hectares) in extent and having a capacity of 160 million gallons. Three 12-inch (300mm) diameter pipes were incorporated in the dam wall to allow for the future abstraction of water for use in the north Dublin county.

Dublin Corporation had constructed a 22,000m³ (5 million gallon) reservoir at Ballycoolen near Blanchardstown in 1954 to serve the developing Finglas area that was not capable of being supplied directly from the city system. A pumping station on the Finglas Road delivered water to this reservoir at night through a 600mm rising main which functioned as a gravity supply main during the day.

Construction of the new Leixlip treatment works and pumping station for the North Regional Scheme commenced in 1965 and was completed in 1967. The treatment plant was of conventional design and featured hopper-bottomed upward flow sludge blanket clarifiers and rapid gravity sand filters. Treatment wastes were discharged untreated back to the Liffey. Three 350 hp single stage pumps were installed and the supply was delivered to the Ballycoolen reservoir through a 9km-long 685mm steel rising main.

At this time the Ballymun housing complex was being built and to provide a water supply for it a temporary filtration plant and pumping station was constructed on a part of the treatment works site in 1965. This plant would serve Ballymun until the new Leixlip works came into use. It employed rapid gravity filtration and was rated at 5,000m³/day. A second 600mm main was now laid from Ballycoolen reservoir to Cappagh and thence around north Finglas to Ballymun. The Ballymun complex had its own reservoir and a pumping plant to service the high-rise flat blocks. The 600mm main was continued to Santry to replace the supply then being pumped from Whitehall.

The city was now absorbing the maximum

**Plaque at Ballymore
Eustace showing
boundary of the Pale.**
*The famous Pale, the
outer defences of the
English-ruled territory
surrounding Dublin at
the end of the fifteenth
century, ran through the
site of the Ballymore
Eustace Treatment Works.*

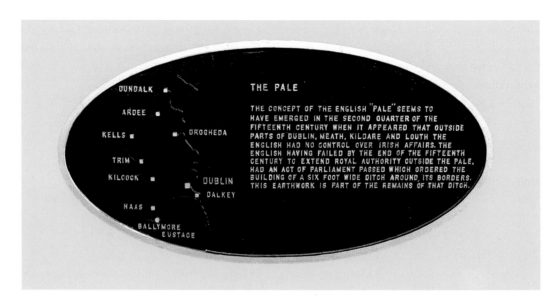

output of the new Leixlip works plus the contribution of the temporary plant, with only the modest needs of Blanchardstown, Castleknock and district going to the county council. Approval for an expansion of the Leixlip works was obtained and the work was completed in 1973, doubling output to 68,000m³/day. Three more 350 hp pumps were installed and a 1,000mm diameter pre-stressed concrete main was laid from Leixlip to Ballycoolen to operate in parallel with the existing 27-inch steel rising main.

In 1971 work had commenced on the supply to the north county area. An arterial main varying in diameter from 900mm to 675mm was laid from Ballycoolen to a terminal reservoir at Jordanstown, near Balbriggan. This main was of pre-stressed concrete on the Australian Rocla system and was manufactured in County Antrim by Macrete. These main pipes were used almost exclusively over the next fifteen years for pipelines of greater than 600mm diameter throughout Ireland. From this arterial main, branches were laid under a series of contracts to serve the entire north county. The council's direct labour force laid most of the smaller distribution mains and by the end of the 1970s virtually every premises in the north county was connected.

Leixlip was now supplying 12 million gallons per day to the city and serving north Kildare as well as all of north County Dublin. A new service reservoir with a capacity of 70,000m³ was constructed at Ballycoolen to provide adequate storage for the rapidly developing new town of Blanchardstown and provide balancing storage for the increased rate of pumping.

The rapid spread of development along the north fringe in the early 1970s was on lands above the service levels of the city trunk mains. A 600mm (24-inch) branch main was therefore laid from the terminus of the 600mm main at Santry to Clonshaugh to serve this area, and a parallel main was later completed along the old main road from Santry to Forrest Little (Swords). In contrast to the pumping required from Leixlip to Ballycoolen, the elevation of Ballymore Eustace treatment plant over Datum enables water to flow from there by gravity almost as far up as Ballymun. One result of this can be found at Killester where a water tower built to serve the area became redundant and was removed.

By 1985 increased demand necessitated a further addition to the Leixlip plant, raising treatment capacity to 107,000 cubic metres a day. This new section of the plant was of a different design, with flat-bottomed upward flow clarifiers equipped with lamella plates and deep bed single size rapid sand filters. A second raw water inlet main and a new chemical preparation block were also provided. The existing filters were refurbished and pneumatic controls replaced the outdated hydraulic gear. It now became possible to dispense with the 'temporary' plant after twenty years of service.

The original intake at the Leixlip dam was not far below crest level and to ensure continuity of supply in the event of the reservoir level having to be lowered for essential maintenance of the sluice gates, an auxiliary pump had been provided just down-stream of the dam. The increased output of the works eventually required the full-time operation of the pumped supply to supplement the normal gravity flow. The location of the intake on the dam face also gave rise to problems from floating debris and leaves which blocked the screens. A new intake upstream of the dam and capable of abstracting water, by pumping when necessary, was a pressing requirement by the mid-1970s.

In 1994 a review of hydrology of the River Liffey catchment confirmed that a refurbished plant at Leixlip could safely increase the treatment capacity to 175,000 cubic metres per day. The work comprised four elements. There is a new intake system, an upgraded and refurbished treatment plant, a new clearwater tank and pumping station and a sludge processing and dewatering unit. The upgraded and refurbished plant was officially opened on 1 February 2002. A brochure produced to mark the event contains detailed technical information. Operated by Fingal County Council, Leixlip is the second largest water treatment facility in Ireland. Like Ballymore Eustace it has its own laboratory, which oversees water quality.

There is an inherent risk associated with this waterworks. The Liffey passes through a highly developed catchment area, including the towns of Naas and Newbridge, and is at constant risk of being rendered unusable for an extended period from an accidental spillage or similar mishap. Such an event could interrupt the supply of water to all of the Fingal area and large parts of the north city,

without any possibility of a substitute supply. The consequences are unimaginable. This has not happened in nearly forty years of operation, but Murphy's Law still applies!

Good waterworks practice requires off-river storage of at least seven days' supply to cope with such a risk. Such storage could have been provided on the site of the adjoining Weston airfield had funding been available in the 1970s, but this option seems no longer possible. The problem remains!

THE NEW LIFFEY AQUEDUCT

The original aqueduct from Ballymore Eustace to Rathcoole had a maximum carrying capacity of about 86,000m³/day. It required periodic brushing to remove surface deposits of alum floc to maintain capacity. The aqueduct was a non-pressure conduit with a horseshoe cross-section, constructed to a uniform gradient over its full length. A number of valleys were crossed with inverted siphons and it transpired that these were under-designed. The siphons were duplicated in the 1970s to gain a sorely needed increment in carrying capacity.

The increased production capacity at the Ballymore-Eustace treatment plant now required additional trunk main capacity to bring the water to the city. It was decided to provide this by means of a pressure pipeline, 1,620mm in diameter and 25km long, laid north of the original aqueduct. An advance contract was placed for the manufacture and supply of the pipes in pre-stressed concrete with the Macrete company. At this diameter the only available alternative would have been steel pipe at a much higher cost. An agent was appointed to oversee the manufacture and ensure that quality control was maintained. The 1,600mm butterfly valves for in-line use were also procured in an advance contract.

Three separate contracts were prepared for the laying of the pipes. The pipeline required careful design in view of the enormous thrust forces resulting from unbalanced pressures at valves and bends. Pipe specials were manufactured in welded steel and suitably protected against corrosion.

The placing of the pipeline contracts was delayed inordinately by the unwillingness of Dublin County Council to pay what had now become the going rate to compensate landowners for wayleaves. Four years were wasted in fruitless negotiations until the council officials eventually bowed to the inevitable. The delay totally disrupted the programme for the development of the water supply system, with consequences that persisted for many years. Frustrated at the delay, one engineer engaged on the project ruefully recalled the powers vested in Maurice Fitzgerald for the 1244 Poddle scheme which, if available nearly 750 years later, would have expedited the urgent work considerably.

The maximum discharge capacity of the new aqueduct was well below expectations. Investigation of this and other pipelines showed that the manufacturer's claims regarding pipe roughness factors were quite optimistic.

A new 14,000m^3/ reservoir and a 600mm pipeline to Belgard had been constructed in the early 1970s to provide an interim water supply to the rapidly developing Tallaght area. The new aqueduct discharged to this reservoir.

SOUTH DUBLIN COUNTY SUPPLIES: TALLAGHT–RONANSTOWN

From Saggart reservoir a 1,000mm trunk main was laid to the Ballyboden works, in parallel with the older 600mm main, to provide an auxiliary supply to the Ballyboden supply area. This pipeline was extended to Stillorgan reservoir in 2001 to replace the diminishing Vartry supply, in accordance with the development policy outlined earlier.

The county council's design staff prepared detailed plans for the future distribution systems for Tallaght and Ronanstown. The sizes and routing of the principal pipelines were identified and the designs refined by computer modelling. The mains were installed by the county council's direct labour units as the need arose and were usually financed from development levies.

A major new service reservoir with a capacity of 100,000 cubic metres was constructed at Belgard to serve both Tallaght and Ronanstown. This reservoir is of unconventional design as a measure to save construction costs and is flexible to accommodate the considerable blast vibrations from the adjoining Roadstone quarry. Ongoing records of blast effects are maintained in collaboration with the quarry owners. This is believed to be the largest service reservoir in these islands.

FURTHER DEVELOPMENT AT BALLYMORE-EUSTACE

Plant wastes at Ballymore-Eustace, mainly filter washwater and clarifier sludges, were discharged untreated to a marshy area near the Liffey, and the periodic cleanout of the old clarifiers, involving a massive release of sludge, had become a serious pollution risk. Following pilot plant studies the corporation designed a sludge treatment plant using sludge thickening followed by dewatering in multi-chamber presses. The press water was recycled and the sludge cake disposed of to a licensed local landfill.

The original twin 900mm raw water mains were now at the limit of capacity. A new 1,600mm pre-stressed pipeline was installed to enable the abstraction agreed with the ESB to be delivered to the treatment works.

M. C. O'Sullivan, consulting engineer, was appointed in 1983 to devise a long-term development plan for the expansion of the Ballymore-Eustace works. His report was received in 1985 and approved. His core recommendation was to develop the plant as two independent treatment units, operating in parallel, retaining the existing filters and the recently constructed upward-flow clarifier. The incoming raw water mains were led to a manifold house from which the two treatment lines would be supplied. Because clarifier capacity was again the limiting factor in water production, a new clarifier of 180,000m^3/day was included in the next phase of development. The layout of the treatment units and pipelines was carefully planned to ensure that their construction would not interfere with the normal operation of the works. This phase also provided new chemical storage and handling facilities and a service water tower.

TELEMETRY

The desirability of having centralised surveillance of the operation of the far-flung water supply network was recognised in the mid-1970s. Existing instrumentation was sparse and not always maintained in reliable working condition. As a prerequisite to the acquisition of a telemetry system a programme was commenced to install primary instrumentation throughout the entire existing system. As new facilities – Belgard Reservoir for example – were being constructed, they were equipped with all the necessary flow, level and pressure sensors. These were connected to a central panel to enable them to function as outstations when it became possible to acquire the communications system and a central control room. This was finally achieved in the late 1990s.

DUN LAOGHAIRE

Steady development in Dun Laoghaire and its hinterland up to 1939 accelerated in the years following the Second World War. The original Kingstown supply in 1867 was through a 15-inch pipe from Stillorgan reservoir to near Monkstown Castle, from where a branch main was laid to Dalkey. From Loughlinstown (The Silver Tassie) a supply was taken from the Callowhill-Stillorgan 24-inch main laid between 1891 and 1907 to serve Ballybrack and Killiney.

To serve the new housing estate at Sallynoggin in the 1940s a new 9-inch main was laid from the 24-inch trunk line at Cornelscourt. A 12-inch diameter supply from Cabinteely to cater for the expanding Glenageary and Dalkey areas was laid from Cabinteely to a new reservoir at Ballinclea in the

1950s. A new intermediate level reservoir was constructed in Killiney Hill Park adjacent to Killiney Village. This was designed to serve the higher areas around Killiney and received a pumped supply from Ballinclea.

At that time there was a small, older high-level reservoir near the Killiney Obelisk which was supplied from Loughlinstown through a pumping station to the south of the village. In a total re-organisation of services in the Borough area a tunnel was laid down Brewery Road from Stillorgan works. Falling pressures in the Killiney-Ballybrack distribution system resulted in insufficient pressure at the pumping plant during the day and pumping was possible only during the night. This high-level reservoir, which served the highest developed land around Killiney, obtained a fresh pumped supply from the new intermediate-level reservoir.

Rising demand, poor pressure, untraced leakages and uncertainty about linkages led to the appointment of consultants in the mid-1980s to examine the Dun Laoghaire water supply and make recommendations. Among other things they recommended a new supply from Stillorgan reservoir, and a new reservoir off Church Road on the western side of Roche's Hill. The extensive programme of work was divided into four contracts.

A new valve, metering and control chamber was constructed in the embankment of the lowest reservoir at Stillorgan and existing infrastructure was reorganised. In Brewery Road a 1,200mm-diameter steel main was laid in a tunnel excavated by blasting in granite as far as the Bray (N11) Road. A major valve chamber was constructed within the traffic island at the bottom of Brewery Road to allow for making additional connections. A 900mm-diameter supply main to Dun Laoghaire Borough continued in tunnel under the N11 into the grounds of the School for the Deaf. These works were designed to provide a secure water supply to a wide distribution area; they were finished in Spring 1996.

A major mains laying programme provided for linking the main trunk main from the Brewery

Road tunnel to Church Road (Killiney) reservoir via an 800mm pipeline to a new pumping station at Kilbogget. This station pumps directly to the Church Road reservoir through an 800mm rising main. A 39,000 cubic metre reservoir was constructed above Church Road between Killiney Golf Club and Roche's Hill, with much blasting through solid rock. This contract also included pumping plant, secondary sterilisation and metering, and the laying of a 300mm rising main across Killiney Golf Course to the boundary with Roche's Hill.

Improvements in the intermediate and high-level distribution systems included the building of a new pumping station, metering and valve house. This is adjacent to the intermediate-level reservoir near Killiney village. The intermediate-level reservoir was refurbished, the high-level one reconstructed, and the 300mm rising main was continued across Roche's Hill to the high-level reservoir.

PLANNING ON A WIDER SCALE

The development plans prepared for Dublin City and county in the late 1960s greatly improved the ability to anticipate future water supply needs over the entire area. What was not known was exactly when or where particular developments would take place. Furthermore the explosion of development during the 1970s together with the long times required to provide extra capacity resulted in demand constantly outstripping supply – and this was in spite of the fact that the delivery of water had doubled within a relatively short period.

Kevin O'Donnell, on whose writing this chapter is overwhelmingly based, was chief engineer in charge of water and drainage for both Dublin city and county during the 1970s and 1980s. He was better placed than anybody else to set out what happened during those years and his account of contemporary problems and their solution is therefore invaluable.

THE NORTH DUBLIN DRAINAGE SCHEME

An obstacle to the expansion of Dublin's north side prior to their abolition in 1858 was the large number of toll-gates north of the Liffey. These were a serious deterrent to builders, who had to pay for every load of material they brought through, and also discouraged potential residents who would travel into the city regularly. The resulting negative image of the north side persisted for many decades and development was therefore slow. As late as the 1930s, significant improvements in public services were an essential prerequisite to any large-scale extension of the northern suburbs and villages. Up to a dozen villages, some of them already inside the city boundary, needed greatly improved drainage, as did the many houses and institutions served by septic tanks.

P. J. McGovern read a paper entitled 'Proposed Main Drainage of Finglas, Coolock and Raheny', to the Institution of Engineers in May 1941. In it he envisaged an interceptor sewer running eastwards from Finglas to discharge to the foreshore at Bettyglen. The proposal was developed during the years 1943–1950, the North Dublin Drainage Scheme being planned to cater for a population of 265,000 people. Construction of this project, usually referred to simply as 'The North Dublin' or NDDS, began in March 1952 and took more than six years to complete. Its purpose was to alleviate overloading in the north city sewers and serve the growing northern suburbs, together with Portmarnock, Baldoyle, Sutton and Howth. Raw sewage outfalls across beaches, as at Kilbarrack and Sutton, were also in urgent need of interception.

A trunk sewer, increasing along its route from a diameter of 3 feet 6 inches (1,067mm) to 5 feet (1524mm), was laid from Blanchardstown via Navan Road, Cabra, Finglas Bridge, Griffith Avenue, Donnycarney, Killester, Raheny and Sutton. This North Dublin trunk sewer flows by gravity as far as Raheny (Watermill Road). It siphons under the Royal Canal at Cabra (Reilly's Bridge) and the River Tolka at Finglas Bridge, opposite The Royal Oak. The section from Old Finglas Road to Mobhi Road is a 1,200mm (4 feet) diameter tunnel. A third siphon takes the line under the railway at Killester and on via Howth Road and St Anne's to Watermill Road, Raheny.

The interceptor flows as a normal gravity sewer as far as Raheny. From Raheny to Howth the sewer was laid to a continuous falling gradient and with normal dry-weather flow and low tidal levels it flows partly full as an ordinary gravity sewer. As tidal levels increased the sewer was backwatered up to Kilbarrack at the highest spring tides. High tides coinciding with storm flows extended the surcharged section towards Raheny to enable the flow to discharge against the prevailing tidal level. A maximum pressure of 1.4 bar in the sewer occurred at Kilbarrack should the surcharged section extend back to the inlet of the pressure line at Raheny. The manholes on the pressure section were designed to withstand the pressure conditions and were fitted with bolted-down covers.

The Raheny-Howth section has pumping stations at Kilbarrack, Baldoyle Road, Sutton (Burrow Road) and Howth Screen House. There are further pumping stations on major subsidiary sewers at Portmarnock, Mayne Bridge, Baldoyle Village, Warrenhouse Road (Moyclare) and Strand Road.

The last mile of the North Dublin main line is a tunnel 6 feet in diameter, with a valve house and access shaft at Balscadden. At more than 55m (180 feet) this is the deepest structure on the Dublin drainage network. From the bottom of the Balscadden shaft the tunnel was driven at a rising grade to a point some 60m (200 feet) off the Nose of Howth. It terminates in a vertical shaft to exit on the seabed about 25m (82 feet) below sea level. The sewage was discharged untreated except for rough screening. The tunnel was constructed in 1955 and 1956, the contractor being Kinnear, Moodie and

Company Ltd. Developments to follow the Dublin Bay Project, largely completed in 2003 (described in Chapter 13), will minimise the use of this outfall, with obvious major benefits for the environment and amenities of Dublin Bay.

Much of Drumcondra, Marino and Fairview, as well as parts of Killester and Clontarf lying south of the North Dublin interceptor are considerably lower than the NDDS main line. Previously drained to the Eden Quay siphon via Clontarf pumping station (Chapter 8), they were connected to the North Dublin system when this was commissioned. Rising mains were laid northwards from Clontarf and Vernon Avenue pumping stations (formerly ejectors) to the NDDS main line at Killester (Collins Avenue) and Sybil Hill Road respectively.

A small area on the south side of the Howth peninsula, known as the Baily or Earlscliffe catchment, was omitted from the North Dublin scheme. This was due to the difficult local terrain and the likely high cost of connection; it still discharges, via a septic tank, to the sea at Doldrum Bay.

Two of the North Dublin pumping stations – Clontarf and Howth – were staffed around the clock. In time Clontarf, which has instruments recording flows and other information from stations further along the line, itself became automated. The grounds of this station, which also contained a rain gauge, were developed as a beautiful garden which was lovingly tended for several years by the late Paddy Cadwell.

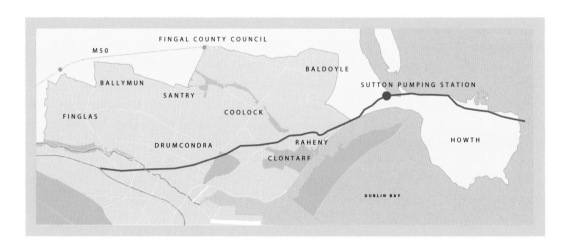

Diagram showing the North Dublin Drainage Scheme.
Construction of this project began in March 1952 and took over six years to complete.

Kilbarrack Promenade
New housing schemes
constructed in
Kilbarrack during the
1950s were served by the
North Dublin Drainage
Scheme and enabled
people to move from city
centre slums to a healthy
seaside location.

LIFE IN THE 1950s – THE 1953 BOUNDARY EXTENSION

While the North Dublin scheme was under construction a large expansion of the municipal area took place in April 1953. On the north side the new city boundary brought Baldoyle, Coolock and Finglas under the jurisdiction of the corporation. Districts added on the south side included Ballyfermot, Drimnagh, Walkinstown, and yet another part of Rathfarnham.

Crushing poverty was the lot of too many people in Dublin during the 1950s despite every effort to improve the lives of the disadvantaged. As well as the long-established Sick and Indigent Room Keepers Society and St Vincent de Paul Society many people relied on the Lord Mayor's Coal Fund and the Evening Herald Boot Fund. Barefoot children were a common sight the 1960s, many residing in the foul tenements that were not finally eliminated until later in that decade.

Much of the new housing that replaced the tenements – in Finglas, Kilmore, Coolock,

Kilbarrack and Ballymun – was served by the North Dublin Drainage Scheme. People who would at one time have been disparagingly called the

lower middle classes were also moving into the new housing estates facilitated by the NDDS. An indication of how far most people had yet to advance materially can be gleaned from the fact that if someone bought a car or had a telephone installed, it was a topic for conversation – and a cause for envy – in the area for several days.

The prevailing harsh economic circumstances in the Republic of the 1950s were made even worse by a serious recession in the middle of the decade. Although this retarded progress on many projects, the 1953 boundary extension was followed by more rapid building development than had been initially envisaged. Because development was denser and more extensive than was anticipated in the sewer design, and due to the 'partially separate' system of drainage, the capacity of the NDDS was being reached within a comparatively short time.

To conserve the remaining sewer capacity it was decided that all future development would be drained on the 'separate' system. Some developments were completed prematurely, necessitating special interim drainage arrangements. An example was a large septic tank built at Ardcollum Avenue in Artane as a temporary expedient to serve the extensive Maryfield Estate, then in the course of development. Part of this structure, which discharged to the adjacent Nanniken River, was uncovered during ESB ducting work in 2001.

Following completion of the North Dublin project a programme was undertaken to connect to the sewers the many premises on septic tanks within the catchment area. Most of the tanks were bridged, emptied out and broken down or backfilled, but a few isolated survivors were found to be operational up to thirty years later.

During the early 1960s, arrangements were made to divert drainage in the West Cabra area from the overloaded city centre system to the North Dublin system. An interceptor sewer was laid from Ratoath Road, starting as a 9-inch diameter pipe, increasing in size as it followed a necessarily circuitous route around the geometric West Cabra road layout. From Bannow Road it crossed under the railway and canal at Liffey Junction with a diameter of 30 inches, continuing along Blackwater Road in the Dublin Industrial Estate. It joined the North Dublin main line at Slaney Road in the Dublin Industrial Estate.

The North Dublin Drainage Scheme was completed in 1958 at a cost of £2m, well within budget. Built in the light of the best information available at the time, it encountered increasing diffi-culties when it had to cater for areas never intended for development at the system's design stage. The continuing use of the interim control powers conferred by the flawed 1934 and 1939 Town and Regional Planning Acts compounded the problems. The Planning Acts did not specify when a develop-ment plan would have to be produced and, until this was done, interim control powers could continue – as it turned out, with no end in sight. In the absence of a development plan, planning for whatever development might be approved could, at best, only be based on educated guesses. Several

years elapsed before this defect was remedied under fresh legislation in 1963.

The city sewers and main drainage department staff carried out all the detailed design work and supervision of construction on the North Dublin scheme. By the standards of the time it was a gigantic undertaking and a great achievement for a total design and supervisory team of less then a dozen professional, technical and administrative staff. They were based in site offices and in the city engineer's primitive headquarters at 28 Castle Street. This condemned industrial building had been acquired by the corporation in 1913 and adapted to accommodate the staff pending the building of new civic offices. At his retirement presentation in Castle Street in the mid-1970s Michael Sinnott recalled that when he joined the corporation staff around 1931 he was told that he would work in Castle Street for a very short time until the new civic offices were built.

In a city startlingly less affluent than it is today the drawing boards in the Castle Street design office were propped up on broken concrete blocks and continued thus until the 1986 move to the present civic offices. The primordial state of the telephone service when the North Dublin was being built required calls between Castle Street and Howth to be booked through a manual public telephone exchange. Even interdepartmental calls had to be routed through the corporation's manual exchange. In that era of widespread inequality the women who operated the telephone system, and all other female staff, were required to resign from their jobs when they got married, an injustice not remedied until 1972.

Several roads that are now main arteries were unlit and poorly surfaced country lanes when the North Dublin drainage system was under construc-tion. Thoroughfares such as Kilbarrack Road or Skelly's Lane had drainage ditches at each side and minimal public lighting. Outside the city, even in the villages, all street lighting was extinguished at midnight. As a concession to those attending Christmas religious services such as Midnight Mass,

The Howth Tunnel.
This forms the last mile of the North Dublin Drainage Scheme and at 55 metres/180 feet below ground, it is the deepest structure on the Dublin drainage network.

or socialising around the New Year, the lights were kept burning throughout the night during the festive season.

This Ruritarian scenario changed rapidly during the 1960s and 1970s when large corporation housing estates were built in the northern outskirts of the city. Areas such as Kilbarrack, Edenmore, Coolock and Kilmore were developed rapidly, all draining to the North Dublin system. Construction

of these estates hastened the end of the slum conditions that it had been the lot of so many people in Dublin to endure for several generations.

Much of the North Dublin construction work was carried out by direct labour. At its peak the project employed 115 men, several of whom were recruited externally and afterwards remained with the corporation as highly respected members of the permanent staff. Some frustrating delays were

Vernon Avenue Pumping Station, Clontarf. *Designed for Dublin City Council by De Paor Architects, this distinctive modern building was the recipient of an Opus Construction Award in 2004.*

experienced in the early days of the scheme when the delivery of plant and equipment on order was delayed. Machine operators, tradesmen and other specialists were transferred from various corporation departments as their services were required by the sewers and main drainage department. Much of the equipment taken for granted today was not available at the time of the NDDS. Cement, when it was batched, was transported to where it was needed on tippers – mixer lorries had not yet arrived, and mobile cranes, so much part of modern construction projects, were both primitive and scarce.

In 1953, the second year of work on the North Dublin scheme, the average wage for industrial workers was just under 2s 5d (15.2c) per hour. For a 45-hour week, the pay was £5 8s (€6.86). By 1958, when the North Dublin was completed, pay rates had increased by about 25%, the workers now earning 3s per hour, which worked out at £6.75 (€8.57) per week.

During the 1950s there was an almost constant shortage of workers in Britain and most other European countries but not in Ireland. This decade was the independent state's worst in terms of unemployment and emigration. So bad was the situation

in Dublin that many skilled workers emigrated, either bringing their families with them or sending for them as soon as they secured reasonable employment and accommodation.

An unprecedented situation arose when people who were forced to emigrate simply walked out of houses they had been buying with corporation or county council loans. These houses reverted to the local authority when the occupiers left. Seen against this background, the value of the employment afforded by the North Dublin scheme can be readily appreciated. Many of the houses abandoned by the emigrants remained unoccupied for long periods and were ultimately let as local authority tenancies or sold to people who were prepared to clear the arrears of payments and take over the existing mortgages.

Initiatives to tackle unemployment and stifle protests in the 1950s included the establishment of a special works department in the corporation. This provided badly needed employment on desirable schemes that would otherwise be deferred or considered unessential. Among the projects undertaken was river culverting: most of the remaining open stretches of the Wad between Ballymun and

Clontarf are an example of this. The special works department continued to operate into the 1960s when the employment situation improved with the onset of industrialisation. In special works projects the labour element had to account for at least 80% of all costs.

Brendan Murphy, Andrew Whelan and Dermot Coyle – all corporation engineers engaged on the North Dublin project – were acutely aware of a contemporary mindset that had little time for preserving the minutiae of engineering work. Therefore, when they presented detailed papers on various aspects of the scheme, even the plant – every item used on the project – was carefully recorded. Some 700 North Dublin drawings, most of them elegantly delineated and lettered on linen, survive in the drainage division's records.

ENGINEERING AND MANAGERIAL CHANGES

Although planned during the regime of Norman Chance, who retired as city engineer in 1950, construction of the North Dublin scheme was carried out under the direction of his successor, Edmond J. Bourke. There were two changes of city manager

during the construction of the project. The long-serving Dr P. J. Hernon retired in 1955 and was succeeded by John Keane, who retired in 1958 and was in turn replaced by T. C. O'Mahony.

In 1967, towards the end of E. J. Bourke's tenure in office, the first change in the city engineer's title and function in over a century took place. During this period, the city manager also had responsibility for Dublin County Council and for the Borough of Dun Laoghaire, both of which were administered by assistant managers. Some city and county services, already closely co-ordinated, were amalgamated to achieve savings and greater efficiency. Assistant managers could be in charge of an entire local authority area or of a function or group of functions covering both city and county.

In an extension of this policy, some duties of the Dublin city and county engineers were merged to cover both jurisdictions. From 1967 until his retirement in 1971 E. J. Bourke, while retaining the title of city engineer, became responsible for all drainage and water services in the city and county, the roads functions going to the county engineer, Michael Dee. Bourke was succeeded by Kevin O'Donnell whose title was Dublin Chief Engineer, Sanitary Services.

Further managerial changes occurred during the 1960s and 1970s. T. C. O'Mahony retired in 1965 and was replaced by Matthew Macken, who occupied the post until 1976 when he, in turn, was succeeded by James Molloy. Molloy enjoyed only three years in office because of ill-health and was followed in 1979 by Frank Feeley who was city manager until 1996.

THE SANTRY VALLEY SEWER – DUBLIN AIRPORT

In 1953 work began on the Santry Valley sewer, which parallels the Santry River to Raheny where it joins the North Dublin trunk sewer. This line opened up considerable areas for development including the sites of the large housing estates at Kilmore, Bonnybrook and Coolock. The Santry

Edmond J. Bourke, Dublin City Engineer 1950–1971. *Among his other achievements, Bourke supervised the construction of the North Dublin Drainage Scheme.*

Valley sewer has a number of storm overflows, because it was designed to serve an area drained on the partially separate system, and these have caused serious pollution of the Santry River.

Dublin Airport, established in 1940, was drained initially to a small private treatment plant which discharged to a local watercourse. Later the treatment was replaced by a pumping station which discharged to the county council's pumping station at Santry via a 100mm rising main. To meet the requirements of the rapidly growing airport complex, a new gravity connection was made to the sewers at Darndale in 1974 under an agreement with Dublin Corporation. This pipe passed through a large tract of potentially developable land and was eyed enviously by landowners and developers but, because of its status as a drain, Aer Rianta succeeded in repelling all boarders.

DEVELOPMENT STRAINS CAPACITY: THE NORTHERN SUBURBS

As stated earlier the North Dublin system was intended to cater for developments drained on the partially separate principle. This allows surface water from the rear of premises to discharge to the foul sewer, while front roofs, gardens and roads drain to separate surface water lines, which outfall to the nearest stream or watercourse. This practice was standard from the 1930s onwards but after 1961 complete separation became a universal requirement for new developments and every effort has since been made to divert as much surface water as possible from foul sewers. The benefits of the 'separate' system are the conservation of local sewer capacity and the avoidance of pollution of local watercourses by storm overflows. Energy savings are made through not having to pump storm water. A separate system also means fewer and smaller pumping stations and shorter pipe runs for the surface water as it goes to the nearest watercourse.

Intensive efforts to remove surface water from the North Dublin system were made over the years, but any spare capacity thus created was quickly overtaken by new development. Lack of capacity in the system over time became so critical that even the most modest additional drainage requirements had to be examined minutely.

The history of the North Dublin system highlights a recurring dilemma in the planning of drainage schemes in former times. In the absence of any long-term development plans, sewer designers had to make a best guess as to the extent of the catchment area and the type and density of development to be served. The projection forward of past or current trends could lead to woeful inadequacy in coping with unforeseen and unforeseeable expansion. The North Dublin system was conceived in the hungry 1940s and in the wake of the war years and the 'economic war' that preceded them. The explosion of development that commenced in the 1960s and still continues was unimaginable in the 1940s.

In the case of the North Dublin system, not only was development more intensive than anticipated, but several major additions were made to the catchment area. In 1967 the government commenced the construction of a large-scale high-rise housing project at Ballymun. For Ballymun, a major new line, increasing from 18 to 24 inches in diameter was laid south-eastwards to connect with the North Dublin line at Elmhurst Lane off Griffith Avenue.

Shortly after that the corporation was forced to construct the Kilbarrack pressure sewer to permit housing at Grangemore and Donaghmede. This sewer was subsequently extended to allow major housing development north of Tonlegee Road and at Darndale, between the Malahide and Clonshaugh Roads. The system was further extended to serve a major industrial park west of Clonshaugh Road. Dublin Airport, the drainage of which was explained earlier in this chapter, drains to the sewer that serves north Darndale. The flow from the Kilbarrack pressure sewer entered the interceptor at a point where it seriously aggravated the prevailing pressures in a pipeline of dubious integrity. The Sutton pumping station commissioned in 2003 now relieves the problem

Baldoyle Road Pumping Station. *In contrast to the modern edifice at Vernon Avenue, this simple structure is typical of pumping stations built in Dublin during the 1950s.*

of overpressure in the interceptor.

Other large housing developments took place in the years 1967–1975 including Baldoyle, Sutton and Finglas South. To serve Finglas South, a sewer was laid along the north bank of the Tolka from Scribblestown to Finglas Bridge. Beginning at 9 inches in diameter, this reaches 15 inches before entering the pumping station at The Royal Oak. From there, a rising main brings it into the North Dublin interceptor.

Much of this Tolka Valley sewer (not to be confused with the 1926 line of the same name from Drumcondra to Ballybough) runs under the linear Tolka Valley Park. Deposition of municipal refuse over the sewer has buried it to a depth of 11 metres (36 feet) and caused problems from the ingress of methane gas. This gas is highly explosive at low concentrations and was the cause of a fatal accident in the area. In the past, methane gas has ignited on the surface, a phenomenon also recorded at Edenmore (Raheny) where conditions similar to the Tolka Valley existed. The numerous spurting flames coming from the ground were likened to a gigantic gas cooker with all its jets alight.

12 Planning 1960–1985: New Schemes – Ringsend, Dun Laoghaire, Shanganagh and Bray

In April 1964 Professor Myles Wright was commissioned to prepare an advisory regional plan for Dublin. This was to establish a co-ordinated framework for the development plans local authorities would have to produce as required by the 1963 Planning Act. The Wright report, submitted in 1967, was intended to provide a long range strategic framework for the future expansion of the metropolitan area and thereby avoid the haphazard and poorly planned developments of earlier years.

Wright's plan envisaged four new towns – at Tallaght, Clondalkin, Lucan and Blanchardstown – each accommodating around 100,000 people. The plan was accepted and the first statutory development plan for County Dublin was based on it and adopted in 1972. The only significant change made at the detailed planning stage was to coalesce the Lucan and Clondalkin towns into a single unit, later called Ronanstown.

The development plans made it possible to assess future infrastructural needs accurately and to plan for their provision. The routes and sizes of major pipelines for water supply and sewerage could be determined and plans laid for their timely provision. The execution of the plans however depended ultimately on the allocation of sufficient financial resources by the state, on which local authorities are almost wholly dependent for capital expenditure.

The flow of capital was perennially inadequate and erratic and Dublin never received its fair share of the capital funds available. Because of this the provision of services was often outpaced by development, which was only made possible by devising special arrangements. Blanchardstown was temporarily connected to the North Dublin Drainage Scheme until it had attained a population of some 30,000 persons. The initial phases of Tallaght were connected to the city sewers at Orwell, and Ronanstown was connected via a temporary pumping station on the Naas Road to the Dodder Valley sewers at Greenhills.

All developments in the thirty years between 1960 and 1990 took place against a background of oscillating fortunes for most Irish people. Industrialisation in the 1960s raised living standards and created a widespread feel-good atmosphere accompanied by expectations of even better times to come. Ireland's accession to the then European Economic Community in 1973 resulted in an influx of funds that improved many public services but progress was uneven and there were alternating periods of prosperity and recession, leading to the severe economic conditions of the 1980s.

Harsher times culminated in the swingeing cutbacks that were imposed in the late 1980s. A reduction in the numbers employed in the public services was sought, severance and early retirement packages being offered in an attempt to achieve this. Some services were reduced or abandoned: drain clearance by the corporation was a case in point. Before the cutbacks a person whose drains were blocked could request help from the local routemen in any of the six drainage areas into which the city was divided. Blockages were cleared free to private householders and for a small fee in commercial premises. This widely appreciated service became a victim of the cutbacks in the 1980s and is now provided by commercial firms. But, paradoxically, despite cutbacks and setbacks, some progress was made in extending and improving infrastructural services.

GOING METRIC
– MORE MANAGERIAL CHANGES

February 1971 saw Ireland successfully changing from antiquated units of currency to the decimal system when the pound was divided into 100 pence instead of the shillings and pence hitherto used. The change from imperial units to the metric system also began, but here that change has been very gradual. In January 2005 speed limits and some weather data changed to metric units, but experience so far suggests that it will take a long time to divest ourselves fully of the old system. From 1972 all drawings and measurements were designated in millimetres and metres in the SI system, which officially recognises millimetres but not centimetres.

Except for those prepared in imperial units (some of which have been quoted in both systems here to ease the transition) all new dimensions quoted from this point forward are metric. There are however people who have not bothered with the metric system more than thirty years after it was officially adopted in Ireland and the equivalent imperial dimensions are often requested instead of metric ones. Also younger people who have been educated in an exclusively metric environment sometimes seek help from older colleagues about imperial dimensions, particularly the more obscure ones found in legal documents.

THE DODDER VALLEY
DRAINAGE SCHEME

Following publication of the Wright report there was intense pressure from the late 1960s onwards to provide additional drainage capacity in the areas of the county south and southwest of the city

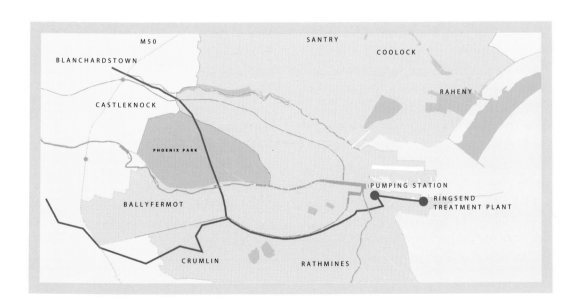

Diagram showing the Greater Dublin Drainage Scheme.

All of the city's principal sewage schemes drain into the pumping station at Ringsend and go on to receive tertiary treatment at the modern Ringsend Treatment Plant.

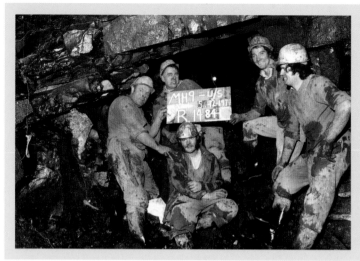

Construction of the Grand Canal Tunnel.

Built during the 1970s, this tunnel runs parallel to the canal and under its southern bank. The first full-face tunnel-boring machine ever used in Ireland was employed on this contract. Great difficulty was experienced in driving this tunnel due to the semi-fluid ground conditions.

boundary. Extensive tracts of land outside the city boundary were purchased by the corporation on which great numbers of houses would be built within a few years. Speculators when they saw what was happening also began to acquire land, starting the era of astronomical prices that prevails today.

Before the Wright report was commissioned Dublin County Council was in fact already developing a proposal for a new trunk sewer called the South Dublin Drainage Scheme along the Dodder Valley to Templeogue. An extension northwards via Greenhills was planned to drain the development occurring outwards from the city boundary along the axis of the Naas Road.

The county council undertook the South Dublin Drainage Scheme to relieve the branch sewers extending outwards from the city by intercepting the sewage from Templeogue, Rathfarnham, Ballyboden, Willbrook, Churchtown, Windy Arbour, Dundrum, Ballinteer, Roebuck and Goatstown. Often referred to simply as the Dodder Valley Drainage, this should not be confused with the former Rathmines and Pembroke sewer laid alongside the river in the 1880s.

The Dodder Valley scheme was adapted to serve the new town of Tallaght by extending the main trunk sewer westwards from Templeogue along the Dodder River to central Tallaght. Various principal

tributary sewers were laid as required to service sub-catchments, all by gravity.

Downstream of Templeogue the 1,520mm-diameter trunk sewer follows the Dodder to Mount Carmel Hospital from where it is in tunnel under Milltown Golf Course to Patrick Doyle Road (beside the Nine Arches). En route it intercepts the sewers serving the areas listed earlier, leaving Mount Merrion as the only remaining part of the southern suburbs still draining to the city sewers. A new branch sewer was laid along the then disused Harcourt Street-Bray railway (now the Luas tramway line) to serve the Churchtown area.

Because the older areas were drained on the partially separate system, it was necessary to position a storm overflow in Milltown at Patrick Doyle Road. Tallaght and the other new towns are drained on the separate system. Generally however it has been found difficult to achieve total separation of foul and storm flows and to maintain separation because house extensions are sometimes drained incorrectly, with dishwashers and washing machines mis-connected to the surface water drainage system.

From a point east of the Clonskea Road, where the Clonskea and Goatstown flows enter, the sewer was laid in open cut to a valve chamber near University Lodge. From here it continues in twin

pressure pipes 910mm and 1,370mm in diameter via Greenfield Park and Nutley Lane to the foreshore. The twin pipes then proceed parallel to Strand Road in an embankment at just over beach level to the Ringsend treatment works. The embankment provides a much-used amenity for strollers as well as car parking for beach users. The total length of the Dodder Valley interceptor is 16km, and it was completed in 1973 at a cost of £3m (€3.81m)

In what are now South County Dublin and Dun Laoghaire/Rathdown county councils, there are several interconnections with Dublin city systems. Rathcoole-Saggart (already mentioned and now connected to the Grand Canal sewer) and Mount Merrion in Dun Laoghaire/Rathdown are at present drained to the city sewer network. The large industrial estate complex at Leopardstown, together with some adjoining housing developments, is drained to Stillorgan and into the Dun Laoghaire main drainage system.

Work on the Grand Canal tunnel and all other projects carried out in the 1970s took place against a background of considerable change and unrest. Ireland became a member of the European Economic Community, as the EU was then known, on 1 January 1973. Considerable benefits were expected from membership but these took longer than hoped to filter through to all sectors of the population.

Meanwhile there were several negative forces at work throughout the 1970s and 1980s. Civil unrest and terrorism, north and south, affected the social and economic life of the country. There was considerable industrial unrest, with frequent strikes and catastrophic job losses. At the end of June 1976 unemployment was stated to be the highest since 1940 and the rate of inflation was 18%. Yet despite this unhappy scenario, work on the tunnel and associated projects proceeded.

THE GREATER DUBLIN DRAINAGE SCHEME (GDDS)

This major project was developed in parallel with the studies leading to the Myles Wright report, and underlies the proposals made in that document. The Greater Dublin Drainage Scheme (GDDS), also known as the Grand Canal Scheme, bigger and far more sophisticated than the North Dublin Drainage Scheme of only two decades earlier, caters for drainage from several major catchments. Another difference from the era of the North Dublin scheme was that industrialisation, with extensive estates of factories on a scale undreamed of in the 1950s, would have to be catered for in future. It provided for the foul drainage of three new towns, for suburban areas south of the Grand Canal and for the relief of flood-prone watercourses in the inner city area. A new main pumping station would be constructed at Ringsend and a modern sewage treatment plant built at Poolbeg.

THE GRAND CANAL TUNNEL

The key element in the Greater Dublin scheme was the provision of conduits to bring the foul drainage of the new towns of Lucan, Clondalkin and Blanchardstown through the city to Ringsend for treatment prior to discharge into the Liffey estuary, and to divert surface water from the south county area from the inner city.

Originally it was proposed to provide two pipes or culverts in open cut under the bed of the Grand Canal from Dolphin's Barn to Grand Canal Street. This proposal was vigorously opposed by those who saw it as a ploy by Dublin Corporation to close the canal permanently and use the route to form a new urban highway. It was therefore decided to drive a tunnel along this route, parallel to the canal and under the southern bank.

The 3.65m internal diameter tunnel – the same size as a London Tube – is 5km long and divided into two compartments for foul and surface water. Along its route, the tunnel intercepts foul drainage from Walkinstown, Drimnagh, Crumlin, Terenure and part of the Rathmines and Pembroke areas. The surface conduit intercepts the River Poddle and other streams and relieves flood-prone areas in Crumlin, Mount Brown, Harold's Cross, Rathmines and the south inner city. A trunk foul sewer that starts at Blackhorse Bridge runs along under Davitt Road to the head of the tunnel, which is just west of Herberton Road.

The downstream end of the tunnel is at Grand Canal Street (Maquay Bridge). From this point a short tunnel was driven to bring the surface water to the western end of the Grand Canal Basin. A high capacity siphon overflow was designed for the blind lock channel at the basin outlet, to discharge the maximum anticipated inflow within acceptable level variations. The overflow was in fact never provided and the blind lock has now been equipped as a functioning lock. The Office of Public Works, now responsible for the canal system, requires the removal for environmental reasons of the discharge from the basin, and at the time of writing it is planned to bring it directly to the Liffey through the basin and part of the former gasworks site.

A second tunnel, of 2,743mm internal diameter, was constructed from Grand Canal Street through Bath Avenue under the River Dodder at Londonbridge Road and the Ringsend housing estate to convey the foul drainage to a new main lift pumping station at Ringsend. The first full-face tunnel-boring machine ever used in Ireland was employed on this contract. Great difficulty was experienced in driving this tunnel due to the semi-fluid ground conditions. A short spur tunnel 1,500mm in diameter linked the redundant Londonbridge Road pumping station with this tunnel.

BLANCHARDSTOWN

Virtually all of Blanchardstown lies in the catchment of the River Tolka and drains by gravity to a trunk sewer laid along the riverbank from the Dublin-Meath border to Ashtown. It is prominently visible where it passes over the M50 motorway in a 1,500mm steel pipe just north of Junction 6 with the N3 (Navan Road). Foul drainage from the County Meath towns of Clonee, Dunboyne and Ashbourne enters at the head of this sewer. Prior to the construction of the Grand Canal scheme the Blanchardstown sewer formed part of the North Dublin Drainage Scheme which continued from Ashtown to Howth (Chapter 11).

At Ashtown the Blanchardstown sewer was diverted into a new line flowing south through the Phoenix Park and into the Liffey catchment. Near the Papal Cross this conduit enters a control chamber from where it continues as a twin pressure sewer across Chapelizod Road, under the Liffey

below Islandbridge Weir, through Memorial Park and then in tunnel under Con Colbert Road, the Camac, Emmet Road and the Grand Canal to discharge into the trunk sewer in Davitt Road.

LUCAN-CLONDALKIN (RONANSTOWN)

This town is partly in the Camac catchment, the remainder draining to the Liffey or its tributaries. From the end of the Grand Canal tunnel the trunk foul sewer continues west along Dolphin Road and Davitt Road to meet the 1,800mm sewer from Blanchardstown. At the western end of Davitt Road, the sewer is in the Lansdowne valley where the flow from Drimnagh enters. It continues to the Naas Road where the 450mm Greenhills and 750mm Ballymount lines join. The latter sewer drains Walkinstown and the Kingswood area of Tallaght. The trunk sewer then leaves the Naas Road to follow the Camac valley to Yellowmeadows, near Clondalkin. At this point the flow from the old Clondalkin sewage works was diverted into it.

A 750mm branch sewer crosses under the canal and runs northwards to the watershed with the Liffey near the Liffey Valley shopping centre. Two sub-catchments are pumped to this point from pumping stations at Quarryvale and Johnstown. Just north of the canal crossing another principal branch sewer runs west along the north bank of the canal to near the Ninth Lock and then north-westwards to the head of the Camac catchment at Ballyowen, where the flow from Lucan joins. A major pumping station at Esker, near Lucan, pumps the foul flows from the portion of Ronanstown that lies in the Liffey catchment. Two main sewers from the Ballyowen and Griffeen sub-catchments flow directly to the Esker station which also receives the flow relayed to it from the Lucan low-level station. The latter serves Lucan village and the areas along and west of the Lucan-Peamount road.

From Yellowmeadows the main interceptor continues to the Ninth Lock road to drain the areas south of the canal along the Nangor Road. It finally extends along the Camac River to pick up the Citywest development and the towns of Saggart and Rathcoole which have been linked in since 2002.

MV Seamróg II. *This 450-ton vessel replaced the original TSS Shamrock. Registered on 23 December 1958, the Seamróg remained in service until 1984, when it was sold for use as a barge.*

THE NEW MAIN LIFT PUMPING STATION

The Main Lift pumping station, which replaced the original plant commissioned in 1906, is one of the largest foul sewage pumping stations in Europe. It has a maximum capacity of 323 million gallons (1.468 million litres) per day, serving an ultimate population of 708,000 people. The station, a circular building 25,800mm in overall diameter and 15,500mm deep, derives its shape from the circular cofferdam used to construct the underground pumping chamber. Great difficulty due to ground-water was experienced in its construction. The original cofferdam was deepened in an unsuccessful attempt to achieve sufficient cut-off. Finally a 30-metre deep slurry trench was installed and the inlet and screening chambers were constructed by diaphragm walling. The station was commissioned in July 1985 after a delay of four years and a 100% cost overrun.

After coarse screening the combined flows from the diverted Rathmines and Pembroke system and the city centre pass directly to the pumps, which deliver to a high level gallery. Six pump sets are installed, four rated at 34m³/sec and two at 1.7m³/sec. From the gallery the flow passes to the new treatment works at the Pigeonhouse through a pair of 2,290mm diameter inverted siphons.

Ringsend pumping station has its own standby electricity generating station. The equipment consists of three diesel driven Duvant generators, each rated at 1,400 KVA, speed 1,500 rpm, the engines being V16s. The generating station is on a piled foundation and is acoustically treated to limit the external noise level. This and the other buildings in the complex are of a high architectural standard.

TRAGEDY AT RINGSEND

Following the commissioning of the new Main Lift pumping station, consideration was given to the future of its predecessor, the external appearance of which was very different to that it presented in 1906. The change was caused by the events of 10 February 1969 when the worst accident in the history of the city drainage division occurred.

The Dublin Gas Company at that time was using naphtha, a dangerously volatile substance, in the production of town gas. Following an unreported overflow from the naphtha tank near the Grand Canal tidal locks, a quantity of naphtha found its way into the sewers during the early hours. It travelled to Ringsend, escaping into a staff room at the main pumping station. William Dixon, the fitter in charge at the station, evacuated his three colleagues (James Beggs, Larry Gilmore and Joseph Murphy) when they all complained of feeling ill.

At around 6.15 a.m. just after Joseph Murphy had returned to retrieve his coat there was a massive explosion (possibly triggered by a spark from an electric switch) which demolished most of the building and its 120-foot chimney. Joseph Murphy was buried in the rubble and died later in hospital from extensive burns and blast injuries. Two fire brigade officers, Colin Smart and Christy Brennan, were injured. The tragedy at Ringsend was one of those incidents that led to the introduction of strictly codified safety standards in the drainage service

The pumping station, a fine example of early twentieth-century industrial architecture, was repaired. However because of financial restraints and the strong likelihood of its early replacement, its architectural features were not reinstated. Eventually, following fruitless efforts to find a use for the building, it was demolished in the 1990s. Had its character not been destroyed in 1969 it would probably have been listed for preservation as one of Dublin's few Edwardian public service brick structures.

RINGSEND TREATMENT WORKS

The sewage treatment works provided at Ringsend as part of the 1906 drainage scheme has been described in Chapter 7. The addition of the new towns to its catchment required that additional treatment be provided, and the modernisation of the works was also overdue. In 1970 it was generally

MV Sir Joseph Bazalgette. *Built in 1963 with a capacity of 2,000 tonnes, this vessel was acquired from the Thames Water Authority for a very reasonable £250,000 in 1983. It was already named after the eminent engineer who had a close connection with Dublin's 1906 Main Drainage Scheme.*

accepted that primary treatment alone was adequate where large dilution was available for the effluent in estuarine or coastal waters.

A basic plan for the Ringsend works provided for coarse screening followed by grit removal and primary sedimentation in horizontal flow clarifiers. The primary sludge would be thickened by gravity and stored prior to removal to a marine disposal area by tanker. Flows in excess of three times dry weather flow would be diverted to the old works which would, after refurbishment, function as storm tanks. This refurbishment was delayed because of the restraints on capital spending in the 1980s and it was eventually overtaken by events.

The construction of the new works took place in two phases – each providing six clarifiers – and included a new administration building with staff facilities, a laboratory and a lecture room. A new workshop and stores were also built. A new jetty was constructed, designed to accommodate a 1,000-ton tanker to replace the 450-ton *Seamróg II*, by now of inadequate capacity and due for retirement.

The appropriately named *Sir Joseph Bazalgette* (more fully described in Chapter 15) replaced the *Seamróg II*.

The new Ringsend works provided preliminary treatment to serve a population of about one million, including effluent from Dun Laoghaire which was pumped across the bay to join the Dodder Valley flow at the inlet to the works. The suspended solids and Biochemical Oxygen Demand (BOD) content of the effluent were reduced by 50% and 25% respectively and the former grossly offensive pollution along the Great South Wall was terminated.

DUBLIN COUNTY COUNCIL DRAINAGE SYSTEMS

In the 1950s the South Dublin Drainage Scheme was undertaken by Dublin County Council to alleviate flooding in the Carysfort and Blackrock areas. The Brewery and Priory streams were intercepted and re-routed to join the Deansgrange stream at the Kill Lane-Clonkeen Road intersection.

Part of the diversion was in a tunnel through the St John of God lands.

The county council made independent provision for the foul drainage of various towns and villages, for example Donabate/Portrane, Lusk, Rush, Skerries, Balbriggan, Swords and Malahide in the area north of the Liffey now called Fingal. These self-contained systems are not connected to the city networks and are therefore outside the scope of this history. The impact of large-scale speculative building in the ten years 1967–1976 was felt sharply in these smaller centres; they developed rapidly to the limit of local drainage capacity, whether determined by the treatment works or the receiving waters.

From what are now South County Dublin and Dun Laoghaire/Rathdown county councils there are several connections with the Dublin city drainage system. Rathcoole-Saggart in the South Dublin County Council area (already mentioned and now connected to the Grand Canal sewer) and Stepaside in the Dun Laoghaire/Rathdown area both drain into the city sewer network.

DUN LAOGHAIRE DRAINAGE: BULLOCH INTERCEPTOR SEWER AND OUTFALL

Postwar housing developments, particularly in the Glenageary area, caused overloading of the Glasthule drainage system which resulted in the pollution of the sea at Scotsman's Bay. The then Dun Laoghaire Borough Corporation therefore engaged the consulting engineering firm John Taylor & Sons to advise on the matter in the 1950s. The resulting scheme involved the construction of an interceptor culvert along the foreshore from Newtownsmith to Sandycove. The culvert was extended in tunnel under Sandycove Point and along the foreshore to Bulloch Harbour. Here a screening station and sea outfall were constructed to the seaward side of the harbour. Float surveys were carried out to determine the optimum location, length and depth of the outfall. The pumping plant at Eden Road, which had heretofore lifted the sewage to the sewer constructed along the Metals in

the 1890s, was decommissioned and the flow was diverted to this new sea outfall and away from the West Pier.

The Bulloch culvert was designed as a 'tank sewer' which stored the discharge and released it on the falling tide. The screened effluent was discharged through a tidal flap valve via a 4,600mm long outfall pipe into deep water. The 42-inch diameter outfall pipe was duplicated to cater for discharging the high storm flows over a weir that bypassed the screens. The mechanically raked screenings were passed by conveyor through a macerator chamber and delivered back into the effluent upstream of the screens. Drainage from the Dalkey area was also collected into the Bulloch system, although the small direct foul discharges to the sea in the Coliemore remained.

FOXROCK-KILLINEY
JOINT DRAINAGE SCHEME

A few centres of development in the south county such as Foxrock and Loughlinstown had small sewage works discharging to local watercourses. In the late 1950s the county area south of Foxrock and the Killiney-Ballybrack district in Dun Laoghaire began to experience pressure for the development of housing estates as the areas nearer to the city were becoming fully developed. Dublin County Council therefore decided to provide, jointly with Dun Laoghaire Borough Corporation, a drainage scheme to facilitate development of the districts of Foxrock, Cornelscourt, Cabinteely, Deansgrange, Loughlinstown, Ballybrack and Shankill. The consulting engineering firm P. H. McCarthy was engaged to examine the drainage requirements in the Deansgrange Stream catchment area of the south-east county. The resulting scheme provided for the construction of a small sewage treatment works near the mouth of the Shanganagh River together with a tank sewer in the valley of the Deansgrange Stream to cater for development in the Ballybrack, Johnstown, Cornelscourt and Foxrock areas.

About the same time, the South Dublin Drainage

Scheme was undertaken by Dublin County Council to alleviate flooding in the Carysfort and Blackrock areas. The Brewery and Priory Streams were intercepted and re-routed to join the Deansgrange Stream at the Kill Lane-Clonkeen Road. Part of the diversion was constructed in tunnel through the St John of God lands. The capacity of the Deansgrange Stream was improved around the same time and it was culverted under what is now Kilbogget Park to facilitate the provision of adjoining landfill sites for Dun Laoghaire and Dublin County Council. In the 1970s the Carrickmines Stream was culverted to provide a similar facility at Ballyogan when the Kilbogget facility became exhausted.

THE SHANGANAGH OUTFALL WORKS

Commencing at Deansgrange a trunk sewer was laid along the route of the Deansgrange Stream and Shanganagh River to the outfall of the Loughlinstown River into the sea. Here a sewage works provided primary treatment in a set of three horizontal clarifiers before discharge through a short submarine outfall. A second main sewer was laid running northwards to the treatment works from Shankill.

Rapid development took place in the catchment during the 1960s and it became obvious that the sewage works was now coping with a multiple of its design capacity, estimated at 70,000 by 1970. Subsequent development in the county area caused overloading of the joint treatment works and in 1972 Dublin County Council commissioned John Taylor & Sons to submit proposals to remedy the situation. The council accepted the consultants' proposals in 1975 and approval in principle was received from the Department of Local Government in 1977.

The treatment works was abandoned and the effluent was discharged through a 1.86 km-long sea outfall to Killiney Bay by way of a new inlet works equipped with communitors and grit removal plant. A new pumping station was also constructed to enable the effluent to be discharged at high tide. This had enough capacity for the ultimate develop-

ment of the catchment and was designed to disperse the untreated discharge so as to achieve acceptable bacterial standards along the shoreline. In the absence of any long-term planning objectives for the catchment it was assumed for design purposes that it would develop from the shoreline to the steeper foothills of the Dublin Mountains and accommodate a population of about 200,000. Provision was made for discharging storm flows through holding tanks, which were part of the previous treatment works, and through a short outfall at the southern end of Killiney beach.

In the former Killiney-Ballybrack area much of the original development concentrated on septic tank drainage. Before the Second World War, however, part of Ballybrack appears to have drained to the Deansgrange Stream where it is culverted under the Shanganagh Road. In addition some developments in the coastal area extending southwards from Killiney Village were served by sewers and combined drains which discharged foul and surface water to the sea at Killiney beach. Dun Laoghaire Corporation engaged the firm of P. H. McCarthy to prepare a small local drainage scheme to deal with these untreated discharges. An interceptor sewer was laid which collects the majority of the effluent into a pumping station on the beach near Killiney railway station. A small supplementary interceptor and pumping station serves the south end of the beach. Both pumping stations now discharge to the Shanganagh outfall works through a sewer in Seafield Road.

Dun Laoghaire/Rathdown County Council inherited the Carrickmines to Shanganagh drainage scheme when the new local authorities came into being in 1994. Pressures for development in the Ballyogan area had resulted in a temporary drainage arrangement, with pumping stations at Merville and Cabinteely relaying the sewage to the trunk main in the Shanganagh valley. Existing plans were revised 'in house' and Mulcair Contractors commenced work in March 1996. A revised and accelerated construction programme saw the works substantially completed by December in the same year. About six

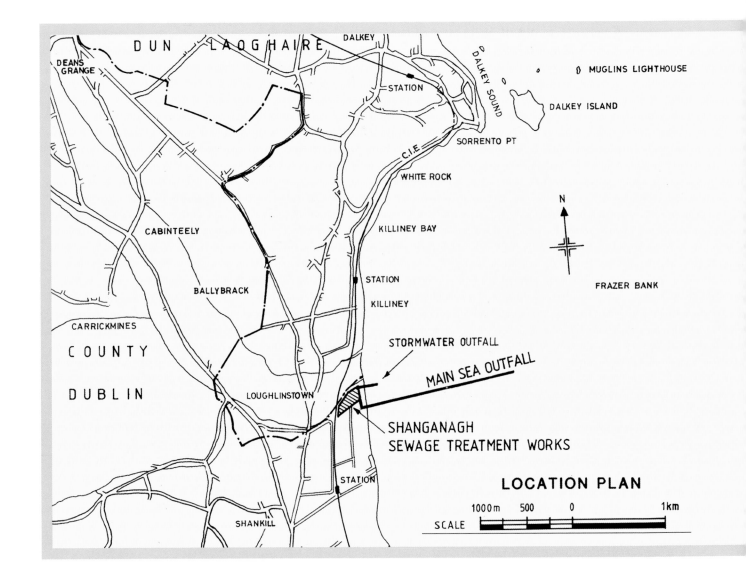

Diagram showing the Shanganagh Outfall Works. *Originally, a trunk sewer was laid along the route of the Deansgrange stream and Shanganagh River to the outfall of the Loughlinstown River into the sea. This system was substantially up-graded during the 1970s.*

kilometres of trunk sewers varying from 525 to 1,200mm in diameter were laid. The scheme included pipe-jacking under the railway line at Shanganagh and under the N1 roadway, the Cherrywood Road and the Carrickmines River at Loughlinstown. The scheme provided for the proposed new developments in the Carrickmines River catchment and the elimination of the unsatisfactory temporary pumping station at Merville, Ballyogan. A branch to Cabinteely Park along the line of the St Brigid's Stream permitted decommissioning of the temporary pumping station at that location.

At the end of 2004 design work was in progress on the proposed new waste water treatment works at Shanganagh to provide full treatment and comply with the EU Urban Waste Water Directive and work was expected to begin early in 2006. This scheme also provides for collecting the untreated discharge through the sea outfall at Bray and pumping it approximately five kilometres along the coastline to Shanganagh. The combined works will cater for a population of between 150,000 and 200,000 as estimated in 1970 and when completed will be one of the largest treatment plants in the country.

DUN LAOGHAIRE DRAINAGE
IMPROVEMENT SCHEME

The current Dun Laoghaire Drainage Scheme dates back to the 1960s when new developments and catchment expansion caused overloading of the nineteenth century drainage system described in Chapter 6. This gave rise to overflows of untreated sewage to the foreshore at Williamstown and Blackrock and to the deterioration of water quality at the popular local sea bathing area at Seapoint due to overloading of the West Pier system. The consulting engineering firm P. H. McCarthy was employed by the then Dun Laoghaire Corporation to advise on the subject.

The consultants proposed an additional Blackrock interceptor sewer to relieve the nineteenth-century system and to divert sewage from the Booterstown and Blackrock areas directly to the West Pier. It was also proposed to construct a new and larger tidal holding tank and a longer sea outfall at this location. The interceptor sewer extends from Upper Booterstown Avenue via Cross Avenue and Mount Merrion Avenue to the Rock Road. It continues along the line of the Blackrock Bypass and on to Seapoint Avenue via a tunnel under Temple Hill. It then passes along Seapoint Avenue through the Beach Gardens and crosses under the railway to the east of Salthill station.

The Blackrock interceptor sewer, together with several small pumping stations and collector sewers recommended by the consultants, was completed in 1972. A temporary pumping station was provided at the West Pier to lift the effluent into the existing tidal holding tank. When approving the scheme, however, the Department of Local Government omitted the new holding tank and outfall pipe proposed by the consultants.

During the 1970s Dun Laoghaire Corporation and Dublin County Council undertook a joint scheme which drained parts of Mount Merrion and Blackrock to the Dun Laoghaire system. Concern was being voiced with increasing frequency about the worsening coastal pollution caused by the

Shanganagh Treatment Works.
The modern treatment works were developed by Dun Laoghaire Borough Council during the 1970s to cater for a rapidly-growing population.

growing volume of sewage discharging from an expanding catchment that had been considerably extended into the county council area. In addition, during adverse weather conditions, a number of serious pollution incidents arose along the adjacent Salthill to Seapoint beach, giving rise to considerable public disquiet. The consultants were therefore asked in the early 1980s to re-examine the West Pier arrangements.

Three options were considered, two of which involved sea outfalls and the third proposed pumping the sewage to the Dublin Corporation treatment works at Ringsend. This option, which was not the cheapest, was accepted by the council, agreed by Dublin Corporation, approved by the Department of the Environment – and implemented. In the light of a future EU directive prohibiting the discharge of untreated sewage, this proved to be a very significant decision. Later, in the mid-1980s, this brief was extended to cover the elimination of the discharges at Bulloch and at the smaller Coliemore outfall.

This scheme in the South Bay area proved to be the template for the elimination of local untreated foul discharges to the sea. Subsequently, following an environmental study and recommendations for cleaning up the Bay, the Ringsend waste water treatment works (WWTW) was modernised and the discharge of untreated sewage through the Howth outfall eliminated. Like the Dun Laoghaire scheme in the South Bay, the Howth effluent is now pumped across the North Bay from Sutton to Ringsend for full treatment (Chapter 13).

All this happened against a background of heightened environmental awareness and an increasing realisation of the need to protect water resources. The 1975 Council Directive Concerning the Quality of Bathing Water and the 1977 Water Pollution Act gave local authorities new powers, responsibilities and standards in relation to water pollution control. Subsequently the 1991 Council Directive Concerning Urban Waste Water Treatment made it mandatory to treat all significant sewage flows before discharge to waters. The result is that existing sewage discharges through sea outfall pipelines now require appropriate land-based treatment. Simple and cheap 'marine treatment' of crude sewage is no longer an option!

Detailed design of the first phase of the Dun Laoghaire Drainage Improvement Scheme, consisting of separate contracts for the West Pier pumping station and the marine pumping main connecting it to the Ringsend treatment works, was approved in 1988. Walls/Dutch Dredging JV commenced construction in the spring of 1989 on the 940mm-diameter, 7 kilometres steel pumping main across Dublin Bay. A suction dredger excavated a wide trench, on average 3.5 metres deep, into the seabed

and in water up to 11 metres deep. The excavated material was deposited about 100 metres away and parallel to the trench by means of a floating pipeline. The operation continued night and day with three crews working 12-hour shifts.

While the pipes were being manufactured and coated in Germany and Holland, assembly areas were being prepared at both the West Pier and Ringsend. When delivered, the 12-metre pipe lengths were welded together in strings at the assembly areas and moved into the trench by a pulling barge which only stopped working to allow each successive string to be joined and protected. About one-third of the pipes were pulled from the West Pier and the remainder from the Ringsend assembly area and the ends of the pipelines were joined by divers. The excavated seabed material was collected and replaced over the pipeline by the suction dredger.

On completion of the pipeline, Uniform Construction began its work on the new West Pier pumping station. This contract included the refurbishment of the tidal holding tank and sea outfall to provide storm flow balancing and an emergency overflow. As part of this scheme the end of the

Diagram showing Dun Laoghaire Drainage system.

This was created during the 1960s when new developments and catchment expansion caused overloading of the nineteenth-century drainage system.

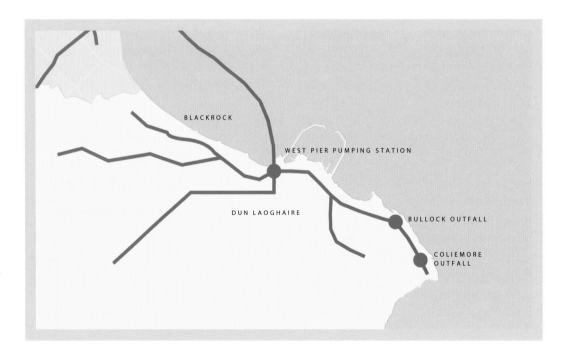

old sea outfall is marked by a navigation buoy. Also included in this contract was the laying of a 2,100mm-diameter pipeline under the adjoining railway lines with minimal headroom. This was achieved by building a support structure under the track ballast while each line was closed, removed and reinstated between midnight and 9.00 a.m. on successive Sundays. This subsequently allowed the trench to be tunnelled, the pipe laid and surrounded with concrete while the twin rail lines remained in operation.

THE WEST PIER PUMPING STATION

Because of its prominent location special care was taken in the conception and detailed design of the West Pier pumping station which houses the screening and odour control plants together with the wet and dry pumping wells. Air and gases, treated by ozone and scrubbing, pass out through stainless steel roof-top louvres, which also admit fresh air. Three variable speed pumps are installed, one duty, one assist and one standby, each capable of delivering 800 litres per second and powered by 185 Kw motors. All air from possible odorous areas where potentially dangerous gases could arise is collected and passed through an ozone treatment and scrubbing plant. Expelled air passes out of, and fresh air passes in through, the stainless steel roof-top louvres.

The three square buildings, with pyramidal roofs and linking blocks with flat roofs, reflect the form and function of the L shaped substructure. Against the background of Dublin Bay the deeply overhanging roof structures appear to float on the lighter-coloured building, which is faced with Wicklow granite. The consultant architect of these much-admired structures was Paul O'Toole, who received the 1991 Sunday Independent/Irish Life Arts Award for his work on the project. A ceramic artistic work by Hugh Lorigan symbolising the function of the drainage scheme is exhibited in the entrance lobby of the pumping station.

The pumping plant was commissioned in April 1991, ending the daily discharge to the marine environment of the untreated sewage from a population of 55,000. As a result of the elimination of the West Pier discharge there was a significant improvement in the quality of the bathing water in the South Bay area. It has consequently been possible in most years to satisfy the stringent water quality standards required before a Blue Flag may be flown at Seapoint. The cost of this phase of the drainage scheme was £15m.

Drainage from other sea outfalls at Bulloch and Coliemore harbours, catering for 15,000 and a few hundred people respectively, was provided for in the design of the West Pier station. Bulloch Harbour was connected to the West Pier station in June 2000 and at the time of writing Coliemore was expected to follow in the near future.

EASTERN INTERCEPTOR SEWER

The second phase of the Dun Laoghaire Drainage Improvement Scheme was to eliminate the Bulloch outfall and also to make provision to end the Coliemore discharge. An eastern interceptor sewer was laid to collect and divert to the West Pier approximately 80% of the flows discharging through the Bulloch outfall. Flows from the Dalkey area, which could not be intercepted, were collected into a new pumping station at Bulloch and transferred to the eastern interceptor sewer at Newtownsmith through a pumping main laid within the existing Bulloch Culvert.

Sorensen Engineering carried out the Bulloch Culvert works. The culvert, which was cracked in places, thereby allowing the ingress of seawater, was cleaned out and repaired. A plastic rising main was inserted, the internal dimensions being carefully measured and the annulus grouted to enclose the rising main. This work was all carried out in a live sewer subject to high storm flows.

The interceptor sewer extends from the former Ibex Works on Dunleary Road along the seafront and through Glasthule to Castlepark Road. It was conceived as a 'tank sewer' to store the large volume

**Dun Laoghaire
Pumping Station.**
*The modern West Pier
Pumping Station was
built for Dun Laoghaire-
Rathdown County
Council by Uniform
Construction.*

of surface water which enters the drainage system
every time it rains. This additional capacity is
necessary because the pumping plant at the West
Pier was not designed to deal with the great
variation in the rate of flow on such occasions. The
depth at which the sewer is laid along the chosen
seafront route, and the need to minimise traffic
diversions and disruption to local residents,
required that the construction would be in tunnel
in this area.

During the design stage a major site investigation
was undertaken along the proposed line of the
sewer from near the West Pier to Castlepark Road.
This established the nature of the ground and in
particular the depth and character of the underlying
rock, together with the location of underground
services. Blasting trials were carried out to study
ground vibrations in order to assess the feasibility of
controlled drilling and blasting as a method of
tunnel excavation. The consultants put considerable
effort into the detailed design and geotechnical
engineering issues during the preparation of the
contract documents. Among the sensitivities that
had to be taken into account while implanting
this major engineering works were the heavily

trafficked nature of the urban area, the proximity
of the DART rail line, period dwellings and essential
utility services.

The contract was awarded to Ascon and satisfactory arrangements were concluded with local
residents and other interests for blasting. Twelve
tunnel shafts were sunk to facilitate the construction
of some 1,800 metres of tunnel in two sections
which vary in diameter from 1,200 to 2,100mm.
Coleman Tunnelling assisted Ascon in this work.
The rate of progress was determined by the need to
limit the blasting effects on the DART and adjacent
buildings and services. The safety and security of
the railway was a major issue requiring procedures
to be agreed with Irish Rail that confined blasting
to specific times. The effects were all carefully
recorded, monitored and successfully controlled
and no significant damage occurred. All dwellings
along the route were independently surveyed in
advance of blasting and any defects were noted
and photographed and copies of the reports were
supplied to the owners.

The project team recognised that the use of
explosives would give rise to a certain amount of
public disquiet and complaint and it was decided to

adopt a policy of complete transparency throughout. Before blasting commenced an information circular was distributed to all local residents and meetings were held with community groups. A written log of all complaints and follow-up actions was maintained. In general, good co-operation was received from the public and most issues were resolved quickly as a result of following the positive public relations policy adopted. Virtually identical procedures were followed by Dublin City Council on the North Fringe Sewer Project (Chapter 13).

Work began in June 1995 and was completed early in 1998. The entire length of tunnel has a secondary concrete lining to provide a smooth finish. Extensive relaying and repairing of existing sewers, conversion of the former Board of Works culvert into a surface water sewer which now discharges at the back of the West Pier, and diversions

of flows into the interceptor sewer, were all part of the contract.

Bulloch pumping station was constructed by Clonmel Enterprises on the site of the screening station, work being finished in 1999. The refurbished culvert provides storage for storm water and the outfalls are used as emergency overflows. The new station was designed by Paul O'Connor to compliment its surroundings. On completion of the Bulloch work, the discharge into the sea of effluent from a population of approximately 16,000 ceased.

Detailed design of the next phase of the scheme was in progress early in 2005. This will eliminate the sewage discharge at Coliemore Harbour and other minor outfalls in the area. When this work is implemented the regular discharge of untreated sewage to the marine environment in the south Dublin Bay area will have ceased.

13 New Boundaries and Major Projects

NEW COUNCILS AND BOUNDARIES

A momentous change in the pattern of local government in Dublin city and county was initiated in June 1986. Extensive boundary changes transferred Howth, Sutton and Baldoyle from the corporation area to that of the county council. At the same time the city became responsible for extra territory along the north fringe, including Ballymun, Priorswood and Darndale. On the south side, areas such as Rathfarnham beyond the Dodder went to the county council, the corporation taking over some additional districts to the southwest. The overall result was the first reduction in the area of the city in Dublin's history.

The administrative changes of the 1980s took place in a very unhappy period for the people of Ireland. Terrorism continued on its murderous and destructive course in an unstable political atmosphere during a decade that saw no fewer than five general elections. Unemployment was rife and emigration levels were horrific, with young people leaving the country in droves. There were reports that in some rural parishes it had become impossible to assemble a football team and television news bulletins routinely showed bleak family partings at sea and air ports.

The Irish pound, which had been floated in 1979, was worth only 78 pence sterling in January 1981 and by September inflation had reached 20%. At that time the Republic was, unsurprisingly, regarded as one of the most disadvantaged areas in Europe. The country was crippled by interest repayments on foreign loans and taxation was a particularly sore subject, as it would continue to be into the 1990s. Workers were accused of living beyond their means and bore a constantly growing burden of the taxes needed to finance government programmes. The savage cuts in public services introduced in 1987 were accompanied by a pay agreement under which the workers, who bore the brunt of every cut and thrust of financial policy, put the economy on the road to recovery. The pace of change from a primarily agricultural economy to an industrial one also quickened during this period.

Conditions generally improved during the 1990s and led to the more affluent country that we know today. Financial and social changes on a scale never before experienced saw improvements in some public services, including water and drainage, being tackled more radically. Reorganisation became an imperative during the decade of the successful nineties. It took time to reorganise various services and assign responsibilities for those that served two or more local authorities. The final stages of a prolonged reorganisation process took place on 1 January 1994 when Dublin County Council ceased to exist and three new local authorities came into being. What was previously the north of the county came under the control of the new Fingal County Council, which established its headquarters in Swords. The western portion of the county south of the city area was henceforth to be managed by South Dublin County Council, with headquarters in Tallaght. The south-eastern portion of the erstwhile county was amalgamated with the borough of Dun Laoghaire to form Dun Laoghaire-Rathdown County Council, having for its head office the former town hall in Marine Road, Dun Laoghaire.

When the new councils finally came into being the boundaries originally proposed in 1986 were modified slightly to take cognisance of contemporary developments and in the light of experience. At the time of writing the newest event as far as the city is concerned was the change of name from Dublin Corporation to Dublin City Council on 1 January 2002. This was one of several initiatives, including the division of the city into five areas, intended to deliver better local government and raise the standards of public service. The programme of reorganisation was fully implemented by 2003.

Widespread alterations to the local government structures were accompanied by significant changes in the functions and titles of senior officers during the transitional years from 1986 to 1994. Kevin O'Donnell, who had been chief engineer (Sanitary Services) since 1971, retired in 1991 and was succeeded by James Fenwick, whose role and title changed two years later in 1993 when he became city engineer, a post revived to cover all functions for the first time since 1967. He retired in 1997 and was succeeded by Michael Phillips. Each of the other three local authorities in the Dublin area now has its own autonomous engineering organisation.

The creation of the new councils necessitated the formation of a self-contained management structure for each of the four local authorities. In 1996 Frank Feely retired and was succeeded as city manager by John Fitzgerald, who had been county manager in South Dublin since its establishment. The management structure of the city council has evolved since 1994 and the water and drainage divisions currently have Matt Twomey as assistant city manager, with Con Coll as executive manager. The same team are also responsible for Planning and Waste Disposal.

At the time of writing, the city engineer, Michael Phillips, has six deputy city engineers, who are responsible for particular services, and each one manages several sections dealing with specialised functions. Brian Smyth and Bartholomew White are in charge, respectively, of the water and drainage divisions, while Tom Leahy, Tim Brick (roads) and Kieran O'Sullivan (roads and traffic) are the other deputy city engineers. The sixth post is vacant.

THE DUBLIN BAY PROJECT AND THE ENVIRONMENT

During the nineteenth century – and well into the twentieth – the vast majority of citizens struggled with poverty, malnutrition and disease in appalling living conditions. Care for the environment was a concept they would never have heard of or understood, let alone worried about. As factories were established and sewers laid, therefore, Dublin's rivers were widely regarded as convenient conduits into which sewage or other waste matter could be discharged. And, although the 1906 main drainage scheme ameliorated pollution in the Liffey, it did not improve the problem in Dublin Bay which was already taking untreated sewage from the Rathmines and Pembroke outfall at Whitebanks and from several other places around its coastline.

Like the rivers up to 1906 the bay and the sea beyond it were regarded as open depositories, not only for sewage but also for waste of every description. Prior to 1907 much of Dublin's refuse was barged out to a sea discharge in a manner very similar to that applied to sewage sludge until 1999.

Several public bodies exercised some degree of authority over the bay but none had overall responsibility – nor did they seem to care – for its wellbeing.

Shortly after the completion of the Howth outfall in the late 1950s, awareness of everybody's accountability for the welfare of our natural environment began to slowly dawn. In the 1970s and 1980s, as more intensive industrialisation proceeded, concern escalated into anger. Increasingly critical and more frequent articles and letters appeared in the newspapers and those who were worried about the environment regularly confronted various public bodies and commercial interests. The deepening environmental consciousness as more and more people became better informed resulted in an almost universal acceptance of Dublin Bay as a pre-eminent natural amenity.

Dublin Bay is a unique resource for more than a million people who live in the greater Dublin area. More than half of this population is believed to enjoy the amenities of the bay every year, engaging in swimming or water sports, or simply walking along its shores and beaches.

Full compliance with best practice by all concerned is essential to the preservation and enhancement of this wonderful gift of nature. Many pollution and environmental control measures are already in operation and these are reinforced by EU directives. Minimum requirements in every aspect of environmental care will inevitably be raised to higher levels in the future in the light of experience and new research. Visual standards are also improved whenever possible; the relocation underground of the formerly very obtrusive north Dublin pumping station at Kilbarrack is an example.

An early benefit arising from the interim arrangements at Ringsend was the disappearance of the former Rathmines and Pembroke untreated drainage outfall at Whitebanks. This was diverted to the Ringsend treatment works, and Londonbridge Road pumping station became redundant, closing in 1985 after 104 years of service. Another, very different, development of this period concerned the former station superintendent's house at Londonbridge Road. This attractive Victorian building, unoccupied for some time and badly vandalised, was thoroughly restored and returned to use as a residence.

SUTTON-RINGSEND SUBMARINE PIPELINE

The untreated Howth sea outfall of 1958 was the final and most unpleasant feature of the North Dublin drainage network. It certainly did not, and could not, comply with the EU Urban Wastewater Treatment Directive which demanded a standard for secondary treatment. One of the biggest drainage schemes tackled in the Dublin area for many years was planned to eliminate this nuisance. A number of alternatives were considered, including treatment works at Sutton and Howth, but these were not taken up, a Sutton-Ringsend pipeline going to the existing treatment works being chosen as the best option. From the end of the roadside embankment or promenade opposite St Fintan's School at Sutton the North Dublin trunk line was to be diverted to a new pumping station beside the DART line, adjacent to Tramway Court. A submarine pipeline was designed to take the sewage from there across to Ringsend treatment works.

The 10.5km Sutton-Ringsend submarine pipeline, which is 1.4m in diameter and weighs 25,000 tonnes, was laid during the summer of 2001. Despite the discovery of an uncharted seventeenth-century shipwreck and bad weather conditions, the work was completed on time. Dublin City Council protected the site of the shipwreck and the pipeline trench was re-aligned to bypass it.

Pipe pulling began in August 2001 when two massive barges, led by the *Jimmie Mac*, began hauling the future conduit from the Ringsend foreshore. The pipeline was prefabricated in twenty-five strings on the site at Ringsend. Dredgers had excavated two million cubic metres of sand earlier in the summer to make a deep trench along the sewer's route, which traversed

the shipping channels that serve Dublin Port.

Steel wires were attached to a pull-head at the front of the concrete-coated steel pipes in order to winch the pipe necklace along the bottom of the pre-dredged trench over to the Sutton foreshore. The process stopped every 384 metres for a new string to be welded on. Working around the clock during the most propitious hours on either side of high tides, the next 384m string was welded to the end of the pipe at the shore and was, in turn, pulled into the trench at high tide. This continued until all twenty-five strings were connected and the pipeline stretched the whole way from Ringsend to Sutton. The contractor for the Dublin Bay pipeline was the Pierse, McAlpine and Tideway consortium.

Ringsend treatment works remained largely unaltered from its 1906 inauguration until the 1970s when a complete new plant was built on the opposite side of the road. This new wastewater treatment plant has superseded the interim arrangements described in Chapter 12. The new complex provides primary, secondary and tertiary treatment for rainwater, sewage and other effluents. The treated matter is converted into three products: Biofert, a high grade agricultural fertiliser; Biogas to supply 60% of the plant's energy needs; and clean water in Dublin Bay.

The preliminary and primary treatment system, which began operating in March 2001, provides 6mm screening. FOGG (an acronym for fat, oil, grit

Ringsend Treatment Plant. *Opened in 2003, this is a key part of the Dublin Bay Project, Europe's largest waste-water treatment scheme. It cost €300 million, was financed by the EU Cohesion Fund and is managed by Dublin City Council.*

**Sutton-Ringsend
Submarine Pipeline.**
*This pipeline, which is
10.5km in length, 1.4m
in diameter and weighs
25,000 tonnes, was laid
during the summer
of 2001. Dublin City
Council protected the
site of an uncharted
seventeenth-century
shipwreck, which was
discovered during
construction, and the
pipeline trench was
re-aligned to bypass it.*

and grease) is removed in aerated tanks and sludge
is taken out in lamella-equipped primary tanks. In
addition, twenty-four secondary treatment tanks
remove organic material and nitrogen from the
settled wastewater which then undergoes ultraviolet
disinfection during the bathing season (May-
September) before discharge to Dublin Bay. These
tanks operate on a 'fill and draw' basis, as did the
tanks of the 1906 scheme, and are believed to be the
largest aggregate of such tanks yet constructed.

The Dublin Bay Project, Europe's biggest wastewater treatment scheme, includes the Ringsend
treatment works, Sutton pumping station and the
submarine pipeline. It cost €300m, was financed by
the EU Cohesion Fund and is managed by Dublin

City Council. It benefits Dublin city and the greater
Dublin area generally, including Dun Laoghaire,
west Dublin, the airport and parts of Meath county.
Contributions to the project costs were also made
by the Department of the Environment, Heritage
and Local Government, and by industry on the
'polluter pays' principle.

Dublin City Council operates a comprehensive
and continuous water monitoring programme at its
central laboratory in Marrowbone Lane. This
involves chemical and bacteriological analysis of
water samples to ensure that drinking water quality
meets the highest national and EU standards. It also
monitors the quality of bathing water, river water
and trade effluent discharged to the sewer system.

The laboratory, which is accredited by the Irish National Accreditation Board, performs around 300,000 tests every year. Samples from the Liffey Estuary and offshore waters are continuously taken and analysed.

Lord Mayor Dermot Lacey and Taoiseach Bertie Ahern formally opened the Ringsend wastewater treatment works – a design, build and operate venture – on 30 June 2003. ABA, a consortium of Ascon, Black & Veatch and Anglian Water, designed and built the plant. ABA is responsible for operation of the works for twenty years; this includes the sludge drying plant which had been designed and built by Swiss Combi Technology as an advance contract to enable dumping at sea to cease in the year 1999 in accordance with EU directives.

THE NORTH FRINGE SEWER

The North Dublin Drainage Scheme, more than adequate when constructed in the 1950s, was in time overwhelmed by the sheer volume of new and unforeseen development adjoining its catchment area. Despite several modifications over the years, it became increasingly clear that new arrangements were necessary to achieve two important objectives. One was to intercept and divert existing flows at various points out of the North Dublin system, thus relieving both overloading and pollution in adjacent streams and watercourses. The second was to make lands available for development in both the Dublin city and Fingal county areas.

Designed in the mid-1990s, the North Fringe/Northern Interceptor Sewer Project was intended to fulfil these urgent requirements. This joint Dublin City Council/Fingal County Council project was estimated to cost €61m. Work began in the year 2000, managed by Dublin City Council and divided into three main sections.

The Northern Interceptor Sewer (Ballygall Road and Glasnevin Avenue), with pumping stations at Mellowes Park and Ballymun Road, is 6km long. The 4km Meakstown-Poppintree sewer flows from the M50/North Road junction through Poppintree,

Storm water tanks at Ringsend.
The Ringsend Treatment Plant benefits Dublin city and surrounding areas, including Dun Laoghaire, west county Dublin and parts of county Meath.

Ballymun, Sillogue Road and Ballymun Road. The new North Fringe Sewer, 17km long, runs parallel to the M50 and its N32 feeder road towards Sutton via Baldoyle. The North Fringe/Northern Interceptor discharges to the Sutton pumping station alluded to earlier.

Sutton pumping station has four main 450kW pumps, each capable of pumping 1.5 cubic metres per second. There is a ventilation and odour control system and Sutton station has its own standby generators. The wet well in the station has a capacity of 1,500 cubic metres, while the storm water storage is capable of dealing with a further 4,000 cubic metres. Stored water can be pumped over a period so as to even the demand on the equipment in the station. Like the Main Lift station at Ringsend and the West Pier buildings at Dun Laoghaire, Sutton is an architecturally pleasing building. Ascon and Bowen Water Technology were responsible for the construction and commissioning of Sutton pumping station. This most important of projects was completed in 2003, Sutton pumping station being ceremonially opened on 8 September by Taoiseach Bertie Ahern.

When the Sutton-Ringsend pipeline was commissioned, only sewage downstream or east of Sutton continued to discharge from the Nose of Howth outfall. A new sewer to be laid westwards from Howth by Fingal County Council will reverse this flow back to Sutton pumping station. The already much reduced Howth outfall will then cease to operate but the redundant trunk line from Sutton

Official opening of Ringsend Treatment Plant, 2003. *The Lord Mayor of Dublin, Councillor Dermot Lacey, welcomes An Taoiseach Bertie Ahern TD, and Minister for the Environment and Local Government, Martin Cullen TD.*

to the Nose of Howth will be retained as an overflow.

An especially satisfactory event that followed the most recent stage of the Dublin Bay Project was the award, in 2005, of a Blue Flag to Dollymount Strand. Within the Bay, this was the second award of a Blue Flag – Seapoint had achieved this distinction on completion of the Dun Laoghaire-Ringsend pipeline.

WATER CONSERVATION

Water loss – the difference between the quantity extracted from the canals and that delivered to the consumers – was described in Chapter 1 as serious at the turn of the nineteenth century. It continued as an irritating low profile problem for the next 200 years, occasionally achieving more prominence, as when wanton but temporary waste followed the inauguration of the Vartry scheme in 1867. But the issue continued to grow as the water system expanded and it became a prime cause of concern in the last quarter of the twentieth century.

A survey commissioned by the Department of the Environment and Local Government in 1996 found that in 1994 more than 40% of all the water produced in the Dublin area could not be

accounted for. At that time of unprecedented growth the four Dublin local authorities, together with Bray UDC and Wicklow and Kildare county councils, now had an urgent motivation to systematically locate and eliminate this haemorrhage of such a precious resource.

The first step to eliminating the problem was the creation of the Dublin Region Water Conservation Project (DRWCP). This £37m (€47m) project, co-funded by the EU, was led by Tom Leahy and Brian McKeown of Dublin Corporation. When the team assessed the enormity of the task and the need for full co-operation from every individual and organisation involved, a partnership was established. Anglian Water, one of the privatised UK water companies, was appointed as main contractor and it set up a subsidiary company called Anglian Water Ireland to carry out the enormous programme that lay ahead. A good industrial relationship was established between local authority teams and those of Anglian, the first outside contractor to work closely with unionised city council personnel.

Sub-contractors were appointed to carry out repair work on leaking mains and by early 2000 more than 16,000 leaks had been repaired and daily water savings of 30 million litres effected. New equipment and methods – computer network models, a geographical information system (GIS), a telemetry (remote monitoring and control) system and water distribution meters – expedited the work, which would have taken decades using traditional procedures and tools.

A fundamental stage in setting up an effective water monitoring, leakage detection and repair system was the delineation of more than 500 District Meter Areas (DMAs) throughout the Dublin region, each containing between 1,000 and 1,500 properties. The DMAs were grouped to form larger Water Supply Areas (WSAs) each of which was metered and could be checked against output meters at the water plants. More than 600 meters have been installed and are connected to the telemetry system. Readings identify abnormal water usage, enabling teams to be sent to the district concerned.

Pinpointing the exact location of a leak can be a frustrating experience. The approximate location of some leaks can be found when water oozes through road or footpath surfaces, but these can be as nothing compared to some much larger discharges into the surrounding ground. Leaks are traced by listening for water escaping from a main, using one of the oldest items in the waterworks toolbox. This is the listening stick, the bottom of which is placed on a pipe, valve, stopcock or hydrant. The top end is put to the operator's ear, but the loudest sound heard is not necessarily the most prolific leak.

If the traditional detection method fails, the next stage is a Step Test, in which sections of the District Meter Areas are shut down. This enables the section with the greatest leakage to be singled out – but the exact location of the loss has still to be established. Step tests are performed at night because usage is at its lowest, water pressures are at their highest and households suffer less inconvenience. However, hospitals and industries operating around the clock have to be provided for in advance.

Leakage had been reduced from 42% to 30% by early 2000 and to get as near as possible to total elimination of leaks is an objective of the city water services division. Meanwhile, fewer leaks have resulted in increased pressure and an end to night-time pressure reduction which in the past adversely affected 150,000 customers. Water saved has also allowed for 40,000 new homes to be served and 5,500 new jobs to be created.

NEW BYE-LAWS

New bye-laws adopted in 2003 set high water conservation standards for all new housing and commercial developments. Every new development must now have a water conservation plan, while large commercial users must submit a water conservation policy statement and an annual water audit. All water fittings must be to an approved standard and be of a type that contributes to water conservation. The use of hosepipes is prohibited during dry spells and low-flush toilets must be installed in all new developments or where an existing WC is being replaced.

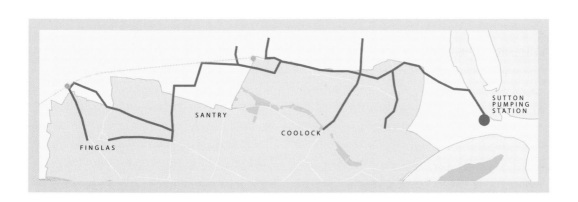

Diagram showing the North Fringe Sewer. *Work began in the year 2000 on this joint Dublin City Council/ Fingal County Council project, which is designed to relieve over-loading and pollution on the existing system.*

**James Fenwick,
Dublin City Engineer
1993–1997.**

*Jim Fenwick was
in overall charge of
developing the
North Fringe Water
Supply Scheme.*

BALLYBODEN WATER TREATMENT WORKS

The Ballyboden filter beds installed as part of the
Rathmines water supply system in 1887 are referred
to in Chapter 6. Following the incorporation of
Rathmines into the city in 1930, Ballyboden
achieved greater importance when it became part of
the larger Dublin Corporation network. A new
water treatment plant was constructed in the 1950s
and the slow-sand filters taken out of service. This
was upgraded in the 1980s when its sedimentation
tanks converted to upward flow operation.
Polyelectrolite was also added to assist precipitation.
The 18 million litres (4 million gallons) per day
coming from Bohernabreena is mixed with 9
million litres (2 million gallons) per day from
Ballymore Eustace water treatment works to meet
the demand of the Ballyboden water supply district.
In the mid-1990s a new lime plant introduced the
dilution of highly concentrated liquid lime. This
reduced the labour element of mixing bagged lime
and led to a more uniform lime solution.

A possible source of an extra 9 million litres per
day is the Owendoher Stream which passes within
400 metres of the treatment works. This extra
quantity would be assured in the winter months but
not every summer; it would, however, make the
plant at least partially independent of Ballymore
Eustace water.

THE NORTH CITY ARTERIAL WATER MAIN

Until the early 1990s all the large arterial water
mains coming into Dublin city from the Roundwood
and Ballymore Eustace water treatment plants
underwent pressure reduction to the south of the
city centre at various locations along the Grand
Canal. This saved significantly on leakage within the
city but when the pressure-reduced mains crossed
the Liffey they could only service north city properties up to a level of approximately 30m Malin Head
Datum (about 100 feet). This level corresponds to
most of the length of Griffith Avenue.

The circumstances just described left the northern
portion of Dublin County Council (now Fingal
County Council) to supply areas north of Griffith
Avenue from its Leixlip treatment works and
Ballycoolen storage reservoir. This led to an unusual
situation in which the corporation supplied south of
Griffith Avenue with 18-inch and 24-inch water
mains and the county council supplied the north
side of Griffith Avenue with mainly 15-inch arterial
mains. These arterial mains were connected by 9-
inch and 12-inch mains crossing Griffith Avenue.

The idea of having an arterial water main that
maintained its pressure through the city to the
north side with pressure reducing valves only on its
branches was born; it was called the North City
Arterial Water Main (NCAW). It was decided to use
the pressure from the Cookstown storage reservoir
in Tallaght for this new main. This pressure could
be boosted in emergencies to that of the Saggart
storage reservoir.

Work commenced in 1985 with a 1,200mm
ductile iron water main being laid from the
Cookstown reservoir under the Belgard Road (in
tunnel), down Kilnamanagh, under Ballymount
Road Upper, under Greenhills Road (in tunnel) and
across the Walkinstown Roundabout. The line then
continued down Bunting and Balfe Roads and

through the Lansdowne Valley Park to Davitt Road. At Davitt Road a 750mm spur connects to a 30-inch arterial main coming from Ballymore Eustace at the Naas Road, while a 1,000mm concrete main (now a 1,000mm ductile iron pipe following Luas diversions) went eastwards down Davitt Road to James's Walk. At Thomas Court it reduces to an 800mm pipeline that goes to Bridgefoot Street.

An incident that happened in the late 1990s will give some idea of the pressure in this new water main. It was struck by an excavator in Bridgefoot Street which caused a small breach in the main, sending a jet of water 7.5 metres into the air.

Leaving Bridgefoot Street the main crosses Mellowes Bridge as two 500mm pipes which join again as an 800mm pipe in Queen's Street. From here it makes its way through Church Street, Constitution Hill, Western Way and Dorset Street to the junction of Lower Drumcondra Road and Clonliffe Road. A 600mm branch goes from here up Drumcondra Road and via Home Farm Road and St Mobhi Road to Griffith Avenue Extension where it connects to previously existing 24-inch and 12-inch mains, the latter supplying Ballymun.

Reverting to the 800mm line: from Drumcondra this goes down Clonliffe Road and Poplar Row and reduces to a 600mm ductile iron pipe across Annesley Bridge. It then turns into Fairview Park where it connects to a previously existing 24-inch water main. The principal contractor for most of the sections of this project was Clonmel Enterprises, while direct labour was responsible for most of the remainder.

In the mid-1990s there was an opening ceremony to mark the joining of Vartry and Pollaphuca water in Fairview. Lord Mayor John Gormley, in true Green Party style, arrived on a bicycle, locked the bike to the park railings and asked a corporation engineer who was standing nearby to keep an eye on it. He then delivered his speech, followed by Jim Fenwick (deputy city engineer at the time) and Frank Feeley (city manager). A stone monument near the southern entrance to the park commemorates the event.

The 600mm arterial water main left in Fairview Park was being extended in 2004 along Clontarf Road and James Larkin Road to Kilbarrack Road (400mm branch). There is also a 400mm branch up The Stiles Road to boost the pressure on Howth Road. This final stage of the North City Arterial Water Main is now part of the North Fringe Water Supply Scheme.

The rest of the North Fringe scheme has five components. First is a new 800mm main from Cappagh Cross to Ballymun and down to the 600mm main on Griffith Avenue Extension mentioned earlier. There is also a new 600mm main from Ballymun to Donaghmede and a 450mm main from Donaghmede to James Larkin Road. At Sillogue there is a new storage reservoir with water tower and pumps. Lastly, existing water services in the Finglas area are being upgraded.

PUMPING STATIONS

Water pumping stations are required to increase pressure in areas within the city that gravity water pressure cannot reach. These areas can be quite small, perhaps as little as a few dozen houses. The pumping stations need to be carefully located because the pressure downstream of them will be reduced when the pumps are in operation. Another option is to use a pumping station to supply a storage reservoir, preferably at night, which the low pressure can drain down during the day. Howth is an example of this water system.

REHABILITATING LOCAL WATER MAINS

Another initiative, carried out on a pilot basis by the city water division in the 1980s and 1990s, was to completely re-lay sections of the city mains that were known to be in poor condition. These sections, which typically supplied between 200 and 500 houses, usually had as their main water source 3-inch (76mm) or 4-inch (105mm) mains. These pipe sizes can become almost completely blocked by corrosion, particularly over a 100-year period.

Kevin C. O'Donnell,
Chief Engineer
1971–1991.

Kevin O'Donnell was
chief engineer in charge
of water and drainage
for both Dublin city
and county during the
1970s and 1980s.

The house connections, normally ½-inch (12mm), and some of the water mains were installed by the then ground breaking technology of directional drilling which reduced costs.

Some of the existing house connections were in twos and threes, which led to a few 'neighbours from hell' scenarios. As a result, the corporation offered all the residents the option of an individual connection to the edge of their properties. Leakage in the areas in question was monitored before and after it was re-laid with usually great reductions in consumption. A large number of lead connections were also replaced.

The improvement in pressure did not suit everybody. One woman in Ranelagh who lived at the end of a long laneway was used to filling up her kettle by putting it in the wash-hand basin below the tap, then going into the living room to watch her favourite soap and returning to turn off the tap over her half-filled kettle at the end of the TV programme. After the water was rehabilitated in the area, she followed her normal procedure only once.

Disconnecting a row of houses from the old water main and connecting the houses to the new one resulted in the supply being cut off for a few hours. One local resident, again in Ranelagh, complained about this injustice to the resident engineer. The engineer pointed out that the residents affected would be warned well in advance so that they could fill bath tubs etc and that other sources of potable water would be available. Still upset, the resident cautioned that 'whatever about cutting me off you certainly can't cut my next door neighbour off'. When the engineer asked her to clarify this statement she replied 'She's Ken Doherty's mother'.

IMPROVING THE DUN LAOGHAIRE
WATER SUPPLY

In the mid-1980s the firm of M. C. O'Sullivan, consulting engineers, was appointed to review Dun Laoghaire's poor water supply situation in the borough and advise appropriately. The firm recommended a new supply from Stillorgan reservoir, a

new reservoir off Church Road on the western side of Roche's Hill and reinforcement of the trunk mains distribution system together with improvements to the intermediate and high-level supply areas around Killiney. Also included were proposals to refurbish or replace local distribution mains where, due to corrosion or poor structural integrity, capacity and water quality were unsatisfactory. It was also recommended that provision be made for zone metering of the networks.

The proposed new supply from Stillorgan reservoir, the new Church Road reservoir, the trunk mains distribution improvements and the upgrading of the intermediate and high-level systems were approved by the Department of the Environment and Local Government and were part-funded by the European Union Cohesion Fund. These extensive works were split into four contracts.

Contract No. 1 was carried out between the autumn of 1994 and spring 1996 and covered work on Stillorgan reservoir and the Brewery Road tunnel. It involved the construction of a new valve, metering and control chamber in the embankment of the lowest reservoir at Stillorgan, together with the reorganisation of the existing pipe and valve infrastructure to facilitate future improvements. This was a difficult operation because of the risk to the stability of the old Vartry structure which had stood for over 130 years. The earthen embankment, founded directly on granite that lay very close to the surface, had a typical clay-puddle core to prevent leakage. Any significant movement of the embankment could have fractured the clay, with serious consequences for the integrity of the reservoir. In the event, it was successfully and economically accomplished as a result of an innovative king-post structure suggested by Denis McCarthy, senior resident engineer.

Because of the multiplicity of old water mains in Brewery Road, a new 1,200mm-diameter steel main from the new valve, metering and control chamber was laid in a tunnel excavated by blasting in granite as far as the Bray (N11) Road. This pipe has the capacity to discharge all of the flows from the Stillorgan reservoir. A major valve chamber was built within the traffic island at the bottom of Brewery Road to facilitate Dublin City Council in making additional new connections. A 900mm-diameter supply main to Dun Laoghaire Borough continued in tunnel under the Bray Road and into the grounds of the School for the Deaf to near Ardagh Court. These works were designed to provide a secure water supply to a wide area. The contractors were Murphy International and Murphy Pipelines JV.

The second contract, catering for primary mains and Kilbogget Park pumping station, was carried out between the spring of 1995 and autumn 1996. It was also the one most likely to cause disruption. It provided for the linking of the main trunk pipe from the Stillorgan reservoir through the Brewery Road tunnel to Church Road reservoir. Initially a 900mm-diameter pipe was laid to Blackrock at Newtownpark Avenue from where it continued as an 800mm line to a new pumping station at Kilbogget. This station pumps directly to the Church Road reservoir through an 800mm rising main.

Work on this phase of the development was the most intrusive from a traffic management viewpoint. The contractor however was required to minimise the duration and intensity of disruption along main traffic routes and advance warning was provided on radio of upcoming work likely to cause public inconvenience or delays. Some blasting for removal of rock was also necessary. The route traversed by this scheme included Ardagh Park, Newtownpark Avenue (with a branch to Temple Hill, Blackrock), Lower Kill Lane and Church Road. Distribution mains were also laid from Church Road reservoir via Thomastown Road and Upper Glenageary Road to Castle Street in Dalkey. Ascon was the contractor for these works, in the course of which a young man sadly lost his life in an accident.

Executed between early 1995 and autumn 1996, Contract No. 3 involved building a reservoir with a capacity of 39,000 cubic metres above Church Road, adjacent to Killiney Golf Course. About half of the excavation for this reservoir was through dense granite rock, making noise inevitable. Earthen and rock embankments were formed between the construction area and adjoining properties, greatly reducing the effects outside the working area. The contract also included pumping plant, secondary sterilisation and metering, and the laying of a 300mm-diameter rising main across Killiney Golf Course to the Roche's Hill boundary. The contractor was Jons Civil Engineering Ltd.

Contract No. 4, covering the intermediate and high-level distribution systems, called for the construction of a new pumping station, metering and valve house close to the intermediate-level reservoir near Killiney village, refurbishment of the intermediate-level reservoir and reconstruction of the high-level reservoir. It also continued the 300mm rising main across Roche's Hill and via Clarement Road to the intermediate level reservoir. New rising and distribution mains were laid to the high level reservoir, together with new distribution mains in Killiney Hill Road. This work was carried out by RTJ Ltd and was completed in 1998.

Completion of these works greatly improved the

security of the water supply throughout the former Dun Laoghaire borough and the immediately adjoining areas. The follow-up Dublin area leak programme, described earlier in this chapter, has addressed most of the other outstanding issues raised in the consultants' report. The aggregate cost of the Dun Laoghaire Water Improvement Scheme and the Drainage Improvement Scheme (Chapter 12) was of the order of £90m (€114.3m) and was funded largely by the EU Structural and Cohesion Funds. Larry Brassill, as borough engineer and later as project engineer from the beginning of 1994, played a significant part during the initiation and progress of these schemes.

THE DOCKLANDS PROJECT

The Custom House Docks Development Authority was set up in 1986 to develop the Financial Services Centre and revitalise the extensive run-down and obsolete areas on the North Wall. This body has since evolved into the Dublin Docklands Development Authority (DDDA) with responsibility for development on both sides of the river. The authority's massive projects continue the eastwards expansion of the city that began with the completion of the Custom House in 1791.

When the authority came into being, the berthing of merchant ships became increasingly concentrated in the port area to the east of East Wall Road. The Dublin Port Company, successor to the Port and Docks Board, transferred some of its responsibilities, especially those relating to the Liffey and its bridges, to the city council and to a lesser degree to the DDDA. Surface and foul drainage arrangements are agreed between the three bodies and the city council provides water supply, drainage and pollution monitoring for the entire port area.

Over 5,000 new residences and 500,000 square metres of commercial and industrial units were proposed for the docklands area of the city. A special project was initiated to ascertain the extra water and drainage facilities that would be needed

to serve this large volume of development. The water services to the area would require only minor improvement, but the existing drainage could not cope with the proposed developments. Consultants were therefore appointed to produce a drainage plan for the area.

Time was so pressing that three elements of a programme for the north docklands area were advanced to the pre-construction stage. The first element is a new 2.5m-diameter Liffey services tunnel, west of the Eastlink Bridge, designed to carry drainage rising mains, a 600mm water main, electricity cables etc in both directions. The second element is a large new drainage pumping station at Spencer Dock that will pump effluent via two rising mains through the new tunnel to the pumping station at Ringsend and to the treatment works on the Poolbeg Peninsula. The third element is a large new arterial drainage main from East Wall Road to the Spencer Dock pumping station.

Construction of the tunnel is expected to begin in 2005. Many other pipelines and storage tanks will be needed to complete the drainage requirements of this portion of the city. These are expected to be highlighted in the consultants' final report, which was awaited as this chapter was being written.

FUTURE WATER SOURCES

Drinking water is a scarce commodity. Five hundred million litres of water are produced every day for more than 1.3 million customers in the greater Dublin region. As the population grows and usage increases, an ever greater burden is placed on the sources of supply.

The long-term strategy to meet this ever increasing demand for drinking water is based on the Greater Dublin Water Strategic Study commissioned by the Department of the Environment and Local Government in 1996 and reviewed in 2000. The findings, which allowed for the latest demand projections up to 2016, can be summarised as requiring the following:

↝ a reduction in leakage levels to 20%

↝ the implementation of a major water mains rehabilitation programme

↝ the introduction of demand management measures such as a new set of water bye-laws

↝ a capital investment programme to include:
  - the construction of the north fringe water main
  - the provision of additional strategic storage
  - the covering of existing treated water storage areas to safeguard water quality

↝ the maximisation of existing water treatment sources to include:
  - the expansion of the Ballymore Eustace treatment plant to its full permitted capacity of 318 million litres per day
  - the expansion of the Leixlip water treatment plant to its full permitted capacity of 170 million litres per day.

In addition to the above, the study concluded that due to finite potential for developing the existing water sources there was a need to consider other alternatives to meet the interim and longer-term needs of the region. To this end two further studies were commissioned. The first was to look at possible short-time solutions, for example the construction of a new treatment plant at Islandbridge or the development of the Grand Canal as a source. The second study will seek to identify the options available to provide a major, long-term solution to the needs of the region, options for example such as possibly conveying water from as far away as the River Shannon.

The former Rathmines waterworks on the Grand Canal at Gallanstown (described in Chapter 6), purchased by Dublin Corporation in 1893, will be brought back into service and modernised. It is expected that this plant will provide up to two million gallons per day. The possibility of using desalination plants will also be examined and the renewal of the existing distribution network, much of which is now very old, will continue.

THE GREATER DUBLIN STRATEGIC DRAINAGE STUDY

The Greater Dublin Strategic Drainage Study was initiated in 2001 to analyse the existing drainage system in the greater Dublin area and advise on future policy. The core area was defined as all of Dublin county, northeast Kildare, east Meath and part of northeast Wicklow. Dublin City Council is the contracting authority acting on behalf of Dun Laoghaire-Rathdown, Fingal, Kildare, Meath, South Dublin and Wicklow county councils. The study was carried out by a consortium that included Hyder Consulting (formerly Welsh Water), McCarthy Consulting and M. C. O'Sullivan.

The greater Dublin area is 150,000 hectares in extent and has a population of some 1.3 million people. The topography of the region dictates that most of the sewage generated by extensive future development will go to the wastewater treatment plant at Ringsend. The increased flows will utilise existing trunk sewers, none of which was designed to cater for the scale of development now envisaged.

In the past the design and capacity of the sewer networks needed to drain particular catchments were painstakingly determined on paper with slide rules and primitive calculators. While invariably accurate for the immediate areas under consideration, the effects on the wider network were impossible to forecast. There was always the possibility of a future major storm causing havoc in downstream areas. While such instances have thankfully been extremely rare up to now, the danger of future occurrences is more probable.

Computer-based hydraulic modelling has been used in the United Kingdom since the early 1980s. This greatly eases the task of drainage planners in looking at what would happen to a sewer network in the event of simulated sets of circumstances arising at any point on the system. Hydraulic modelling was applied in the 1990s to Dublin Corporation's North Fringe and Rathmines

& Pembroke studies. The last major model built by Dublin Corporation was for the Dublin Docklands in 1998–2000.

When the Greater Dublin Study was initiated, it was intended to examine seven rivers in detail. These are the Mayne, Santry, Finglas, Camac, Poddle, Deansgrange and Carrickmines. The Tolka was added to the list following the floods of November 2000. Climate change and the environment, concepts unknown when Dublin's sewer network was under construction in the nineteenth century, are but two of the factors to be considered in the new study. This will also make extensive use of geographical information systems (GISs) and is intended to plan as far ahead as 2031. An essential is a sophisticated flood early warning system and this has the highest priority.

The €10m Greater Dublin Strategic Drainage Study, intended to recommend the regional drainage infrastructure required for up to 2031, was published just as this book was about to be printed. Hydraulic models, already alluded to briefly, will shape all major foul and storm drainage.

The study confirmed that the drainage systems in the Dublin area will need major improvement and expansion to cater for population and industrial growth in the coming years. The Ringsend wastewater treatment plant will be extended, but will not be able to cope with all the further anticipated increases in effluent. The existing Fingal treatment plant at Portrane, north of Dublin, which currently serves Portrane and Donabate, is seen as the location for a major new facility that will relieve pressure on Ringsend. It would be half the size of Ringsend and would take some of the north side sewage that currently flows to Ringsend. Portrane would also take at least some of the sewage currently treated at the Swords/Malahide facility.

Another important part of the report stresses the necessity to rebuild or replace much of the brick sewer network built from 1852 onwards which has been increasingly pounded by ever-growing traffic weight and volumes.

RIVER MAINTENANCE: PUBLIC INTEREST

Several references have already been made to river pollution, particularly in the Liffey. The city drainage division undertakes the cleaning and maintenance of rivers and watercourses in the municipal area. There were fifty rivers and streams within the city in 1986 but this number was reduced to thirty-six with the final implementation of the new boundaries in 1994. All are described in detail and their individual histories comprehensively recorded in C. L. Sweeney's *The Rivers of Dublin*.

The embankment of rivers in urban areas is an important factor in the control of flooding. Before construction of the quay walls began in the late seventeenth century the Liffey estuary occupied a much greater area than it does today. Similarly the Dodder and the Tolka have been progressively contained over the years, as have the Camac and Santry rivers. But all rivers are tidal in their lower reaches, and sometimes this is so further inland than many people might suspect. The Liffey is tidal as far as the Islandbridge weir, the Tolka as far as the Distillery Road weir, and the Dodder up to Ballsbridge.

Some rivers have been diverted or had their headwaters re-directed. Medieval changes to the Poddle and its several courses are a very early instance of this. Modern examples are the diversion of the Tolka in a new channel through the present Griffith Park in the late 1920s and the redirection of the Wad headwaters to a new storm water sewer in Ballymun Road in the 1960s. Similarly the upper section of the Nanniken was diverted to the Santry River during the development of Kilmore West in the mid-1960s.

Over the years several rivers and streams that were once features of the landscape were culverted, some of them becoming part of the foul sewer system. Among the most famous of these was the heavily polluted Swan River which was largely incorporated into the Rathmines and Pembroke drainage system around 1880. On the north side the Bradogue suffered the same fate. Conversely some rivers that served as sewers for a time have been substantially rehabilitated, especially the Poddle and the Camac. The several industries contributing to the pollution of the Camac included no less than four paper mills, all now closed.

There is one instance of a stream that had been diverted into a foul sewer partly regaining its

River maintenance crew at work on the Liffey. *Dublin City Council's drainage division undertakes the cleaning and maintenance of rivers and watercourses within the municipal area.*

original status many years later. When a brick sewer was laid in South Circular Road in 1877 outside St Patrick's Convent, this stream – which has no recorded name and flowed northwards from Rialto Lodge – was connected to the sewer. In 1925–1926, when the sewers from Herberton Road and Crumlin were being constructed in tunnel through the grounds of what is now St James's Hospital, an extra pipe was laid to take the stream to the Camac, east of the point at which it originally joined the river.

Apart from the three major rivers and another dozen or so minor ones, the names of some twenty minor streams that were once features of the landscape are now forgotten. In his conclusion to *The Rivers of Dublin* CL Sweeney records that eighty-seven miles (139km) of Dublin's watercourses are hidden or forgotten. In some cases they are remembered in road or bridge names, like Claremont Avenue Glasnevin or Swan Place at Rathmines. A frequent physical clue to the presence of an underground river is a dip in the road.

Interest in local topography grows as people become more aware of how important local history is. Local historical societies flourish today and much research goes into the preparation of talks delivered at their meetings. Rivers and their catchments often form the subject of research, leading to very detailed presentations at public meetings. Even the most reclusive streams interest people – the Nanniken for example. This little river, culverted all the way from Santry to Killester, emerges into the open at Howth Road (Ballyhoy Bridge) to become an attractive feature of St Anne's Park, itself of great historical as well as environmental importance.

Of all the rivers and streams in the Dublin area the one that has commanded most attention over the years is the Poddle. Students frequently make it the centrepiece of studies or projects, its history as the moat of Dublin Castle and its association with so many episodes in our past making it an especially worthwhile subject. A journey through its culvert from St Patrick's Cathedral to Wellington Quay is described in *The Rivers of Dublin*, with many facts and events recalled. Also mentioned is the little-known fact that one branch of the Poddle flows beneath the Olympia Theatre, prompting comparisons with the Phantom of the Opera.

POLLUTION CONTROL

Accelerated industrial development, more numerous sources of water pollution and growing environmental awareness contributed to mounting concern about the condition of our rivers during the 1970s. Even after the Liffey had been substantially purified, gross pollution from the Camac continued to render it profoundly unpleasant downstream of Heuston Bridge. Several of the industries causing this pollution, including the paper mills at Saggart and Clondalkin, were outside the city boundary.

Grave concern for water quality led to the passing of the Local Government (Water Pollution) Act 1977 and the subsequent 1990 Amendment Act. Under the provisions of this legislation local authorities license discharges to rivers and monitor water quality regularly to ensure that standards are maintained. Domestic drainage arrangements are also inspected to ensure that foul drains are not inadvertently connected to surface water sewers.

The city council drainage division has developed comprehensive and adaptable procedures to deal with environmental contingencies. Rivers and watercourses are cleaned regularly and there are also arrangements to alleviate the effects of storms and flooding. These are reviewed regularly and, where necessary, procedures are modified when the circumstances surrounding every flooding incident are examined. The drainage division acts on the principle that there is something to be learned from every occurrence.

As environmental awareness became ever more acute towards the turn of the twenty-first century, greater attention was given to separate surface water systems. Flows from separate storm systems can include pollutants that include petrol and anti-freeze, animal and possibly human waste, decayed leaves and other vegetable matter. These can build up on roads, particularly during long periods of dry weather – decaying leaves in gullies can produce a very potent effluent. An intense summer shower can wash all this material into a clean river or stream and thereby cause considerable pollution.

Aesthetics is another aspect of drainage work that becomes more important as time passes. Examples are the new pumping stations at Ringsend and Sutton where much effort has been expended on producing buildings of a high architectural standard. Attention is also being directed to older structures that were quite acceptable when they were built but now jar on people's sensitivities. Kilbarrack pumping station is typical, built in the 1950s when money was scarce and aesthetic considerations far less important than they are today. This severely utilitarian structure was replaced by an underground installation in 2002, opening up a panoramic vista of the Bull Island and Dublin Bay from Kilbarrack Road.

Another, somewhat less obvious, structure typical of 1950s public utility architecture was the pumping station on Clontarf Road directly opposite the end of Vernon Avenue. This building has now been given a new appearance more in line with modern architectural aesthetics and in deference to its prominent position.

FLOODING PRIVATIONS AND TRAGEDIES 1950–2005

Flooding caused by a variety of factors from a blocked gully to an abnormal rainstorm has always been of concern to the city drainage division. Meteorological records have already been computerised back to 1850, roughly coinciding with the establishment of the city engineer's department. Drainage division personnel examine in detail the circumstances surrounding every instance of flooding because rainstorms and flooding can vary in their causes as well as their effects. Appropriate action is then taken to prevent or alleviate the consequences of any similar recurrence in the future.

Some floods inevitably become etched in people's recollections, the years 1954, 1963, 1965, 1986, 2000 and 2002 being especially memorable for the city's drainage staff. The earliest remembered flooding is a rolling date, the longest memories usually going back sixty to seventy years. Within the working life

of this writer the floods of 1954, rather than those
of 1931 recalled fifty years ago by older colleagues,
were a reliable and easily understood yardstick. And
very shortly after these words are written, 1954 will
cease to be a year to which drainage staff can personally relate. Unless therefore they were reported
and recorded accurately when they happened, all
details of past occurrences must be treated with
caution. Typically, old inhabitants of an affected
area who lived through some traumatic event in
the past are consulted and their recollections, which
may not always be accurate, become quoted as
indisputable historical fact.

Exceptional rainfall in the catchment of the

Tolka resulted in the river overflowing its banks on
8 December 1954. This led to extensive flooding
in Drumcondra, Ballybough, Fairview and the
North Strand areas. Following continuous heavy
rain throughout the day the railway bridge at East
Wall Road collapsed into the River Tolka. This
blocked the flow, enlarged the flooded areas and
increased the depth of water already causing
extreme distress to so many people.

A lack of heat, light and shelter became particular afflictions for the local people, especially the
elderly and very young children. Emergency
arrangements were quickly introduced by a great
number of officials, men like J. Farrelly, the station

master at Amiens Street (now Connolly) railway station. Members of staff at the station were enlisted to prepare and serve hot meals to many traumatised residents.

The floodwater did not subside for several days, during which the concentration of diverted traffic on Drumcondra Road gave an early although quickly forgotten foretaste of the congestion that would become commonplace thirty years later. While the worst flooding was in the northern suburbs the combination of heavy rain and a high tide also caused the Liffey to overflow on to the Esplanade and Victoria Quay. The latter, lower than most of the other quays, has been flooded from time to time and was again affected on 1 February 2002. The widespread flooding on that occasion, especially in East Wall and Ringsend, was due to the concurrence of strong southerly winds, low atmospheric pressure and some rainfall in the hour before high tide.

How a decision taken with little thought for the future can affect the people of a later generation was demonstrated by a feature of the 2002 North Strand area flooding. In the 1960s the canals were seen by many as anachronisms not worth the cost of maintenance. The Royal Canal, always regarded as inferior to the Grand, was by then in a very sad state and there was little recognition of its potential amenity value. Somebody therefore decided that the lock gates just upstream from its entry to the Liffey at North Wall were no longer needed. And so the waterway became tidal as far as the lock immediately west of Newcomen Bridge and this became a contributory element in the 2002 flooding.

On 11 June 1963 seven inches of rain fell within a concentrated area of the south-eastern suburbs in less than three hours. This caused serious flooding in the Pembroke, Merrion and Ballsbridge districts. Virtually the same thing happened in 1965. As a result of these inundations, which damaged the ground floors and furniture of many expensive houses, a painstaking study of the entire area was carried out and elaborate plans were drawn up to eliminate as far as possible the effects of any future

recurrence. New storm sewers were laid and a pumping station was built at Shrewsbury Park to relieve the affected districts. These arrangements have proved satisfactory.

It was, however, the 1963 rainfall in the inner city and the events surrounding it that were more memorable and dramatic. A tragedy connected with the rainstorm of 11 June 1963 bore more than a passing resemblance to the horrific deaths and injuries caused by the collapse of the Church Street tenements on 2 September 1913 (Chapter 8). Despite the herculean efforts of governments, public officials and numerous welfare bodies over the half-century following the 1913 incident, Dublin still had slum tenements in the 1960s, most of which had inevitably deteriorated since the Church Street disaster.

By 1963 a determined campaign was well under way to eliminate the tenements once and for all. The city's dangerous buildings and housing welfare sections were especially active and worked in tandem with each other; many old houses that were unfit for human habitation on health grounds were also structurally dangerous. In many of Dublin's Georgian streets that had been in continuous decline for more than 150 years there were now gaps where houses had either fallen down or been demolished. One of the city's most notable features at this time was the number of buildings supported by shoring. There was, therefore, unrelenting pressure on accommodation to re-house people displaced by the condemnation and demolition of old buildings.

Public alarm and official activity became acute on Sunday 2 June 1963 when a house collapsed in Bolton Street, killing two people. The sense of shock and outrage became even more intense on 11 June when two more houses, which had shops on the ground floor, fell down in Fenian Street, beside its junction with Holles Street. The weather and flood conditions probably contributed to this second, fatal collapse in which two children were killed. A huge outcry followed, escalating the pressure on the authorities to finally bring to an end the conditions

Riverbank Apartments,
Dodder Park Road,
25/26 August, 1986.

Districts beside the
river Dodder suffered
the worst of widespread
and severe flooding
caused by Hurricane
Charlie in August 1986
– a rare instance of a
tropical storm crossing
the Atlantic and
affecting Ireland.

that had been excoriated over the years by Whitelaw (1798), Aikenhead (1833) and Willis (1845). One result was the construction of the vast Ballymun complex – which later had drainage among its many problems.

Areas adjoining the River Dodder have a long record of flooding – the river falls sharply over its comparatively short course. Before the walling of the river and reclamation of land in the Ringsend area, periodic combinations of high tides and the Dodder swollen by heavy rainfall caused much damage. While the construction of the Boherna-breena reservoirs for the Rathmines water supply in the nineteenth century introduced a method of control and reduced the volume of water in the river, it could still pose serious threats along its course. Serious flooding occurred in the Dodder catchment in 1931 and 1965, and districts beside the river suffered the worst of the widespread flooding caused by Hurricane Charlie in August 1986.

Extensive and continuous land reclamation since

the eighteenth century has extended Dublin's land area considerably over the years. Buildings now stand on what were once beaches. Today many people would be unaware that places such as Strand Street at Irishtown or North Strand Road were so named because at one time they were beside the shoreline. Coastal defences must therefore be capable of preventing the sea from flooding what were once its domains.

The smaller rivers can also create dire local problems, as did the Poddle at Lower Kimmage Road and the Camac at Mount Brown in the 1980s. Because they are merely tributaries of the Liffey, it is sometimes not realised that the Poddle and Camac are tidal. If unusually high tides coincide with heavy rain in the catchments of these rivers, they are capable of creating, albeit on a smaller scale, situations normally associated with the Liffey, Dodder or Tolka. Even rivers that are almost forgotten, of which the Finglas River is an example, can cause havoc when particular sets of circumstances arise.

A report of an occurrence that took place as far back as 1814 illustrates how a combination of a river flood and tidal conditions can interact to produce what, in this instance, had a happy outcome: 'It [the Poddle] occasionally however bursts from its caverns and inundates Patrick Street, Ship Street, the Castle Yard and Dame Street where it is sometimes necessary to use boats'. A boy who fell from an arch being built in the Castle Yard fell into the flooded Poddle and was carried down to the Liffey from which he was rescued.

In areas adjacent to Dublin Bay there have always been concerns about the combination of high tides, heavy rain and easterly winds. The tide originally came up to and sometimes overshot the wall separating the beach from Clontarf Road. This main thoroughfare – and sometimes, adjacent side roads – suffered whenever the three conditions just described coincided. The results of such flooding were so serious that in 1926 a specially adapted tram with its motors mounted above the axles, known to staff as the Submarine, was located 'at the ready' at Clontarf Depot to rescue other trams trapped in flood waters along the seafront between Clontarf Railway Bridge and Dollymount.

To ameliorate the effects of such flooding, work began on a surface water culvert along the sea front in the 1930s. A series of flap valves enables this culvert to store storm water during high tides. Additionally, land was reclaimed along the sea front and the Clontarf promenade was developed in two stages, work being completed during the 1960s. This operation greatly reduced the danger of flooding and created an attractive coastal amenity at the same time.

THE FEBRUARY 2002 FLOODING

The flooding that occurred on 1 February 2002 was unusual in that it was not caused by heavy rain. The weather forecast for the period from midnight to 18:00 hours on 1 February was as follows: 'Stormy conditions are expected overnight and tomorrow, southerly winds with mean speeds 30-40 mph will gust 60-80 mph. Rainfall up to 30mm will give some localised flooding'. While rainfall was not a significant contributor, key factors were a centre of low pressure, 937 millibars, located over County Down, and the southerly winds. Based on the weather report, drainage crews were alerted to monitor the areas with a history of localised flooding.

The predicted level for high tide at 14:00 hours on 1 February was 1.93m (Malin Head). What actually occurred was that the tide level reached 2.91m at 13:30 hrs, then dropped to 2.69m at 14:15 hrs, before quickly rising again to 2.95m. The tide records in Dublin Port state that the previous highest tide level recorded was 2.59m and this occurred in 1924. The fact that the tide rose and fell twice in such a short period is also unusual and noteworthy. In the following days, the tide returned to the normal pattern.

In the region of 1,000 houses in East Wall, North Strand, Ringsend, Sandymount, Clontarf, Sutton and parts of Fingal were flooded. The Emergency Plan for Dublin City was activated. This provides a co-ordination framework within which the major agencies of the state can respond to significant emergencies. Those who responded on this occasion were officials of Dublin city council, the gardaí, the defence forces, the fire brigade, the civil defence, the coast guard service and Waterways Ireland.

In Ringsend the receding tide caused the collapse of forty-five metres of the Dodder wall adjacent to Stella Gardens. The majority of the houses in this area are single storey, so the residents suffered badly because so much personal property was destroyed. A further difficulty presented itself when the floods began to recede. Evacuated residents are always eager to return to their homes and the normal expectation is that the houses will need only cleaning out. Flood affected houses, however, need rewiring, replastering, new floors and all new electrical appliances. As a result it takes a minimum of six months before a sense of normality returns to victims' lives. Additional to these difficulties is the worry of a recurrence and concerns about future

Flood water under Loop Line and Butt Bridges, 1 February 2002.

This flooding was unusual since it was not caused by heavy rain but by the highest tide ever recorded in Dublin Port. Around 1,000 houses in East Wall, North Strand, Ringsend, Sandymount, Clontarf, Sutton and parts of Fingal were flooded and the Emergency Plan for Dublin City was activated to cope with the crisis.

flood insurance cover and house values in the area.

The city council set up a Coastal Zone Risk Assessment Study in order to deal with the impact of the tidal surge. The purpose of this was to review the adequacy of sea defences around Dublin and parts of Fingal. It was also intended to provide an early warning system through the use of a new computer model of the sea off Dublin. This type of model has been used in Britain and continental Europe for some years and the arrangements proposed for Dublin will be integrated into those models.

Since 1997 there have been major floods on the Rhone, Oder and Danube rivers in Europe. Similarly the River Severn in the UK has been experiencing an increased frequency and intensity of floods. One result of these occurrences is that the study of floods and their management has gained a higher profile within the EU Commission. In 2005 the numerous studies being undertaken are highlighting the importance of flood plains, sustainable vegetation and the introduction of Sustainable

Urban Drainage Systems (SUDS). These latter systems involve studying how water runoffs from particular areas affect river flows downstream. With increasing urbanisation it is critical that rivers are studied in a holistic manner and the introduction of retention methods, tanks or permeable surfaces that comply with SUDS principles will minimise the impact on river flows.

Dublin City Council, in conjunction with communities in Germany, Switzerland and Scotland, is currently (2005) working on an EU project called Strategies and Actions for Flood Emergency Response Management (SAFER). This project is expected, over a five-year period, to ensure that Dublin City is actively involved in developing best European practice in flood risk reduction. It is intended that the evolving best practices can then be implemented without delay in areas at risk.

Storm return periods are a worrying factor in planning for floods, partly because reliable records go back only about 150 years. While computer modelling is a great help in providing for the

An inspection under-way in a brick sewer.

A team of highly qualified inspectors has been deployed to examine minutely every man-entry sewer in Dublin. The inspectors recorded their reports on tape as they went along, noting changes, connections, faults, and other useful information.

future, one unpredictable possibility remains. This is that, having taken the steps necessary to cope with a storm with a fifty-year or hundred-year precedent, the planning is overtaken by one with a much longer return period. Meanwhile, work continues on extensive flood prevention measures, close attention being given to areas with a history of trouble.

INSPECTIONS AND RENEWALS

As traffic volumes and the weights of commercial vehicles both increased inexorably, concern grew during the early 1970s about the condition of the brick sewers and those having random rubble masonry walls. A large proportion of the ninety miles of these structures was by then a hundred years old or more, and subsidences had begun to occur. A team of highly qualified inspectors was therefore deployed to examine minutely every man-entry sewer.

Travelling a conduit with headroom of less than six feet, as in most Dublin sewers, is uncomfortable and even hazardous. The smaller the sewer, the greater the discomfort. The commonest size of man-entry sewers in Dublin is the ovoid three-by-two, 3' 3" (990mm) high and 2 feet (600mm) wide at the shoulder, and travelling one of these in a crouched position requires considerable powers of endurance. The inspectors who carried out the examination – John Byrne, William Cramer and James Murphy – recorded their reports on tape as they went along, noting chainages, connections, faults, and other useful information. .

Priorities were identified and a programme of repair, re-lining or replacement was put in hand. Despite the various instances of deterioration or damage encountered during the inspections, the general condition of the network was satisfactory and a remarkable tribute to those who designed and built it all those years previously.

The increase in safety awareness and improve-ments in technology have greatly facilitated this type of work in recent years. Closed circuit television

(CCTV) is now used extensively to identify underperforming or structurally defective sewers. Such conditions can arise from blockages, traffic loading, ingress of water, tree roots, old age or – occasionally – some unprecedented factor. A bizarre and inexplicable example in this category was a telegraph pole that was found to be blocking a sewer in Marino. It had to be cut into sections for removal, and how it got into the sewer remained a mystery.

Prior to being taken in charge by the local authority, new sewers are examined by drainage inspectors who draw up a list of defects. The list is given to the developer and when the faults have been corrected the work is looked at again and if everything is in order, procedures that will result in the take-over are followed. As more and more has been learned about public safety over the years, the procedures have been tightened and contractors' methods have become more professional.

The need for such professionalism was highlighted by an incident that took place in 1971. An industrial estate was completed by a developer who then requested the corporation to take the services in charge. The drainage inspector prepared a list of matters in need of rectification and this was given to the developer, who at that point had liquidated the construction subsidiary that had carried out the development. Rectification was therefore entrusted to a general contractor. The contractor sent two men to begin the work. The cover on the last manhole within the estate was opened and one of the men sought to examine what was inside but could not see because of the darkness. Without thinking he lit a match, which broke and fell into the shaft. A loud whoosh was heard from gas ignited by the match. The blast travelled up the sewer. It passed along a branch serving some factories and blew into a factory drain on the connection from which the usual cap had been omitted. The now mercifully diminished blast then made its way into the factory toilets and caused consternation among the staff. Happily there were no injuries, but the incident demonstrated forcibly

that safety cannot be taken lightly when dealing with sewers and only competent staff should be allowed to work on or in them.

A POETIC RESPONSE

Everybody who works in the public services is aware that many people, especially the poor and elderly, are nervous about asking for things to which they are quite entitled. Fearful of an unfeeling response, some of them approach a third party they trust to seek what they need, and action invariably follows.

Matt O'Brien, former Dun Laoghaire borough engineer, records an unusual communication from the well-known Dr John Fleetwood on behalf of a neighbour:

I write to you about a thing
Which might not sound too great,
In fact I'm sure you have much more
Upon your crowded plate.

The fact which causes me to write
Is Mrs Flood's loo flush,
She only gets when she pulls hard
A squirt and not a gush.

Poor Mrs Flood's not very well
She has to use the loo
More often then her neighbours,
More frequently than you.

She tells me that you fixed it once
But now the yoke is broke,
And when you have to use the jaks
A fault like that's no joke.

She lives in Newtown number five
Not Avenue but Place,
You will not have a dreadful task
Her little house to trace.

I'm sure that she'd be very glad
To see your Fixer-up,
She'd welcome him with open arms
And tea, a steaming cup.

So please send someone very quick
To make the Flood flush flow
Until it's working properly
She's terrified to 'go'.

The engineer lost no time in dealing with
this heartfelt plea and the late Theo Elliott, clerk
of works, replied to Dr Fleetwood on his behalf:

I write to you about a plea
Which came straight from the heart,
Poor Mrs Flood's predicament
Gave us quite a start.

We swung right into action
At this dire emergency
And straight to Newtown number five
The Place, immediately.

We sorted out her problem
With a cistern bright and new,
And now she has a splendid flush
And all the family too.

And now that we have done our bit
In fixing up her loo,
I hope that you in turn have cured
Her other problem too.

ROUTES, GULLIES AND MANHOLE COVERS

Surface water gullies have always been an integral part of the drainage system, but it was not until 6 April 1999 that the city drainage division assumed complete responsibility for their maintenance. In Dublin, gullies are of two main types. In combined drainage areas they were constructed with water seals to prevent odours coming back from the foul sewers to which they discharge. Where surface water is drained separately, the gullies are of the

Routemen at work on a blocked drain.

Using initiative to solve problems quickly has always been a quality of routemen and a crew is always available to deal with any difficulty that might arise over weekends or holiday periods.

plain type. However both types need regular clearing to remove detritus which builds up in the gulley pit. Special attention is necessary after long periods of fine weather when the grids can become choked, leading to surface flooding. An especially difficult period is when fallen leaves can block gullies in the autumn.

Previously performed with right-angled shovels, the 1920s saw gulley cleansing being carried out by a specially equipped steam wagon. This was replaced in 1938 by two petrol driven vehicles, known as Flying Pigs, one of which is now in the National Transport Museum. Today diesel-engined vacuum tankers called Vactors perform this work, but if a gulley needs manual clearing, a traditional right-angled shovel is still available.

For many years the city drainage division has maintained a rapid response service to deal with chokes and local flooding. The city was divided into six areas for this purpose, the inner ones being served by two-man crews on bicycles. The bicycles gave way to vans with radio links to their control depots in the late 1960s, except in the inner city. Here the bicycles were retained for reasons of speed and accessibility as traffic conditions deteriorated steadily. But in 1991 modernisation inexorably overcame tradition when the last bicycle crew (Michael Steers and Sean Curran in the south inner city) was provided with a van.

Using initiative to solve problems quickly has always been a quality of routemen. A crew was always available to deal with any difficulty that might arise over weekends or holiday periods. Late one Saturday night several years ago the emergency crew consisting of Paddy Fitzpatrick and Terry O'Connor was called out to deal with a damaged and dangerous manhole cover in Ballsbridge. Finding that it belonged to the Department of Posts and Telegraphs (P&T), at that time in direct control of the telephone system, they nevertheless made it safe by erecting barriers and hazard lamps. But the P&T, as that incredibly bureaucratic department was widely known, refused to pay the charges involved because the work was unauthorised.

Dealing imperturbably with anything that might arise requires a sense of humour. Routeman Billy Redmond was called to a particularly troublesome blockage in the grounds of a religious institution on St Stephen's Day. Perseverance eventually paid off and, as Billy was about to depart, the priest in charge enquired if he took a drink. On being assured that he did, Billy averred that the clergyman invited him to kneel down so that he could give him the pledge.

The routemen and crews engaged on maintenance have an encyclopaedic knowledge of the numerous types of manhole covers and frames to be found on the drainage system. These covers, of various shapes and patterns, readily recall particular periods in the history of the system. Often referred to as plates, they also record the names of several foundries, most of them now gone, that supplied material to the drainage division over the years. The oldest include some oval covers on the former Rathmines & Pembroke system, and a few circular cast covers with segmental wooden inserts. The latter date from the 1890s and some similar covers survive on telephone ducts that formerly comprised the tramway power distribution system.

In the earliest days of the sewer network, stone slabs were often used as manhole covers. In the late nineteenth and early twentieth centuries many types of cover – square, round and oval – were used, but most of these have been replaced over the years. However, a diminishing number of hinged square covers can be found on some pre-1914 manholes. There is still a wide variety of round and square covers, the latter always a worry in case, when being lifted, they might fall into the shaft. There are several instances of covers being given special names, the reasons for some being obscure. The Chapelizod, a massive round cover with slightly coned sides, is one of the most difficult to lift, and a close second is the Ner-Rok and its derivative, the Tri-Seat. Known collectively as Shamrocks, these covers have three small semi-circular extensions on their circumference and pose challenging problems for any two men using traditional equipment to lift

'Flying Pig' gully emptier. *This was introduced in 1938 to mechanise the process of clearing gullies of debris and leaves which are a major cause of local flooding. Later replaced by the Vactor, the 'Flying Pig' was retired to the National Transport Museum.*

them. Some manhole covers weigh in excess of two hundredweights (224 pounds or 100Kg).

In contrast, ductile iron covers, widely used from the 1970s onwards, have eased considerably the physical effort demanded of work crews. Old manhole covers, much studied by industrial archaeologists, encapsulate considerable municipal and industrial history. Although needing to be matched carefully to their location (covers are sometimes moved) the dates cast into these covers can be extremely useful to historians; the earliest date so far found on a Dublin cover is 1903. In several suburban estates built in the 1950–1975 period the dates on the manhole covers provide a clue as to when development took place.

Manhole covers are also in many instances among the few tangible reminders of what were at one time substantial foundries. The most numerous testify to the Hammond Lane Foundry, Tonge & Taggart, Conway's, Drogheda Ironworks and Shannon Foundry, Limerick.

At an unrecorded date, probably in the early twentieth century, the city sewers and main drainage department erected a small building on a corner of what was then the scavenging yard at Marrowbone Lane. This was one of a number of locations, such as Rowserstown and Cole's Lane, from which localised staff operated for several years. More and more space was taken over at Marrowbone Lane as the years passed and this depot eventually comprised a collection of buildings housing stores and offices, with a large yard for open storage of materials, plant and vehicles.

Marrowbone Lane depot is sandwiched between the much larger water services division and public lighting premises. As it became increasingly congested and the drainage division's operations covered an ever-wider area, the need for another depot, specifically to serve the north side, became more pressing. In the 1980s a disused factory at Bannow Road in Cabra was purchased and became the division's much-needed second depot. The inspector in each depot was responsible for supervision of work on either side of the Liffey – Ray Reid in Marrowbone Lane and Denis Cassidy in Bannow Road.

A Vactor at work.

Today diesel-engined
vacuum tankers called
Vactors perform the task
of clearing gullies, but
if manual clearing is
required, a traditional
right-angled shovel is
still available.

MANHOLES AND CATCHPITS, LAMP HOLES AND VENT SHAFTS

Some features found on the older parts of the Dublin drainage network but not encountered in modern sewers merit explanation. An element of conjectural retrospection is necessary here because (as stated at the beginning of this document) some routines and practices were seen as so mundane a century and a half ago that nobody bothered to record them at the time. In the earliest days, manhole covers and frames were omitted from the items listed on the contract drawings. Moreover the long sections show all manhole shafts terminating just below the road surface, suggesting that instead of having covers and frames they were slabbed over. This practice is said to have been adopted on grounds of weight, cost and reservations about the quality of castings available at the time. Later, most manhole shafts were fitted with cast-iron frames and covers, but some were left in their original state and still exist below the road surface. These are known as dummy manholes.

Catchpits are another feature encountered on older sewers. These are sumps in the inverts of manholes at strategic locations, intended to trap stones or other heavy items that could damage

equipment in pumping stations. There were twelve catchpits in the Rathmines & Pembroke area, sixty-eight on the city main drainage system and four on the North Dublin. In 1931 it was estimated that seventeen tons of material was being removed from the catchpits every week. Today a similar amount of material is removed by jet-vactors.

Some superfluous catchpits were taken out of use with the passage of time, but the majority continued to be cleaned out manually by a specialist crew known as the Catch Pit Gang, nicknamed the Mau-Maus. In later years its Land-Rover and attendant sludge trailer parked above an open manhole marked the presence of the gang, which worked under very difficult conditions. All the catchpits, which are of varied dimensions, were measured in 1972 in the hope that the cleansing process could be mechanised, but no suitable equipment became available until 1995 when lorry-mounted vacuum tankers were introduced.

Another group with a specialised task is the tide-gate gang. These men's original duty was to inspect, maintain and repair the flaps that were fitted to the sewer openings along the Liffey. What had previously been sewer discharges direct to the river became overflows on completion of the 1906 main drainage scheme and these are still inspected regularly by the tide-gate men, who now use a boat for transport and access.

Manholes are normally placed predetermined distances apart, dictated by local circumstances, and (ideally) at junctions or changes in the level, size or direction of a sewer. To minimise the number of shafts, lamp holes (also called the poor man's manhole) were sometimes installed at less important locations, and can still be found in various places. Narrow shafts with cast iron covers about 225mm in diameter, they allowed a lamp to be lowered on a rope and shone towards the next manhole shaft. From there an inspector could scrutinise the section of sewer illuminated by the lamp. Usually installed as an economy measure that obviated the need for a manhole, lamp holes are long redundant, especially since the advent of travelling CCTV cameras. On several nineteenth century sewers the heading or first manhole had a ventilation grating built into the cover or immediately beside it. From the early twentieth century onwards these were superseded by kerbside ventilation columns easily identified by a wire mesh finial intended to prevent birds from nesting in them. These columns usually had decorated cast iron bases, often showing the crest or initials of the local authority and the year in which the sewer was laid.

Many ventilation shafts or columns fell into

disrepair over the years and were progressively removed. Some that were in good condition were taken over by the city's public lighting department as lamp standards; in a few instances the ESB also used them as poles in local low-tension overhead wiring networks.

A ventilation shaft in red brickwork which stood for thirty years beside the north-west corner of McMahon Bridge (at the east end of Pearse Street) was rebuilt in 2003 in stainless steel, twelve metres high, with a violet/blue vertical light shining on it at night.

Over the years several once-familiar activities
and occupations have disappeared, often without
being recorded in any meaningful way. The local
authorities, especially Dublin City Council and its
predecessors, were responsible for many of them.
Such activities and occupations, relating to water
and drainage, that cannot be easily slotted into
any particular period of this history have therefore
been assembled into this chapter.

CORPORATION SHIPS

In Chapter 7, there is a brief reference to the
corporation's first sludge vessel, the TSS *Shamrock*,
the first of three ships that served the city successively over ninety-four years. The *Shamrock*, 148
feet long and costing £11,139, was built at the Liffey
Dockyard and completed in 1906. David Rowan
& Company of Glasgow supplied its two compound
inverted marine engines. The *Shamrock* began work
upon the commissioning of the main drainage
scheme in 1906 and sailed for fifty-two years. In
1953 it was reported to be making 400 trips per
annum, carrying capacity loads of 377 tons.

In 1957, when the *Shamrock* was overdue for
retirement, the keel of its replacement, the MV
Seamróg II, was laid, again at the Liffey Dockyard.
Registered on 23 December 1958, this vessel
remained in service until 1984. The working life of
the *Seamróg II* was only half that of its predecessor.
Obsolescence aside, its lack of carrying capacity to
cater for continually growing and more frequent
cargoes rendered its replacement ever more urgent.
The need for a larger sludge vessel spurred the
corporation to find a successor for the *Seamróg II*
in the early 1980s.

Around that time the Thames Water Authority,
which operated a fleet of sludge vessels, had one
ship, built in 1963, which was surplus to requirements. Happily this 2,000 tonne vessel was named
after the eminent engineer Sir Joseph Bazalgette
who had a close connection with the 1906 main
drainage scheme. The MV *Sir Joseph Bazalgette* was
acquired from the Thames Water Authority for a
very reasonable £250,000 in 1983.

Unlike the *Shamrock*, which had been scrapped,
the *Seamróg II* escaped the breaker's yard for a time
at least, being sold for use as a barge. Before the *Sir
Joseph Bazalgette* arrived, changes were made at the
Pigeonhouse. A new jetty was constructed which

chorus from HMS Pinafore, it opened with the line 'We sail the ocean blue and our cargo is a beauty'.

THE LIFFEY FERRIES

Another drainage division waterborne activity now almost forgotten was the operation of the Liffey ferries. Established under a charter of 1665 (another progressive innovation during the Duke of Ormond's tenure as viceroy) the ferries were of great importance prior to the building of bridges as the city extended eastwards. Until Carlisle (O'Connell) Bridge was built in 1794 there was no bridge downstream of Capel Street (originally Essex, now Grattan) Bridge. The ferries became progressively redundant as more bridges were built and peoples' work and travel patterns changed.

For many years, the corporation franchised ferry operation to private individuals, who were not allowed to charge more than the halfpenny laid down for the first crossing in 1668, and this flat fare remained unchanged for nearly 300 years. The Ha'penny Bridge (also known as Liffey Bridge, the Metal Bridge and Wellington Bridge) got its name when the concessionaire Walsh built it to replace a ferry service in 1816 – and continued to collect the traditional halfpenny charge, which was finally abolished for this crossing in 1919.

After more than 290 years the original passenger fare of a halfpenny was doubled to a penny in the 1950s. At that time 40,000 people were being carried annually, but this fell to about 15,000 in the early 1980s, when the fare was ten pence (12.7c) and there were only two crossing places, at Macken Street and Ringsend. The opening of the Matt Talbot Memorial Bridge presaged the end of the service, the last ferry plying between Macken Street and North Wall on 21 October 1984, the day the Eastlink Bridge opened. The service was virtually redundant by then, its demise also hastened by the decline in traditional docklands work patterns and the closure or reloca-tion of several industries. Detailed drawings of the last three ferries (Nos 9, 10 and 11), built in the 1960s, are in the drainage division archives.

The Liffey Ferry.
Ably steered by Shay Byrne, last of the Ferrymen, the Liffey Ferry retired in October 1984 with the opening of the East Link Bridge. A ferry service had been provided on the river since 1665.

permitted docking and sailing at all stages of the tide. This jetty was equipped with a loading arm fed by pipelines from two sludge loading tanks, a loading rate of twenty tons per minute to the sludge vessel being achieved. The *Sir Joseph Bazalgette* was a familiar sight in and around Dublin Bay until its last voyage in the service of Dublin Corporation on 6 December 1999, following which sludge dumping at sea ceased. The *Sir Joseph Bazalgette* was subse-quently sold for further service as a water tender in the Persian Gulf.

Drawings of all three vessels have been retained in the drainage services division of the city council. A model of the *Sir Joseph Bazalgette* is displayed in a glass case in the division's reception area in the administrative building at Ringsend. The log books also survive, an interesting entry in that of the *Shamrock* for Easter Week 1916 recording the can-cellation of sailings 'due to disturbances in the City'.

The late Eoin Lavelle, divisional engineer in the drainage division in the 1990s, parodied the lyrics of a Gilbert and Sullivan's classic to portray the *Sir Joseph Bazalgette*. Sung to the music of the sailors'

WORKING CONDITIONS, TRANSPORT AND EQUIPMENT

The vehicles and equipment that support our public services are, effectively, mechanical chameleons that merge into the background unnoticed. They are being replaced continuously and imperceptibly but to see pronounced changes it is necessary to compare views of the same streetscape taken at least a generation apart. The biggest single change – from horse to mechanical power – began with the arrival of the corporation's first self-propelled vehicles around 1920, and after that horses gradually yielded to vans and lorries. Except for transport supplied by contractors (usually called hackers by corporation staff) the last regular employment of horses by the waterworks division was hauling the square tank used for maintenance. In drainage, the semi-circular skip used by the catchpit gang was the last equine preserve. Both of these antiquated vehicles were phased out by the 1950s.

A hundred years ago the corporation workshops at Stanley Street were staffed by a variety of craftsmen whose skills though paramount for hundreds of years are almost forgotten today. They included cartwrights, wheelwrights, harness makers, blacksmiths, farriers and other trades associated with the era when the horse reigned supreme. Vast quantities of bedding and feed were bought, transported and stored and the veterinary surgeon can be seen in retrospect as the predecessor of the fleet engineer. Finally there was the business of sweeping up and disposing of the manure the animals produced in abundance.

In the past, repair crews, usually called gangs, pushed handcarts containing their tools and equipment to work sites. When lorries were substituted, travel to sites found the foreman in front with the driver and the rest of the crew travelling in the open body of the vehicle, and holding on to the gantry behind the cab for dear life.

From the second half of the nineteenth century onwards, mechanical diggers, excavators and earthmovers have increasingly replaced manual work, improving the lot of site workers – and greatly enhancing productivity. Ever since the first time a worker had to handle or lift a heavy object, there has always been the danger of suffering an injury, especially to the back, and many men have been incapacitated, always unnecessarily, as a result. Modern handling devices – pallet trucks, forklifts, tail lifts and cranes – have contributed enormously to reducing strains and injuries. Safety codes and training courses have improved all our lives.

Vehicles and plant specially built or adapted for use by the waterworks or drainage divisions began to appear from the 1920s onwards. A Fowler steam-powered gulley emptier was acquired by the then sewers and main drainage department in 1926 and served until it was replaced in 1938 by the two Flying Pigs referred to in Chapter 14. This change was also a manifestation of the wholesale eradication of steam then taking place in road transport generally.

Waterworks was the first corporation department to tackle the needs of staff transport and accommodation when it placed the first waterworks bus in service. This vehicle had a crew cab, behind which there was a van body in which the crew could dine. Further to the back, above the rear axle and overhang, there was an open dropside wagon section to carry large items and equipment. In 1974 the concept was taken further when the drainage division designed and had constructed two sewermen's vans. The crew compartments in these vehicles provided cooking and dining facilities, as well as changing areas, showers and toilets. Later generations of waterworks' buses and sewermen's vans incorporated various improvements, and crew-cabbed lorries are now universal throughout the public services.

Two simple comparisons exemplify the changes that have overtaken public works over the past hundred years. One focuses on the 1904 and 2004 gangs – pushing a handcart or travelling in a lorry with a crew cab. The second is even more striking: the man using a pick, shovel and wheelbarrow or his great grandson seated in the cab of a JCB.

THE WATCHMEN

For many generations, the watchman was part of the night scene surrounding water or drainage works. Road openings were fenced by barriers and guarded by this sentinel, who was also responsible for the security of plant and equipment left overnight at the work site. At dusk, he lit the red warning oil lamps and placed them strategically around the works. He also saw to the danger signs at the approaches to the works and checked during the hours of darkness that the lamps remained lighting. He sat in a sentry box and for heat had a brazier, which in earlier days burned coke or coal but in more recent times depended on bottled gas. At dawn, the watchman extinguished his lamps, replenished the oil for the next night and returned them to their storage place in a site hut.

There was a corporation shed known as the Watching Office facing St Michael's and John's Church in West Essex Street. There the watchmen would gather each afternoon just after two o'clock to be assigned to their posts for the night. The supervisor stood on a raised dais and read out the list of names and the locations to which the men were assigned. At one time there were nearly 500 watchmen in corporation service, many of them elderly or moved from gangs because of injuries or infirmity.

A night watchman's job was a lonely one and a chat with a passer-by was usually a welcome respite. Watchmen were always popular with children, who rejoiced in standing around a fire on a dark cold winter evening listening to the wonderful and highly embroidered stories the watchman would tell them. But these men were vulnerable to occasional gratuitous violence, something that is an ever more familiar feature of life today. Watching gradually gave way to mobile security patrols and more sophisticated safety arrangements at works sites. The last watchmen in corporation service slipped away quietly in the mid-1980s and are now a mere memory.

Stories and anecdotes about watchmen occupy the realms of urban folklore but several had a genuine basis in real events. In Stillorgan reservoir the watchmen were called rangers and their duties included patrolling during daylight hours. The last of these men (inevitably called the Lone Ranger) was startled one afternoon when he came across a dozen fishermen with all the latest tackle and seats, encamped on the bank of the Gray Reservoir. When he cautiously approached the group, the nearest fisherman greeted him in an English accent: 'Cheers mate, we heard from your colleague that the reservoir has been restocked lately. Oh, and he took the money for our entry fees'.

On another occasion a ranger approached a group of about twenty teenagers with swimming gear and towels ready to take a dip in the clear reservoir water on a hot day. The ranger told them that they were on private property and that the water was for the consumption of the citizens of Dublin and not for contamination by people swimming in it. The leader of the teenage band replied 'sure we wouldn't dirty it – we've washed already'.

Tragedy at Ringsend. *Remains of a chimney after an explosion at the old Ringsend pumping station, 10 February 1969. This was caused by an overflow into the sewers of naphtha, a dangerously volatile substance, used then in the production of town gas.*

Drought in Dublin?

A prolonged drought
through the winter
and spring of 1996
caused water shortages
which were eased by
summer downpours.
The Olympic victories of
swimmer Michelle
Smith de Bruin brought
popular demand for
a 50-metre swimming
pool, now available at
the National Aquatic
Centre. [Cartoon:
Martyn Turner,
reproduced courtesy
of the artist]

OFFICES AND THEIR SURROUNDINGS

Nowhere can Dublin's decline and renaissance since 1900 be seen more clearly than in the city council's offices and their surroundings. In the late nineteenth century, the city engineer's offices were in Municipal Buildings, the former bank on Cork Hill opposite City Hall. To the east lay the commercial and financial centre at Dame Street and College Green, where several fine buildings were erected and older ones renovated in Victorian times.

The older and inferior districts to the west would still be readily recognised by Rev James Whitelaw more than a hundred years after his survey of the Liberties. Whole swathes of this area continued to deteriorate through most of the twentieth century, and by 1980 increasing numbers of surface car parks occupied the sites of demolished buildings.

As related in the section of Chapter 11 describing the North Dublin drainage system, the corporation acquired in 1913 a former leather goods warehouse at 28 Castle Street. This was renovated for use as temporary accommodation pending the provision of new civic offices, but lasted for seventy-three years. On his retirement in the mid-1970s, Michael Sinnott recalled being told on his first day with the

corporation in 1929 that he would endure Castle Street for only a few years.

The sewers and main drainage department was housed in 28 Castle Street, having cramped offices on the second floor and storage for drawings in the basement, which was prone to dampness and rodent infestation. A small lobby, used as a primitive canteen by the staff of sixteen, was known as Manhole T.

The lack of new development in the inner city was pointed up by a vista from the Castle Street building, right up to its closure in 1986. Through the rear windows on the upper floors there was a view right across Lord Edward Street to the buildings on its north side. The south side of this important street was substantially derelict a hundred years after its opening in 1886 and the gaps were not filled until 1990. Most of the area around the Civic Offices and Christchurch Place remained a multiplicity of eyesores until the city's millennium celebrations in 1988 and new financial incentives triggered fresh development.

Waterworks office accommodation was, if anything, worse than that of the sewers department. A collection of assorted and dilapidated buildings in Fishamble Street served the waterworks staff until a move to Marrowbone Lane was made in the mid-1970s. Here the new four-storey headquarters came as a boon to all those who suffered for years in the Fishamble Street buildings. This Dickensian accommodation occupied the site on which the Civic Offices and the most westerly section of the Temple Bar developments now stand.

A Mansard fifth floor was added to the Marrowbone Lane building in 1980–1981 to accommodate the laboratory, which deals with all the Dublin region's testing of water and drainage samples.

The equipment in drawing offices made little progress until the opening of the first floors in the new Civic Offices in November 1986. The drainage division drawing boards were still on the concrete blocks on which they had been propped thirty-five years earlier when the North Dublin drainage project started. The preparation of drawings had changed in that hand lettering gave way first to stencilled work and later – in the mid-1960s – to press-on lettering.

Computer-generated drawings have now taken over and the skills of yesteryear are no longer in demand. Engineers, surveyors and technicians use computers and calculators for almost every operation. The slide rule and many other instruments that are now superseded will shortly be found only in museums. Computers develop so rapidly that the disposal of obsolete equipment has become a problem; care, however, has to be taken to ensure the survival of selected artefacts as museum pieces.

Plan printing changed dramatically in the second half of the twentieth century. In the 1950s, drawings were copied by a complicated process known as the copycat system. This involved a light table, photographic chemicals and washing. It was slow and hopelessly unsuitable for quantity production.

The copycat system gave way to ammonia printers. These were reasonably fast and used rolls of paper. The disadvantage of this system was the constant emission of fumes that were always nauseatingly unpleasant and potentially dangerous. Although the drainage division's ammonia printing machine on the top floor of 28 Castle Street was beside a window, operating it was always hazardous. In the water division in Marrowbone Lane, which also had an ammonia machine, a gas mask was issued to the technician responsible for plan printing.

RECORDS AND ARCHIVES

The papers relating to the Vartry waterworks scheme were deposited with the city archivist in December 2001. They provide a comprehensive record of the scheme from Sir John Hawkshaw's inquiry in 1860 to the work carried out in the 1930s. Contracts drawn up by Parke Neville and the consulting engineer Sir John MacNeill are included. Spencer Harty's diary detailing the commencement of the system and its subsequent testing is also in the collection.

The water services division also has a comprehensive collection of Ordnance Sheets showing every area through or within which reservoirs, mains and other installations have been constructed.

As related in Chapter 5, the earliest editions of the 1:1056 (88 feet to one inch) Ordnance Sheets, dating from 1847, showed some water main and sewer lines. By the time the first major revisions of these maps were produced in 1864–1866, these details were no longer shown. The corporation's own sewer recording system, inserted on some of the 1847 sheets, became well established with the advent of the 1864 maps and show not only the lines, but also the dimensions of the sewers and the years in which they were laid or underpinned.

New 1:1056 Ordnance Maps, their gridding now related directly to the 6 inch (1:10560) sheets, appeared during the 1880s and these supplemented the older maps for sewers records. Successive revisions of the 1:1056 maps became available by 1910 and 1930 and these too have been used by the drainage division. Maps of questionable accuracy, to a scale of 1:1250, were utilised later. These were enlargements from the 1:2500 scale, the most modern dating from the 1940s. Any new estates built after the production of these maps were marked on manually and there were frequently con-

**Water-shortages
in Ireland!** *A series
of exceptionally dry
winters and warm
summers during the
1990s led to pressure on
supply with water-levels
receding in reservoirs
and drowned houses
re-emerging from the
depths. Autumn
downpours helped to
restore water-levels.
[Cartoon: Terry Willers,
reproduced courtesy of
the artist]*

Rusted iron water-pipe.
*This is typical of
nineteenth-century mains
which are still in use
and must be re-laid
as a priority.*

siderable differences between the layouts approved
for particular developments and what was actually
built. All the 1:1250 sheets and others from earlier
times have been carefully preserved and are frequently consulted.

From 1970 the 1:1000 sheets became standard.
These too omitted the many estates built from 1970
onwards and details had again to be drawn on to
the sheets. A constant fear for anyone using early
editions of these sheets was that some of them
showed Poolbeg Datum, others Malin Head, the

difference between the two being 2.7 metres.
Another inconsistency was that some of the sheets
showed imperial levels while others had metric.
The fear of an embarrassing construction disaster
caused by some innocent error arising from these
discrepancies was uppermost in the minds of
everybody involved in survey work. This writer,
thankfully, was neither involved in any such
lapse nor heard of anybody else employed by the
corporation who was so unlucky.

Surveyor C. L. Sweeney (1923–1996) worked in
the sewers and main drainage department from 1946
to 1988. Enthusiastically dedicated to whatever task
was in hand, the sense of humour that permeated
his work produced an unofficial Latin motto for the
drainage division: Sercus tibi, mea victualis (Sewage
to you, but it's my bread and butter).

Known to his friends and colleagues as Clair,
C. L. Sweeney was keenly aware of the historical
importance of the drawings and other records
in his care and he saved many worthy items from
destruction in an era when minimal value was

placed on such things. In 1974 he initiated a programme to upgrade the records system and catalogue fully everything in the department. All the drawings stored horizontally in the basement were put on suspension strips and placed in vertical map cabinets, a new index and register being compiled at the same time.

Sewers and main drainage, by then known as the drainage division, was one of the first three departments that moved to the new Civic Offices, which opened on Monday 3 November 1986. All the historic drawings, an invaluable and compre-hensive record of Dublin's drainage since 1852, were accommodated in the new offices. A few items stored in Castle Street were lost in a malicious fire that destroyed the premises in October 1987.

The Dublin city area as existing in 2005 was covered by 224 Ordnance Maps on the 1:1000 scale. The bulk of the drainage records have been comput-erised, with all the manhole details available on a database. The re-survey of the entire drainage network began in 1987 and was completed in 2003. Regular updating of the information to reflect new developments will ensure the continuing accuracy of the database.

NEW TECHNOLOGY

The many benefits conferred by new technology generally and computers in particular have enabled the drainage division to modernise and simplify its work to an extent undreamed of in the 1970s. The following examples illustrate strikingly the revolutionary transi-tion from long-established equipment and practices to constantly evolving new technology.

Until the mid-1980s the method of monitoring the flow in a sewer was by means of a device called a candelabra. This consisted of a length of timber with small cups screwed on at fixed intervals. The candelabra was placed in a manhole shaft, the highest full cup showing the approximate maximum level of flow during a particular period. Candelabras in the various manholes under examination had to be inspected regularly, a time-consuming and not

Workmen clearing a sewer. *Travelling a conduit with headroom of less than six feet, as in most Dublin sewers, is uncomfortable and even hazardous, and the smaller the sewer, the greater the discomfort.*

too accurate process. Computers now record flow measurement, providing constant, accurate infor-mation. Manholes that formerly needed to be opened at least twice a day for candelabras to be checked can now be left untouched for a week while the computer produces precise and continuous readings. Flows can be measured by electro-magnetic or ultrasonic meters which can store the information locally on a small weatherproof computer called an outstation – or the computer may transmit it live by leased phone lines to the main office.

The preparation and printing of drawings has also been revolutionised. Gone are the drawing boards of yesteryear with all their parallel motions and other attachments. The laboriously hand-drawn but beautiful lettering practised from the earliest times gave way to stencilled characters in the 1960s. In the 1970s, press-on lettering sheets took over, yielding in turn to computer-generated work in the 1980s. Cumbersome copycat, ammonia and dyeline printing processes have come and gone. However the sophisticated computers and plotters currently used to produce drawings – which are greatly appreciated by anybody who worked with older equipment – will assuredly be overtaken by even more advanced methods.

New technology is of inestimable value as applied to the drainage division's records. Most of the old drawings have been scanned and are quickly accessi-ble on computer screens. The registers and indices are recorded in a database, making the extraction of information faster and easier than in times past.

Progress into the twenty-first century.

Michael Phillips, Dublin City Engineer and Bartholomew White, Deputy City Engineer, checking progress of works at Sutton pumping station and submarine pipeline project.

Telemetry and remote control of pumping stations are further examples of how developing technology has changed operations in the drainage division. Two of the North Dublin pumping stations – Clontarf and Howth – were staffed around the clock from the inauguration of the system, but Clontarf became automatic in the 1980s and at the time of writing Howth was on borrowed time. Ringsend, East Road and Sutton were still staffed in 2004.

MAKING SIGNS

Until technology overtook many aspects of work in the public services, most city council works departments maintained stocks of standard signs and specials that were displayed at the sites of various works. These involved the services of signwriters, who are now based in the drainage division's workshops at Ringsend and produce most of the material required by the different departments or divisions.

PREPARING FOR THE LUAS TRAMWAYS

When it was decided to re-introduce trams to Dublin, the matter of underground services and their relationship with the new system received close attention. It was agreed at an early stage that steps should be taken to avoid road openings and interruptions to the tram service by work on underground utilities for the foreseeable future. A major programme was therefore undertaken in which sewers would be internally lined or reconstructed where necessary and water mains would be relocated from under the tracks.

The programme began in 2000 and, as the services under each section of the routes were dealt with, the sites were handed over to the contractors who were responsible for track laying and road reinstatement. The Sandyford line opened on 30 June 2004, the Tallaght service following on 28 September. Valuable experience was gained in the planning and construction of the first new tramways laid down in Dublin since 1906. When extensions are made to the Luas system, this experience, especially in dealing with underground services, will be highly beneficial.

The staff involved in the provision of the water supply and wastewater services carry out a wide range of activities every day in order to ensure that the needs of their customers are met. Perhaps the highest compliment that they might be paid is that very few of those customers are aware of their existence and take the availability of the services for granted.

The staff of the city water services division have responsibility for collecting, treating and distributing drinking water to the 1.3 million consumers in the Dublin region every day. The 510 million litres required daily for Dublin city are produced by four water treatment plants, one of which – at Ballymore Eustace – is by far the largest in the state. The city staff maintain 2,700 km of watermains, 600 km of service pipes and associated treated water storage reservoirs, 18,000 valves, 15,000 fire hydrants and ten pumping stations.

Staff control and manage the water distribution network with the aid of sophisticated mapping and telemetry systems. The GIS mapping facility provides vital information on the location of water mains and fittings, while the telemetry system allows the monitoring of water pressures and volumes throughout the distribution area.

The ability to remotely control strategic valves to facilitate the movement of large volumes of water is also now a reality. In addition, the telemetry system allows staff to monitor water usage in the 200 or so district meter areas into which the city has been subdivided. By virtue of this monitoring it is possible to focus the attention of leakage detection teams on areas where there has been an obvious increase in the volume of water being supplied. This has a clearly beneficial effect in assisting staff to reduce water loss by leakage from the system.

Water maintenance staff in an average year carry out 1,000 repairs to broken water mains as well as 3,000 repairs to faulty water service pipes and fittings, while mainlaying staff lay or re-lay 10,000 metres of water main and provide new water connections to developers' sites.

Planning and asset management staff assess approximately 4,000 planning applications a year in relation to their impact on the water distribution network and determine the increased demands for water to be supplied. Inspectors ensure that the water bye-laws and regulations regarding standards of plumbing materials and workmanship are maintained in all new developments.

Sewermen's van.

In 1974 the drainage division designed and constructed two sewermen's vans. The crew compartments in these vehicles provided cooking and dining facilities, as well as changing areas, showers and toilets.

Drainage services personnel provide equally high levels of services to customers in removing and treating waterborne waste and in preventing or dealing with the consequences of flooding in the city. Every day 500,000 cubic metres of wastewater and storm water are collected, treated and disposed of and, under certain conditions, this figure can rise to 2,000,000 cubic metres. Two and a half thousand kilometres of public sewers and 50,000 manholes are continuously monitored using the latest remotely-controlled camera equipment in the smaller pipes and walk-through visual inspections where possible. The result of these inspections direct maintenance crews to areas of the network that require repair or upgrading work.

GIS mapping and telemetry systems are used in managing and monitoring the various aspects of the drainage system in a similar fashion to the water supply network. The drainage division is responsible for thirty pumping stations, the licensing of trade effluent discharges, reporting on the drainage aspects of planning applications and forward planning.

Drainage staff clear debris from rivers and streams in order to ensure that the maximum possible volume of water can be carried in the event of a flood. River gangs are a common and welcome sight for people living close to areas at risk. The maintenance staff have the often unpleasant task of clearing blockages, mostly caused by discharge to sewers of fats, oils and greases (FOG) from both residential and business premises. Although the most up-to-date and efficient 'jetvac' equipment has been acquired by the city council the citizens of

Dublin still owe a great debt of gratitude to the staff that perform this most undesirable of duties.

Road gully cleaning has been likened, quite justifiably, to the task of painting the Forth Bridge in Scotland in that it is never ending. No sooner have Dublin's 52,000 gullies been cleaned than the work must start again.

Sewer reconstruction crews strengthen, replace or newly construct up to 5,000 metres of sewer every year, while staff in the planning section assess the 4,000 or so planning applications received annually for their possible effect on the drainage network. Appropriate conditions are imposed on developers to best manage both foul and surface water drainage arising from their activities. Meanwhile, administration and planning for the future are carried out in the respective civic offices of the city and the adjoining large local authorities. The majority of large projects are designed by outside consultants, and in-house teams review them technically and ensure their safe passage through the statutory procedures. The investment per annum in such projects is currently in excess of €200 million.

More than 300 people are employed in the city water services division, with another 250 in the drainage division, the vast majority of them unknown outside their immediate family and working circles. As in all the other public services, water and drainage personnel are supported by skilled administrators who are, if that were possible, even more anonymous. For several hundred years, successive generations of all these groups have performed their duties with dedication and good humour. Whatever else happens, the water and drainage systems will be there to serve posterity and Jonathan Swift's nameless men – and women – will continue to provide these vital services.

CONCLUSION

The Dublin region has expanded since the 1970s at a pace not experienced in the previous 200 years. The rate of growth greatly accelerated from the mid-1990s to such an extent that the population in

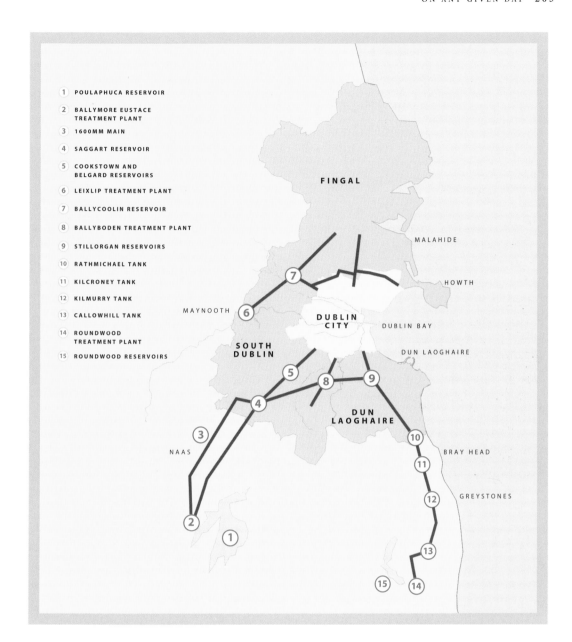

1 POULAPHUCA RESERVOIR

2 BALLYMORE EUSTACE
TREATMENT PLANT

3 1600MM MAIN

4 SAGGART RESERVOIR

5 COOKSTOWN AND
BELGARD RESERVOIRS

6 LEIXLIP TREATMENT PLANT

7 BALLYCOOLIN RESERVOIR

8 BALLYBODEN TREATMENT PLANT

9 STILLORGAN RESERVOIRS

10 RATHMICHAEL TANK

11 KILCRONEY TANK

12 KILMURRY TANK

13 CALLOWHILL TANK

14 ROUNDWOOD
TREATMENT PLANT

15 ROUNDWOOD RESERVOIRS

FINGAL

MALAHIDE

HOWTH

MAYNOOTH

DUBLIN
CITY

DUBLIN BAY

SOUTH
DUBLIN

DUN LAOGHAIRE

DUN
LAOGHAIRE

NAAS

BRAY HEAD

GREYSTONES

Map showing location of reservoirs and treatment plants serving Dublin City, 2005.

the region has grown from 1.4m (1996) to 1.535m (2002) and is forecast to reach 1.71m by 2010. In addition, between 1995 and 2000, regional, commercial and industrial output has grown by 95.3% and while gross domestic product (GDP), which is the measure of industrial output, has dropped below 10% annually since 2000, it remains – currently at 5.25% – a high rate when compared with the remainder of the EU where such growth varies from 0 to 2%.

This expansion has been accompanied by a growth in affluence, and peoples' expectations of the 'quality of service' are much higher than in previous times. When the principles of sustainability, limited natural resources and climate change are taken into consideration, the provision of services presents challenges not previously experienced, and will continue to do so for the foreseeable future.

This becomes apparent in the quality demanded and the conflict between projects for the greater

Ballymore Eustace

The 510 million litres of water required daily for Dublin city are produced by four water treatment plants, and this one at Ballymore Eustace is the largest in the state.

good of the community and the perceived infringements on the individual's rights. The introduction of community gain and extensive public consultation exercises provide a mechanism for managing such situations. The limited availability of financial resources, although not a new problem, to meet diverse and rapidly increasing demands, has resulted in the public and private sectors coming together through public private partnerships (PPP). This form of procurement involves the transfer of risk for the build, design, operate (DBO) and/or finance being transferred to the private sector. The traditional method of procurement was for public sector design and funding with private sector contractors tendering to build the detailed design.

The pace of change has meant that old concepts, as understood by the public and private sectors, have changed dramatically. These sectors now work

in partnership to provide for the requirements of the region. It is essential that strategies for the future are both flexible and yet radical enough to meet the needs of the city. The main difficulty is the difference in pace between implementing public sector infrastructural projects, where the time window is usually twenty years, and private sector industry where it may be as short as five years.

The existing Greater Dublin Water Supply Strategy Plan 1996–2016 and the Drainage Strategy (2005–2031) clearly state what is required to enable Dublin, which will cater for 40% of the nation's population by 2010, to meet the needs of the people and industry, and at the same time provide a high quality environment for all its communities. Dublin has been fortunate up to the present time to have an abundance of water sources and rivers to provide for its citizens. From now on all plans and

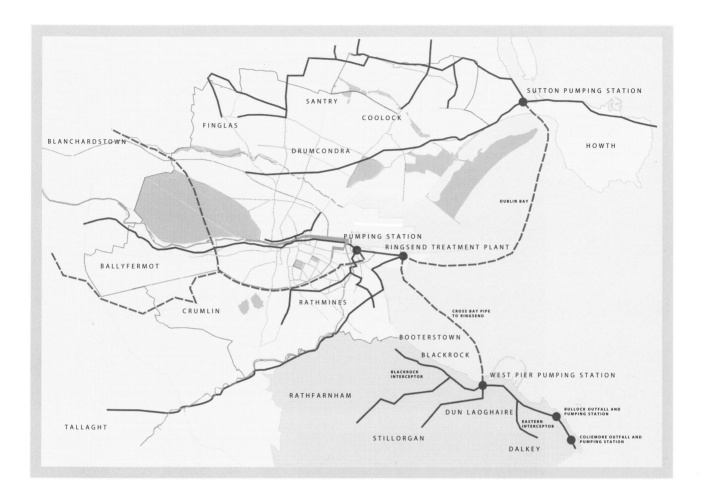

aspirations will increasingly have to bear in mind what was first stated at the Rio Declaration in 1992 and reaffirmed in Agenda 21: that sustainable development should 'meet the needs of the present without compromising the ability of future generations to meet their own needs'. This latter responsibility will present new challenges in managing the environment we live in and setting the priorities for the standard of living that people desire.

WHAT DOES THE FUTURE HOLD?

In the 1770s when Dublin's new water supply began flowing from the Grand Canal and an organised drainage system was being inaugurated, steam power was about to revolutionise every facet of life. That revolution is still rolling on inexorably, with every new technological development leading to

several more. While not everybody has benefited as yet, the resulting progress, especially in public health, has been spectacular, largely thanks to the water supply and drainage services.

Andrew Coffey recognised the advantages of new technology when he proposed using steam pumps in the water service at the beginning of the nineteenth century. Steam still reigned supreme a hundred years later when the Ringsend sewage pumping station opened, but it was already being challenged – by electricity from the neighbouring Pigeonhouse generating station and the internal combustion engines that drove the primordial motor vehicles then coming on to the roads.

For those charged with responsibility for the delivery of water supply and wastewater services the highest priority during the nineteenth and twentieth centuries was given to establishing and

Map showing drainage system for Dublin City, 2005.

**Main Lift
Pumping Station.**
*Opened in 1985, this
state-of-the-art modern
building will help to
ensure that the good
health enjoyed by
the people of Dublin
is sustained into the
twenty-first century.*

meeting quality standards in the interests of public health. Outbreaks of typhoid and cholera were not uncommon and many thousands of people lost their lives to these waterborne diseases. For future generations one of the greatest challenges will be to meet the ever-increasing demand for a clean water supply and a safe and effective wastewater collection and treatment system.

On a macro scale only 2.5% of the water available in the world is non-saline and only 0.17% of that water is available for use by the inhabitants of the globe. The remaining fresh water is trapped in the polar ice caps in inaccessible areas of the world or falls in the wrong place at the wrong time. At the commencement of the twentieth century the world population was 1.6 billion people and this figure reached 6.1 billion by the end of the century. The world population is estimated to grow by 86 million people per annum for the foreseeable future. These major issues, in conjunction with climate change, environmental pollution, government policies etc will significantly influence the availability and use of natural resources.

The growth of transportation and telecoms, followed by the worldwide web and information technology, has shrunk the globe and brought people, businesses and communities much closer together. Globalisation and the pace at which it is happening are not sustainable in the current environment. The emergence of totally new industries, such as the possibility of hydrogen derived from water for cars, will create a critically different environment for water usage. As a result, human ingenuity and creativity will continue to be in demand and we can only gaze into an imaginary crystal ball and speculate on how future generations

Aerial view, Ringsend Treatment Plant
This provides primary, secondary and tertiary treatment for rainwater, sewage and other effluents. The treated matter is converted into three products: Biofert, a high grade agricultural fertiliser; Biogas to supply 60% of the plant's energy needs; and clean water in Dublin Bay

**Roundwood
Reservoir today.**

*Fresh Vartry water
from county Wicklow
is still provided for the
people of Dublin as
it has been since the
mid-nineteenth century.*

will cope with their requirements. The sphere in which ingenuity will be particularly called for will be that of fulfilling the water needs of people, not only for personal use, but most especially for food production.

On a micro scale this ingenuity is today reflected in the rapid developments we are witnessing in water treatment processes such as desalination, the re-use of 'grey' water and the effluent from waste-water treatment works. These processes in conjunction with the conservation of water will play a major part in meeting the needs for future generations.

Andrew Coffey would surely have regarded air travel, jet and rocket engines, landings on the moon and interplanetary exploration as science fiction. Today these advances are seen as mundane by our children and grandchildren, who belong to the new generations that will take science and technology further and faster than we can dream of now. Knowing how posterity will advance the human condition over the next two hundred years would doubtless overwhelm us as surely as our present lifestyles would mystify Andrew Coffey. But one certainty from his time, in our era and even two centuries hence, is that water supply and drainage will still be of prime importance.

**Statue of
Sir John Gray.**

*The hero of Roundwood
Reservoir stands proud
in Dublin's O'Connell
Street, with The Spire,
symbol of the twenty-
first-century city, soaring
skywards behind him.*

Appendix 1

DUBLIN CITY SURVEYORS AND ENGINEERS

Dublin City Surveyors

Name	Dates of service
John Greene, Junior	1679–1687
Barnaby Hackett	1687–1690
John Greene, Junior	1690–1698
Joseph Moland	1698–1718
James Ramsey	1718–1735
Roger Kendrick	1735–1764
Thomas Mathews	1764–1782
Samuel Byron	1782–1795
David B. Worthington	1795–1801
Arthur R. Neville	1801–1828
Arthur Neville	1828–1845
Arthur Neville and Parke Neville	1845–1851[1]
Arthur Neville	1851–1856[2]

Dublin City Engineers

Name	Dates of service
Parke Neville	1851–1886
Spencer Harty	1887–1910
John G. O'Sullivan	1910–1913
Michael J. Buckley	1913–1927
Michael A. Moynihan	1927–1936
Norman D. Chance	1936–1950
Edward J. Bourke	1950–1967

Chief Engineers, Dublin City and County

ENGINEERING SERVICES

E J. Bourke	1967–1971
K. O'Donnell	1971–1991
J. Fenwick	1991–1993

ROADS

M. Dee	1967–1970
M. McEntee	1970–1980
B. Murphy	1980–1986
P. Kellaghan	1986–1991

Dublin City Engineers

J. Fenwick	1993–1997
M. Phillips	1997 to date

1. Appointed as joint city surveyors on 1 August 1845, Dublin City Council Minute Book, Vol 13, pp 161, 252. Parke Neville resigned the office of joint city surveyor on 7 April 1851 and was appointed borough engineer and local surveyor of the city of Dublin, Dublin City Council Minute Book, Vol 15, pp 353-4; Vol 16, p. 231.

2. At the city council meeting of 1 December 1856, there is mention of payment to the executor of Arthur Neville, late city surveyor, of the account due from 1 June 1855 to 1 January 1856, Dublin City Council Minute Book, Vol 19, p. 191

Appendix 2

DUBLIN REGION WATER SUPPLY: CHEMICAL ANALYSES OF WATER 2005

Constituent	Source of supply			
	Vartry	Liffey BALLYMORE EUSTACE	Dodder	Liffey LEIXLIP
Colour (Hazen)	15	5	5	5
Turbidity (NTU)	1.2	0.5	0.5	0.2
Odour	None	None	None	None
Taste	None	None	None	None
pH	7.5	7.1	7.18	7.34
Conductivity (uS/cm)	125	145	148	400
Total Residual Chlorine (mg/1)	0.09	0.04	0.02	0.09
Nitrate (mg N/1)	1.75	0.70	0.0	2.30
Nitrite (mg N/1)	0.00	0.002	0.0	0.002
Ammonia (mg N/1)	0.03	0.01	0.0	0.015
Total Coliforms (CFU/100ml)	0	0	0	0
Faecal Coliforms (CFU/100ml)	0	0	0	0
Heterotrophic Plate Count 22° (CFU/ml)	39	20	23	19
Heterotrophic Plate Count 37° (CFU/ml)	36	2	6	17
Aluminium (mg/l)	0.05	0.05	0.08	0.08
Iron (mg/l)	0.06	0.01	0.02	0.04
Fluoride (mg/l)	0.8-1.0	0.8-1.0	0.8-10	0.8-10
Total Hardness (mgCaCO$_5$/l)	50	55	55	150
Sulphate (mg S04/L)	0	0	0	40

Dublin Waterworks

Map dated 1865 by
Parke Neville showing
course of waterworks
from Roundwood
Reservoir to Dublin.

IMAGE COURTESY
IRISH ARCHITECTURAL
ARCHIVE

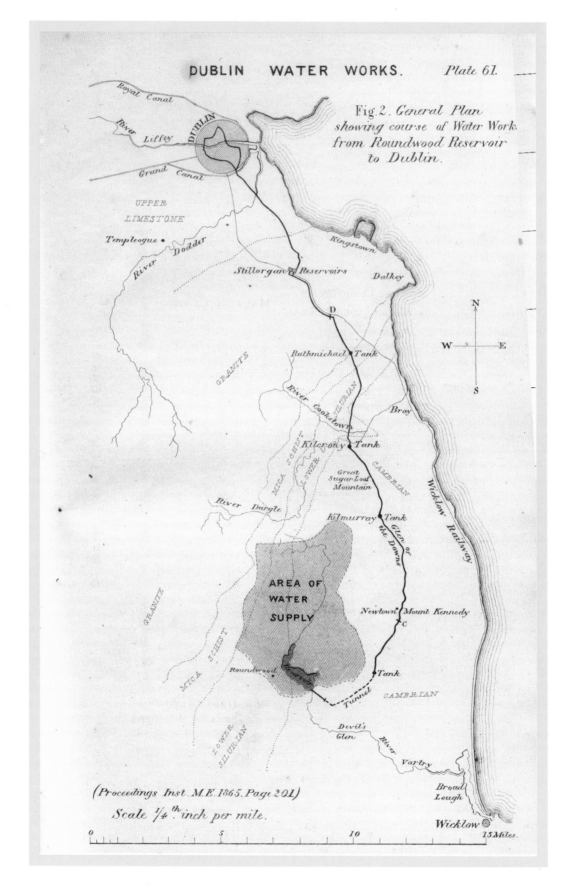

Bibliography

The principal primary sources for the history of Dublin's water supply and drainage are held by Dublin City Council. Dublin City Archives holds the complete records of Dublin City Council and its predecessor body, the Dublin City Assembly, from the late twelfth century to the present, and these include detailed references to both water and drainage. The City Archives also holds records of the Paving Board, which had responsibility for drainage from 1774 until 1851 while minutes of Dublin City Council's Waterworks Committee are available from 1861 onwards, as are log-books for the TSS *Shamrock*. Later materials relating to drainage are held by the Engineering Department as working drawings, since the sewage systems to which they refer are still in use today. However, an ongoing programme of scanning and digitisation should enable these important original records to be transferred to the City Archives in the near future. As can be seen from the illustrations in *Our Good Health* these exquisite drawings are more than triumphs of engineering, they are works of art in their own right, many bearing the signature of luminaries such as Sir Joseph Bazalgette, Parke Neville and Spencer Harty.

The many books, newspapers, periodicals and journals consulted include the following:

J.F. BATEMAN
Letter to the Lord Mayor on the supply of water to the City of Dublin (London, 1860)

MARK BRUNTON (ED.)
Managing Dublin Bay (Dublin, 1987)

PETER CLARKE
Royal Canal: the Whole Story (Dublin, 1992)

MAURICE CRAIG
Dublin, 1660–1860 (2nd edition, Dublin, 1980)

HENRY T. CROOK
'Rathmines and Pembroke Drainage'.
Paper read to the Institution of Engineers of Ireland, December 1881

D.C. COYLE
'The North Dublin Drainage Scheme' in *Transactions of the Institution of Civil Engineers of Ireland*, vol. 90 (1953–54), pp 80, 107–189, 255–270

RUTH DELANEY
Ireland's Grand Canal (Dublin, 1995)

PADRAIG DOYLE
'Greater Dublin Strategic Drainage Study.'
Paper read to the Institution of Engineers of Ireland, April 2003

ARTHUR FLYNN
Ringsend and her Sister Villages (Dublin, 1990)

TOM GERAGHTY
AND TREVOR WHITEHEAD
The Dublin Fire Brigade (Dublin, 2004)

H.A. GILLIGAN
A History of the Port of Dublin (Dublin, 1998)

STEPHEN HALLIDAY
The Great Stink of London (Stroud, 1994)

BRIAN HENRY
Dublin Hanged (Dublin, 1994)

P.H. MCCARTHY
'Sewage Tanks at Howth'. Paper read to the
Institution of Engineers of Ireland, March 1918

MICHAEL A. MOYNIHAN
'Greater Dublin'. Paper read to the Institution
of Municipal Engineers, May 1931

B. MURPHY
'The North Dublin Drainage Scheme –
Construction of Main Interceptor' in *Transactions
of the Institution of Civil Engineers of Ireland*
(December 1954), pp 23–70

PARKE NEVILLE
*A description of the Dublin Corporation
Waterworks* (Dublin, 1875)

MATT O'BRIEN
'Dun Laoghaire Drainage Scheme' in *Local
Authority News*, vol. 7, no. 4, (1992) pp 3–13

DERVAL O'CARROLL
AND SEÁN FITZPATRICK (EDS.)
*Hoggers, Lords and Railwaymen: a History
of the Custom House Docks Heritage Project*
(Dublin, 1996)

K.P. O'DONNELL
*The Dodder Water Supply Scheme,
part 1 (General); part 2 (Technical)*
(Dublin Corporation); 'Dublin's Main Drainage
System, a History' in *Irish Engineer*, vol. 32,
no. 1; 'Protection of Sources – an Overview'
in *I.E.I. Journal*, vol. 41, no. 1 (1988), pp 20-21

SEAMUS O MAITIU
Dublin's Suburban Towns (Dublin, 2003)

DIARMAID O MUIRITHE
*A Seat behind the Coachman: Travellers
in Ireland 1800–1900* (Dublin, 1972)

F.S. O'SHEA
'The Construction of the Howth Tunnel'
in *Transactions of the Institution of Civil Engineers
of Ireland*, vol. 84 (1957–8), pp 49–111, 171–180

JOSEPH ROBINS
Custom House People (Dublin, 1993)

HENRY SHAW
Dublin Pictorial Guide and Directory
(Dublin, 1850)

C.L. SWEENEY
Rivers of Dublin (Dublin, 1991)

THOMAS WILLIS
The Hidden Dublin (Dublin, 1845)

Index

ELEVATION OF SCREEN CHAMBER

PLAN OF SCREEN CHAMBER

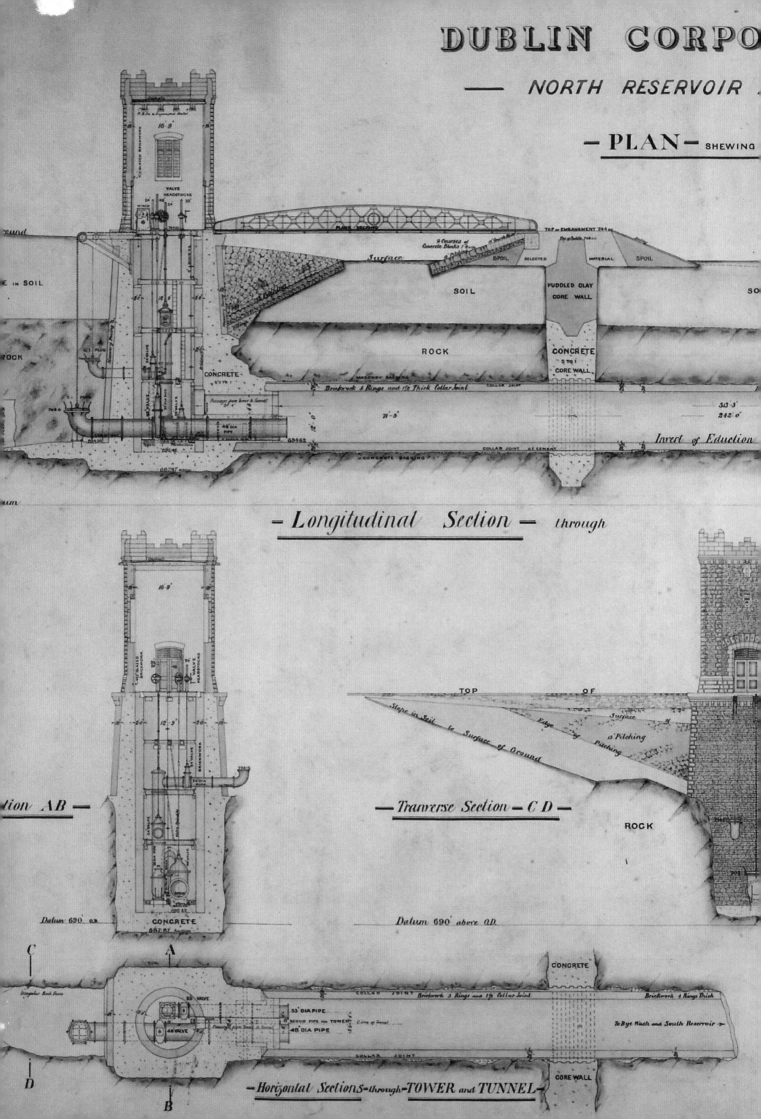